Lecture Notes in Computer Science   10959

Commenced Publication in 1973
Founding and Former Series Editors:
Gerhard Goos, Juris Hartmanis, and Jan van Leeuwen

More information about this series at http://www.springer.com/series/7409

Alejandra González-Beltrán · Francesco Osborne
Silvio Peroni · Sahar Vahdati (Eds.)

Semantics, Analytics, Visualization

3rd International Workshop, SAVE-SD 2017
Perth, Australia, April 3, 2017
and 4th International Workshop, SAVE-SD 2018
Lyon, France, April 24, 2018
Revised Selected Papers

 Springer

Editors
Alejandra González-Beltrán (iD)
Oxford e-Research Centre
University of Oxford
Oxford, UK

Francesco Osborne (iD)
Waltan Hall
KMi, Open University
Milton Keynes, UK

Silvio Peroni (iD)
Department of Classical Philology and
   Italian Studies
University of Bologna
Bologna, Italy

Sahar Vahdati (iD)
University of Bonn
Bonn, Germany

ISSN 0302-9743   ISSN 1611-3349   (electronic)
Lecture Notes in Computer Science
ISBN 978-3-030-01378-3   ISBN 978-3-030-01379-0   (eBook)
https://doi.org/10.1007/978-3-030-01379-0

Library of Congress Control Number: 2018955573

LNCS Sublibrary: SL3 – Information Systems and Applications, incl. Internet/Web, and HCI

This Springer imprint is published by the registered company Springer Nature Switzerland AG
The registered company address is: Gewerbestrasse 11, 6330 Cham, Switzerland

Preface

The scientific world is in dire need of innovative solutions for scholarly communication and dissemination that would take full advantage of the digital world and allow for more efficient use of the research outputs. These innovative solutions should support new forms for sharing and publishing all scholarly outputs, such as data and software, while also facilitating scientists along the research process, with methods and tools from data collection, data analysis, up to dissemination. Thus, it is required to move away from static ways of sharing information (e.g., PDFs) and enhancing the ways of discovering and accessing all scholarly outputs, ensuring science reproducibility and reuse of outputs. There are multiple ways in which scholarly dissemination can be improved. Creating structured and semantically rich metadata about the multiple research outputs and how they are related would support better integration and exploitation of such research data. Providing methods for systematic computational analyses of scholarly outputs would enable us to extract relevant knowledge and reason on this large mass of information. Finally, designing systems for navigating and making sense of scholarly data would allow a variety of stakeholders to understand research dynamics, predict trends, and evaluate the quality of research. The aims of the Semantics, Analytics, Visualization: Enhancing Scholarly Dissemination (SAVE-SD) Workshop series is to highlight solutions in these areas and bring together all the interested parties from academia and industry.

These proceedings report on the two latest events of the SAVE-SD Workshop series: the 2017 and 2018 editions. Following the venues selected by The Web Conference, the SAVE-SD 2017 workshop took place in Perth, Australia, on April 3, 2017, while the SAVE-SD 2018 workshop was held in Lyon, France on April 24, 2018.

For both editions, we had brilliant keynote speakers. In 2017, Patricia Feeney from Crossref presented her talk "Making Connections Between Data." Crossref is an official Digital Object Identifier (DOI) Registration Agency providing persistent identifiers for cross-publisher citations. In her talk, Patricia explained Crossref's plans to capture and share the connections between metadata to form a comprehensive map of research. In 2018, Natasha Noy from Google presented her talk entitled "Facilitating Discovery of Scientific Data" in which she discussed Google's work on facilitating metadata discovery on the Web and their plans to contribute to the creation of a vibrant and open ecosystem of data publishing.

The SAVE-SD 2017 and SAVE-SD 2018 programs presented in this volume include 12 papers: six full papers, two position papers, and four short papers. The workshops received a total of 16 submissions from 13 countries.

For the 2018 edition, we adopted a more open submission process for the first time. The new policy for submissions and the review process was described in the multiple call for papers and on our website (https://save-sd.github.io/2018/submission.html). This new process meant that the submitted papers were made available publicly on the workshop website upon submission (see https://save-sd.github.io/2018/papers.html).

Submissions were not anonymous and thus the authors were known to reviewers. We encouraged reviewers to sign their reviews, although they could decide to remain anonymous. The reviews themselves were also made publicly available on the workshop's website following a CC-BY license upon final notification to authors, together with the final decision. On explicit request by the authors, the rejected papers and their reviews could be excluded from the website. If the reviewers signed their assessments, their names are also available on the website. Among the 55 assessments (including reviews and meta-reviews), seven reviews were signed by six Program Committee (PC) members. In any case, all the reviewers are acknowledged in the PCs, as listed herein. All SAVE-SD workshops have three PCs:

- An Industrial PC, who mainly evaluate the submissions from an industrial perspective – by assessing how much the theories/applications described in the papers do/may influence (positively or negatively) the publishing and technological domain and whether they could be concretely adopted by publishers and scholarly data providers
- An Academic PC, who evaluate the papers mainly from an academic perspective – by assessing the quality of the research described in such papers
- A Senior PC, whose members act as meta-reviewers and have the crucial role of balancing the scores provided by the reviews from the other two PCs

These three PCs are important for our goal of addressing the gap between the theoretical and practical aspects of scholarly dissemination, as the interaction between both aspects happens from the review process onward.

We are very grateful to all the members of the three PCs, who are listed here, for their high-quality reviews and constructive feedback, which improved significantly the quality of the papers contained in these proceedings.

All submissions in both editions were reviewed by at least by one Industrial PC member, two Academic PC members and one Senior PC member. The final decision of acceptance/rejection was made by consensus by the chairs, considering conflict of interest when in existence.

SAVE-SD accepts submissions not just in the traditional formats such as PDF, ODT, DOCX, but also in HTML, encouraging authors to provide semantically rich papers themselves. In order to facilitate the task of submitting articles in HTML, our workshop encourages the use of the systems RASH (https://rash-framework.github.io/) or dokieli (https://dokie.li/) for submissions. RASH stands for Research Articles in Simplified HTML, a markup language defined as a subset of HTML+RDF that can be produced from Open Office documents, Microsoft Word documents, and other formats. Dokieli is a client-side editor for decentralized article publishing in HTML+RDF annotations and social interactions. We are happy to report that the two editions of SAVE-SD presented in this volume received nine out of 16 submissions in RASH (56%).

In both editions we awarded the best paper award to the papers that received the best scores from the reviewers. In 2017, the award was given to "About a BUOI: Joint Custody of Universally Unique Identifiers on the Web, or, Making PIDs More FAIR" by Joakim Philipson. The paper discusses the use of the permanent identifiers (PIDs) on the Internet and their compliance with the FAIR data principles, and suggests that findability may be more important than the resolvability of links by one single authority. In 2018, the award was granted to "Geographical Trends in Research: A Preliminary Analysis on Authors' Affiliations" by Andrea Mannocci et al. The paper presents a study of a conference proceedings dataset extracted from Springer Nature Scigraph that illustrates insightful geographical trends and highlights the unbalanced growth of competitive research institutions worldwide.

Last, but certainly not least, we want to thank our sponsors:

- Springer Nature, who provided a 150-euro voucher to buy Springer Nature's products for the best paper award
- L3S, who provided additional fundings

August 2018   Alejandra González-Beltrán
                                                      Francesco Osborne
                                                      Silvio Peroni
                                                      Sahar Vahdati

Organization

Workshop Chairs

Alejandra González-Beltrán	University of Oxford, UK
Francesco Osborne	The Open University, UK
Silvio Peroni	University of Bologna, Italy
Sahar Vahdati	University of Bonn, Germany

Senior Program Committee

Timothy W. Clark	Harvard University, USA
Ivan Herman	World Wide Web Consortium
Pascal Hitzler	Wright State University, USA
Aldo Gangemi	University of Bologna, Italy
Enrico Motta	The Open University, UK
Cameron Neylon	Curtin University, Australia
Daniel Schwabe	Pontifical Catholic University of Rio de Janeiro, Brazil
Susanna Assunta Sansone	University of Oxford and Nature Publishing Group, UK
Cassidy Sugimoto	Indiana University Bloomington, USA
Simone Teufel	University of Cambridge, UK
Fabio Vitali	University of Bologna, Italy

Industrial Program Committee

Aliaksandr Birukou	Springer Nature, Germany
Anita de Waard	Elsevier, The Netherlands
Scott Edmunds	GigaScience/BGI Hong Kong, SAR China
Patricia Feeney	CrossRef, UK
Maarten Fröhlich	IOS Press, The Netherlands
Anna Lisa Gentile	IBM, USA
Paul Groth	Elsevier, The Netherlands
Laurel L. Haak	ORCID, USA
Rinke Hoekstra	Elsevier, The Netherlands
Thomas Ingraham	F1000Research, UK
Kris Jack	Mendeley, The Netherlands
Christoph Lange	CEUR-WS.org, Germany
Eamonn Maguire	Pictet Asset Management, Switzerland
Michele Pasin	Springer Nature, London
Lyubomir Penev	Pensoft Publishers, Bulgaria
Eric Prud'hommeaux	World Wide Web Consortium, USA

Paul Shannon   eLife, UK
Anna Tordai   Elsevier, The Netherlands
Alex Wade   Microsoft Research, UK

Academic Program Committee

Alfie Abdul-Rahman   University of Oxford, UK
Angelo Antonio Salatino   The Open University, UK
Andreas Behrend   University of Bonn, Germany
Andrea Bonaccorsi   University of Pisa, Italy
Davide Buscaldi   Université Paris 13, France
Paolo Ciancarini   University of Bologna, Italy
Paolo Ciccarese   Harvard University, USA
Oscar Corcho   Universidad Politécnica de Madrid, Spain
Hanna Ćwiek-Kupczyńska   Polish Academy of Sciences, Poland
Mathieu D'Aquin   Insight Centre for Data Analytics, Ireland
Rob Davey   Genome Analysis Centre, UK
Angelo Di Iorio   University of Bologna, Italy
Stefan Dietze   L3S Research Center, Germany
Ying Ding   Indiana University, USA
Said Fathalla   University of Bonn, Germany
Alexander Garcia   Universidad Politécnica de Madrid, Spain
Daniel Garijo   Information Sciences Institute, USA
Behnam Ghavimi   University of Bonn, Germany
Asunción Gómez Pérez   Universidad Politécnica de Madrid, Spain
Tudor Groza   Garvan Institute of Medical Research, Australia
Simon Harper   University of Manchester, UK
Tom Heath   Open Data Institute, UK
Drahomira Herrmannova   Oak Ridge National Laboratory, USA
Leyla Jael García Castro   European Bioinformatics Institute
Tomi Kauppinen   Aalto University, Finland
Sabrina Kirrane   Vienna University of Economics and Business, Austria
Petr Knoth   The Open University, UK
Tobias Kuhn   Vrije Universiteit Amsterdam, The Netherlands
Steffen Lohmann   Fraunhofer University, Germany
Andrea Mannocci   The Open University, UK
Philipp Mayr   Leibniz Institute for the Social Sciences, Germany
Giulio Napolitano   Fraunhofer Institute and University of Bonn, Germany
Terhi Nurmikko-Fuller   Australian National University, Australia
Andrea Giovanni Nuzzolese   Italian National Research Centre, Italy
Steve Pettifer   University of Manchester, UK
Francesco Poggi   University of Bologna, Italy
Philippe Rocca-Serra   University of Oxford, UK
Francesco Ronzano   Universitat Pompeu Fabra, Spain

Contents

Towards a Cloud-Based Service for Maintaining and Analyzing Data About Scientific Events

Andreas Behrend$^{(\boxtimes)}$, Sahar Vahdati, Christoph Lange, and Christiane Engels

Institute of Computer Science III, University of Bonn,
Römerstraße 164, 53117 Bonn, Germany
{behrend,vahdati,engelsc}@cs.uni-bonn.de, math.semantic.web@gmail.com

Abstract. We propose the new cloud-based service OpenResearch for managing and analyzing data about scientific events such as conferences and workshops in a persistent and reliable way. This includes data about scientific articles, participants, acceptance rates, submission numbers, impact values as well as organizational details such as program committees, chairs, fees and sponsoring. OpenResearch is a centralized repository for scientific events and supports researchers in collecting, organizing, sharing and disseminating information about scientific events in a structured way. An additional feature currently under development is the possibility to archive web pages along with the extracted semantic data in order to lift the burden of maintaining new and old conference web sites from public research institutions. However, the main advantage is that this cloud-based repository enables a comprehensive analysis of conference data. Based on extracted semantic data, it is possible to determine quality estimations, scientific communities, research trends as well the development of acceptance rates, fees and number of participants in a continuous way complemented by projections into the future. Furthermore, data about research articles can be systematically explored using a content-based analysis as well as citation linkage. All data maintained in this crowd-sourcing platform is made freely available through an open SPARQL endpoint, which allows for analytical queries in a flexible and user-defined way.

Keywords: Cloud service · Scientific data
Bibliographic information systems

1 Introduction

In computer science, scientific events like conferences and workshops form one of the most important ways of realizing fast publication of papers and bringing researchers together to present and discuss new results with peers. Information about such events is usually provided via web pages which are typically hosted by scientific organizations such as universities, research institutes, etc. Unfortunately, these organizations cannot ensure a reliable archive support, such that

A. González-Beltrán et al. (Eds.): SAVE-SD 2017/2018, LNCS 10959, pp. 1–14, 2018.
https://doi.org/10.1007/978-3-030-01379-0_1

many conference pages just vanish over time. Additionally, many auxiliary services like conference management systems, mailing lists, digital libraries etc. are employed in order to organize and disseminate data about scientific events, but these specialized systems provide selected information or analysis results only. This makes the analysis of scientific events complicated as a complete information record is usually not available. For example, if a researcher searches for a conference with moderate conference fees, a high quality ranking and a continuously growing community interested in the topic 'Graph Databases', a matching event is rather difficult to find.

Therefore, scholars frequently rely on individual experience, recommendations from colleagues or informal community wisdom in order to organize their scientific communication. Often, scholars just simply search the Web or subscribe to mailing lists in order to receive potentially relevant calls for papers (CfPs). Other sources like Google Scholar Metrics[1] or the British Research Excellence Framework are used for assessing the quality and topical relevance of scientific events. So, various internet sources need to be continuously consulted in order to obtain a comprehensive picture about the current research landscape. This complex analysis needs to be complemented by a bibliographic analysis in order to identify the most important research results, related papers, promising approaches as well as the search for the most active groups for a specific research topic. Despite some technical support by digital libraries and repositories on the Web, this analysis typically requires a lot of manual exploration work, e.g., by navigating the citations provided in sets of research articles.

As a solution to these organizational problems, we proposed the cloud-based service OpenResearch[2] for persistently storing, analyzing and maintaining data about scientific events in [7]. OpenResearch manages data about scientific articles, participants, acceptance rates, submission numbers, impact values as well as organizational details such as the structure of program committee, chairs, fees and sponsoring. It is a platform for automating or crowd-sourcing the collection and integration of semantically structured metadata about scholarly events.

In this paper, we introduce a design view for entities in OpenResearch complementing the existing data view. For conferences, this means the possibility to store and view conference homepages along with their factual datasheet. Conference homepages are a good source of metadata that can be used to provide a comprehensive analysis about scientific events or any other scholarly communication metadata. Storing plain HTML conference homepages in OpenResearch makes them accessible for future data analysis, as in future smarter information extraction tools might be developed that would extract from these archived homepages structured data, which would then be fed into OpenResearch's database. In fact, the benefit of the proposed solution is twofold: Having a centralized repository for scientific events supports researchers in collecting, organizing, sharing and disseminating information about scientific events in a structured way. At the same time, the burden of maintaining conference web sites is lifted from public institutions allowing to considerably lower their running cost for providing hosting services.

[1] https://scholar.google.com/intl/en/scholar/metrics.html.
[2] http://openresearch.org/.

OpenResearch is implemented using Semantic Media Wiki[3] (SMW) and provides a user interface for creating and editing semantically structured project descriptions, researcher and event profiles in a collaborative, agile 'wiki' way. By the application of SMW, semantic web features are integrated into the MediaWiki wiki engine best known from Wikipedia, enabling a comprehensive search and organization of wiki content. In particular, OpenResearch ...

1. represents a central storage for information about scientific events, projects and scholars e.g., hosting and archiving conference homepages
2. allows for freely annotating the data (e.g., quality measures, related events) based on results from user-defined queries
3. supports users in finding relevant events and event organizers in promoting their events
4. enables researchers to analyze metadata about scientific events or any other scholarly communication metadata

With the new functionality of providing a design view of the data, more text analysis tools need to be integrated in order to leverage the above mentioned features for data analyzes. In the future, the system will be extended by the functionality to store accepted papers of a given scientific event (e.g., by supporting the semantically structured subsets of HTML such as Research Articles in Simplified HTML (RASH)[4] or the format supported by the dokieli editor) as well as the possibility to store and display entire conference web pages along with their semantically enriched wikis. This way, we hope that a considerable part of research communication becomes freely available and analyzable in a sustainable way.

Section 2 of this paper presents the state of the art of existing approaches and services. Section 3 reviews the background of OpenResearch and the main challenges this project addresses. In Sect. 4 the approach and architecture of OpenResearch is presented and Sect. 5 presents the services that OpenResearch provides to its end users. Section 6 presents the current status of the OpenResearch project and discusses its future perspectives. Afterwards, we summarize and conclude the paper with Sect. 7.

2 Related Work

CfP Classification and Analysis: CfP Manager [4] is an information extraction tool for CfPs from the computer science domain. It extracts metadata of events from the unstructured text of CfPs focusing on keyword detection. Because of the different representations and terminologies across research communities, this approach requires domain specific implementations. CfP Manager neither supports comprehensive data analysis nor data curation workflows involving multiple stakeholders. Hurtado Martin et al. proposed an approach based on user

---

[3] http://www.semantic-mediawiki.org/.
[4] https://github.com/essepuntato/rash.

profiles, which takes a scholar's recent publication list and recommends related CfPs using content analysis [3]. Xia et al. presented a classification method to filter CfPs by social tagging [10]. Wang et al. proposed another approach to classify CfPs by implementing three different methods but focus on comparing the classification methods rather than services to improve scientific communication [9]. Paperleap[5] is a commercial tool for analyzing CfPs and provide recommendations for users. The two well-known digital libraries in the field of computer science provide event support for researchers: ACM[6] hosts webpages for their conferences and IEEE upcoming events with deadlines9.

CfP Dissemination: DBWorld[7] collects data about upcoming events and other announcements in the field of databases and information systems. WikiCFP[8] is a popular service for publishing CfPs on the Web. Like DBWorld, WikiCFP only supports a limited set of structured event metadata (title, dates, deadlines), which results in limited search and exploration functionality. WikiCFP employs crawlers to track high-profile conferences. Although WikiCFP claims to be a semantic wiki, there is neither collaborative authoring nor visioning and the data is neither downloadable as RDF nor accessible via a SPARQL endpoint. CFPList[9] works similarly to WikiCFP but focuses on social science related subjects. Data is contributed by the community using an online form. SemanticScholar[10] offers a keyword-based search facility that shows metadata about publications and authors. It uses artificial intelligence methods for retrieving highly relevant search results but offers no arbitrary user-defined queries.

Quality Estimation Approaches: Google Scholar Metrics (GSM) provides ranked lists of conferences and journals by scientific field based on a 5-year impact analysis over the Google Scholar citation data. 20 top-ranked conferences and journals are shown for each (sub-)field. The ranking is based on the two metrics h5-index and h5-median. GSM's ranking method only considers the number of citations, whereas we intend to offer a multi-disciplinary service with a flexible search mechanism based on several quality metrics.

Data Collections: DBLP, one of the most widely known bibliographic databases in computer science, provides information mainly about publications but also considers related entities such as authors, editors, conference proceedings and journals. Events, deadlines and subjects are out of DBLP's scope. DBLP allows event organizers to upload XML data with bibliographic data for ingestion. The dataset of DBLP is available as an RDF dump. ScholarlyData provides RDF dumps for scientific events. A new conference ontology developed for ScholarlyData improves over already existing ones about scientific events such as the

---

[5] http://www.paperleap.com/.
[6] http://www.acm.org/conferences.
[7] https://research.cs.wisc.edu/dbworld/.
[8] http://www.wikicfp.com/.
[9] https://www.cfplist.com/.
[10] https://www.semanticscholar.org/.

Semantic Web Dog Food ontology. Springer LOD[11] is a portal for publishing conference metadata collected from the traditional publishing process of Springer as Linked Open Data. All these conferences are related to Computer Science. The data is available through a SPARQL endpoint, which makes it possible to search or browse the data. A graph visualization of the results is also available. For each conference, there is information about its acronym, location and time, and a link to the conferences series. The aim of this service is to enrich Springer's own metadata and link them to related datasets in the LOD Cloud.

Other Services: Conference.city[12] is a new service initialized in 2016 that lists upcoming conferences by location. For each conference, title, date, deadline, location and number of views of its conference.city page are shown. The service collects data mainly from event homepages and from mailing lists. In addition, it allows users to add a conference using a form. PapersInvited18 focuses on collecting CfPs from event organizers and attracting potential participants who already have access to the ProQuest service. ProQuest acts as a hub between repositories holding rich and diverse scholarly data. The collected data is not made available to the public. EasyChair is a conference management system allowing organizers to publish CfPs and authors find calls relevant to them. ResearchGate21 is a social networking site for sharing papers and find potential collaborators. Lanyrd[13] is a general service that allows everyone to add or discover new professional as well as scientific events. However, the keyword-based search offered by this service hardly allows for a comprehensive data analysis and the metadata shown for an event is restricted to dates and event locations.

Conclusion: Only Cfplist supports an advanced query search but no free access to their data by means of a LOD set. Free LOD dumps are provided by CiteSeer. ScholarlyData and Springer LOD but no advanced query support. The possibility to advertise events by means of distributing CfPs in a goal-directed way and hosting entire web pages in addition to semantic wikis is not supported at all so far.

3   Open Research Methodology

In [7], we introduced OpenResearch and its general architecture and different views of quality-related queries. In this paper we extend the application range of OpenResearch as a crowd-sourcing platform which provides hosting and archiving services for conference homepages and researcher profiles. Figure 1 depicts the general phases which typically occur during the organization of a conference. With the new extensions, OpenResearch can support conference organizers in various stages with a wide range of features. For realizing these features, the following problems and challenges needed to be solved.

---

[11] http://lod.springer.com/.

[12] http://conference.city/.

[13] https://lanyrd.com/.

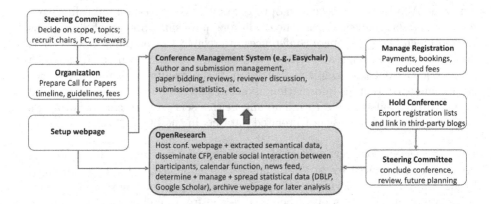

Fig. 1. Role of OpenResearch in the workflow of academic conference management

Promoting Events: Typically, research communities use CfPs in order to promote a scientific event. To this end, various communication channels are used to distribute CfPs like mailing lists or CfP wikis (e.g., WikiCFP). In most cases, CfPs contain unstructured data and the way of distributing them hardly allows for any systematic analysis. Consequently, potential authors or participants easily overlook relevant events and interesting analysis results like changes in topic coverage, fees and PC structure have to be manually explored. Therefore, OpenResearch provides a central repository for CfPs along with extracted semantically structured data for querying them. To this end, we developed assistants that facilitate individual as well as bulk input of CfP related data in a consistent way. Based on that, relationships between conferences and subscription lists for users can be provided in order to simplify the search for relevant events. The relevance and intrinsic complexity of this task is underlined by the fact that the recently founded company Paperleap is solely specialized on this kind of analysis alone.

Diversity of Event Structure: There are structural differences across events, for example, events with many co-located events or sub-events, or new events emerged from multiple smaller ones. One example for the latter is the Conference on Intelligent Computer Mathematics (CICM), which results from the convergence of four conferences that used to be separate but now are tracks of a single conference. In order to support researchers in finding a suitable event, we need to automatically track and present this kind of structural information and developments for events over time. In addition, this information ought to become queryable as it may indicate changes in the underlying community. For example, in the late 90's several logic programming conferences merged into symposiums indicating a decline in the interest from the respective research community.

Tracking Event History: A large number of events are one-off workshops which may be collocated with other events. On the other hand, most scientific events occur in series or are associated with an event series, whose individual editions took place in different locations with narrow topical changes. Researchers often need to explore several resources to obtain an overview of the previous editions of an event series to be able to estimate the quality of the next upcoming event in this series. In OpenResearch, we want to provide a quick overview of past editions and changes over time in order to support researchers in this search. Providing a complete history of event related data also allows for projections into future developments such as likely increases of conference fees or number of participants.

Addressing Different Stakeholders: Event organizers aim to attract as many submitters as possible to their events. Publishers want to know whether they should accept a particular event's proceedings in their renowned proceedings series. Potential PC members want to decide whether it is worth spending time in the reviewing process of an event. Similarly, sponsors and invited speakers need to decide whether a certain event is worth sponsoring or attending. Researchers receiving CfP emails have to distinguish whether the event is appropriate for presenting their work. Researchers searching for events through various communication channels assess events based on criteria such as thematic relevance, feasibility of the deadline, location, low registration fee etc. The organizers of smaller events who plan to organize their event as a sub-event of a bigger event have to decide whether this is the right venue to co-locate with. These examples (for further background see [2]) prove the importance of filtering events by topic and quality from the point of view of different stakeholders. Although, quality of events have huge aspect in the competition of events, the space of information around scientific events is organized in a cumbersome way. Thus preventing events' stakeholders from making informed decisions, and preventing a competition of events around quality, economy and efficiency.

Different Presentation Views: Till now, OpenResearch presents event related information just in the form of wiki pages. The disadvantage of this uniform presentation of data is that the user has no control over the design in which he wants to present his research profile or well-established conference series. Therefore, we are currently extending OpenResearch in order to support two views of the data: a customized presentation view and a semantic data view. Figure 2 shows the two views of the workshop SMWCon 2016 both hosted at OpenResearch. Storing the web pages of an event supports event organizers in archiving their data. In case that not all event related information has been automatically extracted, the stored web pages basically represent original sources from which further information can be subsequently retrieved. In addition, the web presence of a planned or currently active conferences can be directly managed with OpenResearch and no local island solutions are needed. Quite similar idea to GitHub Jekyll[14] which is a static site generator with already existed GitHub Pages, we want to establish links between extracted semantic data and its presentation in order to support the propagation of subsequent changes.

---

[14] https://github.com/jekyll/.

Data View   Design View

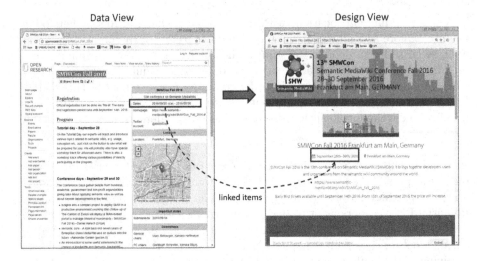

Fig. 2. Two presentation views for SMWCon 2016 conference in OpenResearch

OpenResearch provides a centralized and holistic infrastructure for managing the information about scientific events and researchers. The integration of various services such as ontology based text analysis, user-defined queries and different presentation views, leads to a complex system design with a considerable number of submodules to be coordinated (cf. architecture in Sect. 4). OpenResearch is a cloud service with high requirements with respect to data load and access rates. The latter is not so problematic with respect to simple data access as the amount of event related data is manageable small. In order to provide high access rates for complex query results, however, we need to employ and configure a scaling SPARQL engine with a balanced resource distribution for users. At the moment, we are still using Blazegraph but performance studies (e.g., [6]) already suggest system changes in the future. Finally, a reliable backup service needs to be provided in order to satisfy the quality needs of event organizers and users.

4   Extended System Architecture

OpenResearch is a semantic wiki that balances manual (or crowd-sourced) contributions and (semi)auto-generated content. It follows the semantic wiki paradigm of instant gratification in that it aims to reduce the pain of manual data input by assistants and gives immediate access to visual analyses generated from the data just entered [1]. In Fig. 3 the three layered architecture of the system is depicted. The data gathering layer contains functionality to import event related information. To this end, data extraction tools for analyzing event homepages, web feeds as well as a crawling script for exploring various event related web sources such as WikiCFP or DBLP can be employed. In addition, registered users can create and modify event related content. OpenResearch offers flexible forms for events as well as event related web sites in order to enter data.

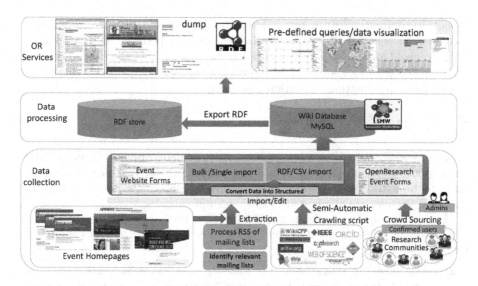

Fig. 3. OpenResearch architecture

In the data processing layer, two database management systems are used to store and query the schema information and generated semantic triples, respectively. The underlying SMW supports various triple stores; we decided to use Blazegraph because of its performance and quality. A MySQL database instance is employed to store templates, properties and forms. OpenResearch applies a comprehensive ontology by reusing existing vocabularies (including the Semantic Web Conference Ontology and the Semantic Web Portal Ontology) and extending them with new properties25. Our ontology is stored and maintained by SMW as properties and categories. The alignment of wiki properties to ontology properties is realized using the SMW mechanism for importing vocabularies.

The service layer of OpenResearch offers various possibilities for consuming the stored data. The underlying SMW provides a full-text search facility and the visualization of their results. In addition, the RDF triple store can be accessed via a SPARQL endpoint or a downloadable RDF dump. Events, CfPs and user profiles are presented as individual wiki pages including a semantic representation of their metadata. Various query results are also visualized, including event locations on a map or event related deadlines using a calendar function.

Aside from wiki articles, OpenResearch is extended for supporting the presentation of the original design of event related web pages. This way, the system becomes an archive of old event web pages and its content which may have not been completely semantically extracted yet. The same service will be offered for user profiles such that researchers can better advertise their achievements in contrast to just presenting a uniform fact sheet about themselves. Aside from just archiving data for presentation, OpenResearch automatically analyzes the HTML code for extracting additional metadata about the given event and maintains this information in the respective fact sheet of the data view. In addition, a component is added which synchronizes changes made to these linked items in order to avoid any inconsistencies between the two views of the data. This way, even the content of a conference web page becomes partly queryable due to the incorporated information extraction mechanism.

5   Use Cases

In the following, we outline a few use cases that demonstrate how OpenResearch can support the analysis of metadata of scientific events. We imagine such services to be extended by interlinking OpenResearch data with other relevant datasets. Prefixes are eliminated from the sample queries.

Event-related: One challenging question that every researcher is interested in is a list of the most competitive, and thus, possibly, highest-quality conferences on their research topic.

```
# Q1:conferences of topic "Semantic Web" ordered based on acceptance rate?
        SELECT ?event ?startDate ?country ?wikipage ?acceptanceRate WHERE {
            ?e a ?EventTypes ;
            rdfs:label ?event ;
            ...
            property:Acceptance_rate ?acceptanceRate ;
            property:Has_location_city ?city ;
            swivt:page ?wikipage.
        FILTER (DATATYPE(?endDate) != xsd:double &&
                DATATYPE(?startDate) != xsd:double)
        } ORDER BY ASC(?acceptanceRate) LIMIT 10
        BINDINGS ?EventTypes {(smwont:ConferenceEvent)}
```

The result of this query is a list of high quality events with their corresponding acceptance rate, location and start date as well as a link to their wiki page. This can be extended to the event series level instead of having the list of individual editions of an event series. Another difficult and time consuming task for researchers, especially young ones, is to get an overview of event series of an given topic.

```
# Q2: Life time of top five event series in the Semantic Web field
        SELECT (AVG(?num_year) AS ?averaged_life_long) WHERE
        { SELECT ?series (COUNT(DISTINCT ?startDate) AS ?num_year) WHERE
        {   ?series a category:Event_series, category:Semantic_Web.
            ...
            FILTER (DATATYPE(?endDate) != xsd:double &&
                DATATYPE(?startDate) != xsd:double)
        } GROUP BY ?series ORDER BY DESC(?num_year) LIMIT 5
        }
```

The result of this query is shown in a default table view as a number representing the average lifetime of corresponding event series in the Semantic Web field, which is 9.5 years. Identifying scientific topic movement is challenging because it is hard to define an objective notion of it [8].

One of the possible ways to get insights on this challenge is to look at the movement of submission numbers for specific topics in their corresponding scientific events. In this way, one can see whether a topic is growing by the interest of active researchers in it. The following query addresses this issue.

```
# Q3: Topic movement?
      SELECT  ?series ?numEvents ?topic ?events ?years WHERE{
        ?series a ?topic.
        ?topic rdfs:subClassOf category:Computer_Science.
        FILTER(?numEvents = 10).
        {
          SELECT  ?series
            (COUNT(?e) AS ?numEvents)
            (GROUP_CONCAT(DISTINCT ?e; separator="; ") AS ?events)
            (GROUP_CONCAT(DISTINCT ?startDate; separator="; ") AS ?years)
          WHERE {
            ?e rdfs:label ?event ;
               a smwont:ConferenceEvent ;
               property:Event_in_series ?series ;
               property:Submitted_papers ?num_papers .
            ...
            FILTER (DATATYPE(?endDate) != xsd:double &&
                    DATATYPE(?startDate) != xsd:double).
            FILTER (?startDate >= "2007-01-01"^^xsd:date &&
                    ?endDate < "2017-01-01"^^xsd:date).
          }GROUP BY ?series
        }
```

Person-Related: In what event did a given person have some role (e.g., chair, PC member or participant). Consider Harith Alani as an example and look for his roles in different events over the last few years. Note that right now these queries are run over OpenResearch's data only; therefore other roles held by this person might not be in this list.

```
# Q4: Researchers's roles in event?
  SELECT ?event ?person ?hasRole WHERE {
    ?e rdfs:label ?event ;
       ?hasRole ?person.
    ?hasRole rdfs:subPropertyOf property:Has_person.
    ?person rdfs:label "Harith Alani".
    ...
  }
```

This way a list of events and roles of the given person is generated. One can add more properties of these events to be shown in the final results. This kind of questions could help researchers who want to attend events to plan their networking when they are interested to meet certain key people in their research field.

History-Related: Recommendations are another service that OpenResearch is aiming to offer. Providing such recommendation services need to have a history of properties and values of them. Basically any property of an event can be used to obtain insights on the upcoming events by extrapolation from the history of that property. Based on the following query one could extrapolate the possible registration fee of the coming edition:

```
# Q5: registration fees of recent events
SELECT  ?series
   (COUNT(?e) AS ?numEvents)
   (GROUP_CONCAT(DISTINCT ?attendFee; separator="; ") AS ?fees)
   (GROUP_CONCAT(DISTINCT ?e; separator="; ") AS ?events)
   (GROUP_CONCAT(DISTINCT ?startDate; separator="; ") AS ?years)
WHERE {

   ...
   ?e property:Attendance_fee ?attendFee.
   FILTER (DATATYPE(?endDate) != xsd:double &&
              DATATYPE(?startDate) != xsd:double).
   FILTER (?startDate >= "2014-01-01"^^xsd:date &&
              ?endDate < "2017-01-01"^^xsd:date).
} GROUP BY ?series
```

The result of this query is a list of individual events with their registration fees. Usually, researchers start searching for possible events to submit their research results as soon as they have made interesting and new achievements. This timing might not be aligned with the schedule of relevant and high quality events. CfPs are typically announced a few months before an event, but researchers might overlook them. A good way of supporting researchers is to give them suggestions of time periods in which they can expect CfPs for relevant events. With the below query we explore over OpenResearch to find periods of year in which most events for a specific field or topic have been held.

```
# Q6: When to submit?
        SELECT ?month (COUNT(?e) AS ?numEvents) WHERE
        {
          ?e rdfs:label ?event;
            ...
            a category:Semantic_Web.
          FILTER (DATATYPE(?endDate) != xsd:double &&
          DATATYPE(?startDate) != xsd:double)
          FILTER (?startDate >= "2016-01-01"^^xsd:date &&
   ?endDate < "2017-01-01"^^xsd:date).
          VALUES ?month {1 .. 12}
          FILTER ( month(?startDate) <= ?month &&
                 ?month <= month(?endDate) )
        } GROUP BY ?month
```

Further extending this query by considering the submission deadline, researchers can effectively plan their activities as well as exporting data about an event into applications such as conferenceLive26.

6   Current Status and Perspectives

OpenResearch, currently in prototype state, is a crowd-sourcing platform with more than 300 registered users. The system has been developed according to the KIDS methodology for evolving applications [5]. OpenResearch has so far been used on the OpenResearch.org site; however, as it is technically a set of plugins and configuration rules on top of MediaWiki and its SMW extension, it could in principle be installed anywhere else as well (using data imported from the OpenResearch.org site, or using other, site-specific data), but this has so far not been documented. There exists a rudimentary GitHub repository hosting the source code of a few import filters and with a few issues being tracked; so far only the core development team has used it.

The project is part of a greater research and development agenda for enabling open access to all types of scholarly communication metadata not just from a legal but also from a technical perspective. In addition to easy and open access to such a knowledge graph, it has the potential to serve as a unique integrated environment for comprehensive analyzes on top of the metadata. The size of the community potentially interested in collaboratively analyzing scholarly communication metadata using the extended OpenResearch software can be estimated from the venues that bring together researchers with related interests: the Semantics, Analytics, Visualization: Enhancing Scholarly Data (SAVE-SD) workshop at the International World Wide Web (WWW) Conference (yearly since 2015; usually involving 35 authors), the Big Scholarly Data (BigScholar) workshop also at WWW (since 2014; 30 authors), the Scholarly Big Data workshop at AAAI (since 2015; 20 authors), the Semantic Publishing Challenge at the ESWC Semantic Web Conference (since 2014; 20), as well as sub-communities of the Scientometrics journal, the OpenSym conference on open collaboration, and of several Semantic Web, Digital Libraries and Knowledge Management conferences.

In order to ensure future sustainability of OpenResearch we are pursuing a two-fold strategy: First, we are planning to establish an OpenResearch Foundation in order to govern the platform. Secondly, we are trying to improve the reusability of the OpenResearch software so that third parties can more easily install and operate it on their own and thus contribute to building a decentral, interlinked knowledge-base about research results.

7   Conclusion

We presented the OpenResearch platform, which supports researchers in finding the most suitable event for their publications according to various criteria. In particular, OpenResearch allows for comprehensively querying semantically structured metadata about scholarly events. Young or even unknown events can benefit from that and can become attractive for authors due to certain quality metrics despite still being poorly ranked in general (e.g. by impact). Organizers can also benefit from our this platform because the quantification of quality becomes transparent and possibilities of positively influencing quality metrics can be systematically explored. In addition, the temporal evolution of the assessment metrics can be investigated, which allows for identifying the stability of certain quality indicators such as the acceptance rate. This plays an important role for sponsors and other long-term partners. As an additional feature, we are investigating the archiving of web pages along with the semantic data extracted from them. First, this would lift the burden of maintaining new and old conference web sites from public research institutions; secondly, it would support evolution and evaluation of information extraction: once better information extraction tools become available, one could re-apply them to the archived conference web sites.

Acknowledgments. This work has been partially funded by the European Commission under grant agreements no. 643410 and the German Research Foundation (DFG) under grant agreement AU 340/9-1.

References

1. Aumüller, D., Auer, S.: Towards a semantic wiki experience - desktop integration and interactivity in WikSAR. In: Proceedings of the 1st Workshop on The Semantic Desktop - Next Generation Personal Information Management and Collaboration Infrastructure (2005)
2. Bryl, V., Birukou, A., Eckert, K., Kessler, M.: What's in the proceedings? Combining publisher's and researcher's perspectives. In: 4th Workshop on Semantic Publishing (SePublica), no. 1155, CEUR Workshop Proceedings (2014)
3. Hurtado Martín, G., Schockaert, S., Cornelis, C., Naessens, H.: An exploratory study on content-based filtering of call for papers. In: Lupu, M., Kanoulas, E., Loizides, F. (eds.) IRFC 2013. LNCS, vol. 8201, pp. 58–69. Springer, Heidelberg (2013). https://doi.org/10.1007/978-3-642-41057-4_7
4. Issertial, L., Tsuji, H.: Information extraction for call for paper. Int. J. Knowl. Syst. Sci. (IJKSS) **6**(4), 35–49 (2015)
5. Liu, Z.H., Behrend, A., Chan E.S., Gawlick, D., Ghoneimy, A.: KIDS - a model for developing evolutionary database applications. In: DATA 2012, pp. 129–134. SciTePress (2012)
6. Morsey, M., Lehmann, J., Auer, S., Ngonga Ngomo, A.-C.: DBpedia SPARQL benchmark – performance assessment with real queries on real data. In: Aroyo, L., et al. (eds.) ISWC 2011. LNCS, vol. 7031, pp. 454–469. Springer, Heidelberg (2011). https://doi.org/10.1007/978-3-642-25073-6_29
7. Vahdati, S., Arndt, N., Auer, S., Lange, C.: OpenResearch: collaborative management of scholarly communication metadata. In: Blomqvist, E., Ciancarini, P., Poggi, F., Vitali, F. (eds.) EKAW 2016. LNCS (LNAI), vol. 10024, pp. 778–793. Springer, Cham (2016). https://doi.org/10.1007/978-3-319-49004-5_50
8. Vahdati, S., Behrend, A., Schüller, G., Lange, C.: A flexible system for a comprehensive analysis of bibliographical data. In: WEBIST 2014, pp. 143–151 (2014)
9. Wang, H.-D., Wu, J.: Collaborative filtering of call for papers. In: IEEE Symposium Series on Computational Intelligence, pp. 963–970 (2015)
10. Xia, J., et al.: Optimizing academic conference classification using social tags. In: IEEE Computational Science and Engineering, pp. 289–294 (2010)

ILastic: Linked Data Generation Workflow and User Interface for iMinds Scholarly Data

Anastasia Dimou[1,2(✉)], Gerald Haesendonck[1], Martin Vanbrabant[1],
Laurens De Vocht[1], Ruben Verborgh[1], Steven Latré[2], and Erik Mannens[1]

[1] IDLab, IMEC, Ghent University, Ghent, Belgium
{anastasia.dimou,gerald.haesendonck,martin.vanbrabant,laurens.vocht,
ruben.verborgh,erik.mannens}@ugent.be
[2] IDLab, IMEC, University of Antwerp, Antwerpen, Belgium

Abstract. Enriching scholarly data with metadata enhances the publications' meaning. Unfortunately, different publishers of overlapping or complementary scholarly data neglect general-purpose solutions for metadata and instead use their own ad-hoc solutions. This leads to duplicate efforts and entails non-negligible implementation and maintenance costs. In this paper, we propose a reusable Linked Data publishing workflow that can be easily adjusted by different data owners to (i) generate and publish Linked Data, and (ii) align scholarly data repositories with enrichments over the publications' content. As a proof-of-concept, the proposed workflow was applied to the iMinds research institute data warehouse, which was aligned with publications' content derived from Ghent University's digital repository. Moreover, we developed a user interface to help lay users with the exploration of the iLastic Linked Data set. Our proposed approach relies on a general-purpose workflow. This way, we manage to reduce the development and maintenance costs and increase the quality of the resulting Linked Data.

1 Introduction

Semantic publishing (i) enhances the meaning of publications by enriching them with metadata, (ii) facilitates its automated discovery and summarization, (iii) enables its interlinking, (iv) provides access to data within the article in actionable form, and (v) facilitates its integration [20]. Scholarly publishing has undergone a digital revolution with massive uptake of online provision, but it has not realized the potential offered by the Web [20], let alone the Semantic Web. Even though the latter allows providing identifiers and machine-readable metadata for the so-called *enhanced-publications* [3], benefits come at a cost.

Ad-hoc solutions were established so far for generating Linked Data from scholarly data. Therefore, even though different data owners may hold overlapping or complementary data, new implementations are developed every time, customized to each publishers' infrastructure. Such approaches are adopted not

© Springer Nature Switzerland AG 2018
A. González-Beltrán et al. (Eds.): SAVE-SD 2017/2018, LNCS 10959, pp. 15–32, 2018.
https://doi.org/10.1007/978-3-030-01379-0_2

only by *individual efforts*, such as COLINDA[1] [21], but also by *publishing companies*, such as Springer[2] or the Semantic Web journal[3], as well as *large-scale initiatives*, such as OpenAIRE LOD[4] [23]. Nevertheless, this leads to duplicate efforts which entail non-negligible implementation and maintenance costs. The DBLP computer science bibliography[5] is one of the few exceptions, as it relies on an established approach, the D2RQ language [5] and its corresponding implementation, which is reusable and the Linked Data set is reproducible.

Workflows that semantically annotate scholarly data from repositories with structured data, generate Linked Data sets which remain independent, whereas the actual publications' content enrichment is rarely published as a Linked Data set. Besides the structured metadata regarding researchers and their publications, additional complementary information might be derived from the publications' actual content by extracting and semantically annotating it. While there are many approaches proposed for identifying entities in publications and associating them with well-known entities, such as [2,19] and others summarized at [11], publishing such metadata as a coherent Linked Data set and, even more, associating them with complementary metadata from repositories with structured data does not frequently and systematically happen so far. In this context, Bagnacani et al. [1] identified the most prevalent fragments of scholarly data publishing approaches: (i) bibliographic, (ii) authorship, and (iii) citations.

In this paper, we present a general-purpose Linked Data publishing workflow, adjusted to scholarly data publishing, which can be used by different data owners. The proposed workflow is applied in the case of the iLastic[6] Linked Data set generation and publishing for the iMinds[7] research institute's scholarly (meta)data. The workflow is complemented by an easily adjustable and extensible user interface which allows users to explore the underlying Linked Data. The scope is to align the Linked Data generation workflow for structured data with the plain text enrichment services developed in particular for iLastic.

The remainder of the paper is organized as follows: In the next section (Sect. 2), the state of the art is summarized. Then, in Sect. 3, the iLastic project is introduced, followed by the iLastic model (Sect. 4), the vocabularies used to annotate the data (Sect. 5) and the details about the generated Linked Data set (Sect. 6). Then the iLastic Linked Data generation workflow is presented (Sect. 7), followed by the iLastic user interface (Sect. 8). Last, in Sect. 9, we summarize our conclusions and our plans for future work.

---

[1] http://www.colinda.org/.
[2] http://lod.springer.com.
[3] http://semantic-web-journal.com/sejp/page/semanticWebJournal.
[4] http://beta.lod.openaire.eu/.
[5] http://dblp.l3s.de/dblp++.php.
[6] http://explore.ilastic.be.
[7] https://www.iminds.be/.

2   State of the Art

In this section, we indicatively mention a few existing solutions for scholarly data enrichment and its corresponding Linked Data set generation and publication.

COnference LInked DAta (See footnote 1) (COLINDA) [21] exposes information about scientific events, like conferences and workshops, for the period from 2007 up to 2013. It is one of the first Linked Data sets published on scholarly data, thus it is a custom solution which cannot be reused by any other data publisher who maintains similar data, as it might occur with the solution we propose. The data is derived from WikiCfP[8] and Eventseer[9]. COLINDA uses as input a harmonized and preprocessed CSV which contains data from the two aforementioned data sources. The CSV is imported into a MySQL database and a batch process is used to generate the corresponding Linked Data, whereas in our proposed solution, the CSV can be used directly and any data process may be applied during the Linked Data generation.

Even though OpenAIRE LOD [23], the Open Access Infrastructure for Research in Europe[10], was recently launched, it still relied on a custom solution to generate its Linked Data set from OpenAIRE Information Space which cannot be reused by any other data publisher. As performance and scalability were major concerns, a MapReduce [7] processing strategy was preferred. The original data is available in HBase[11], XML[12] and CSV[13] formats. Among the three formats, CSV was preferred to be used for the Linked Data set generation as it is not much slower than HBase, but it is much more maintainable [23]. Besides the CSV file which contains the actual data, an additional manually composed CSV is provided with relations about duplicate records.

The Semantic Lancet Project [1] publishes Linked Data for scholarly publications from Science Direct[14] and Scopus[15]. Its Linked Data set is generated relying on a series of custom scripts. Therefore, incorporating a new data source requires writing such a custom script, whereas in our solution, it is only required to provide the resource's description. Nevertheless, it is one of the few Linked Data sets for scholarly data whose Linked Data set is enhanced with more knowledge derived from the publications' content. This is achieved relying on FRED[16], a tool that parses natural language text, and implements deep machine learning.

DBLP computer science bibliography (DBLP) (See footnote 5) is one of the exceptions, as it relies on an established and, thus reusable and reproducible, approach to generate its Linked Data set. The FacetedDBLP (See footnote 5) is generated from data residing in DBLP databases by executing mapping rules

---

[8] http://www.wikicfp.com/cfp/.

[9] http://eventseer.net/.

[10] https://www.openaire.eu/.

[11] https://hbase.apache.org/.

[12] https://www.w3.org/TR/xml11/.

[13] https://tools.ietf.org/html/rfc4180.

[14] http://www.sciencedirect.com/.

[15] https://scopus.com/.

[16] http://wit.istc.cnr.it/stlab-tools/fred.

described in D2RQ mapping language [5], the predecessor of the W3C recommended R2RML [6], and published using a D2R server[17] instance. Nevertheless, D2RQ may only be used with data residing or imported in a database, whereas our solution may also support data in other structures derived from different access interfaces.

The Semantic Web Dog Food[18] (SWDF) contains metadata for the ESWC and ISWC Semantic Web conferences. Its Linked Data is generated from data derived from small size spreadsheets, tables or lists in documents, and HTML pages. The input data after being extracted, is turned into XML format which is further processed (i.e. cleansed) or non-RDF BibTeX and iCalendar documents. The former is produced manually using a generic XML editor and custom scripts were developed to generate the Linked Data. The latter allows to use some more automated tools, such as the bibtex2rdf converter[19] or Python scripts[20]. A detailed description process of the SWDF's generation is available at [18].

Lately, the SWDF dataset was migrated to Scholarly Data[21]. Conference Linked Open Data Generator[22] (cLODg) [14] is the tool used to generate the Scholarly Data Linked Data set. Besides, DBLP, this is one of the tools whose generated Linked Data set may be reproduced and the tool itself may be reused. It uses D2R conversions, as DBLP, but it also requires data derived from different data sources to be turned into CSV files which, on their turn, are ingested into a SQL database. With our proposed approach, we manage even to avoid this preprocessing step and directly use the original data sources [13], reducing the required effort and maintenance costs and increasing at the same time the reusability of our workflow and the reproducibility of the generated Linked Data.

3   The iLastic Project

The iLastic project was launched by the iMinds research institute in 2015 and aims to publish scholarly data which is associated with researchers affiliated with any of the iMinds labs. The iMinds labs are spread across Flanders' universities, thus researchers affiliated with iMinds are also affiliated with a university and their publications are archived by both iMinds and the corresponding university. To be more precise, iMinds maintains its own data warehouse (DWH) with metadata related to its researchers, the labs they belong to, publications they co-author, and projects they work on. The project aims to enrich information derived from data in the iMinds data warehouse with knowledge extracted from the publications' content. To achieve that, Flemish universities' digital repositories were considered, as they provide the full content of open accessed publications.

---

[17] http://d2rq.org/d2r-server.
[18] http://data.semanticweb.org/.
[19] http://www.l3s.de/~siberski/bibtex2rdf/.
[20] http://www.w3.org/2002/12/cal/.
[21] http://www.scholarlydata.org/.
[22] https://github.com/anuzzolese/cLODg2.

The project relies on (i) an in-house *general-purpose Linked Data generation workflow for structured data*, which was used for semantically annotating the data derived from the iMinds data warehouse; (ii) an in-house *publications retrieval and enrichment mechanism* developed for the project needs; and (iii) an *extensible and adjustable user interface* to facilitate non-Semantic Web expert users to search and explore the semantically enriched data.

The project was conducted in two phases:

Phase 1: Proof of Concept. In the first phase, the goal was to provide a *proof-of-concept* regarding the feasibility of the solution and its potential with respect to the expected results, namely showing the target milestones can be reached. In this phase, we mainly relied on selected data retrieved from the iMinds data warehouse, regarding persons, publications, organizations (universities and labs) and projects. Those entities formed the first version of the iLastic dataset.

Phase 2: Enrichment, Packaging and Automatization. In the second phase, two goals were posed: (i) enrich the first version of the iLastic Linked Data with knowledge extracted from the publications' content, and (ii) automate the Linked Data generation workflow to systematically generate Linked Data from the iMinds data warehouse, enrich them and publish them altogether. The complete workflow is now executed in the beginning of each month. In this phase, we packaged the solution, so other research institutes only need to configure their own rules for their data and repositories to generate their own Linked Data.

4   The iLastic Model

The iLastic dataset consists of data that describe (i) people, (ii) publications, (iii) projects and (iv) organizations. More details follow in this section about each type of entity, as well as challenges we had to deal with for the first two.

4.1   People

The iLastic dataset consists of data regarding people who work for iMinds, but not exclusively. They might be researchers, who belong to one of the iMinds labs and were authors of publications. Besides researchers affiliated with iMinds, many more people might appear in the iMinds data warehouse, even though they do not belong in any of the iMinds labs, thus they are not iMinds personnel but they co-authored one or more papers with one or more researchers from iMinds.

People are associated with their publications, their organizations, and, on rare occasions, with the projects they are involved in if their role is known, for instance if they are the project or research leads or the contact persons.

Challenges. iMinds personnel is identified with a unique identifier which the CRM system assigns to each person. However, researchers, who are co-authors in publications and do not belong to any of the iMinds labs, are not assigned such a unique identifier, as they are not iMinds personnel.

Therefore, there were three major challenges that we needed to address: (i) *distinguish iMinds researchers* from *non-iMinds researchers*; and (ii) among the non-iMinds researchers, *identify the same person* appearing in the dataset multiple times, being only aware of the researchers name (and on certain occasions their affiliation). Besides the data from the iMinds data warehouse, integrating information extracted from the papers' content required us to deal with one more challenge: (iii) *associate authors extracted from the publications' content* with the people that appear in the iMinds data warehouse.

4.2   Publications

The iLastic dataset also includes information regarding publications published by researchers when, at least one of the co-authors, is an iMinds researcher. As with iMinds researchers, each publication that is registered in iMinds data warehouse is assigned a unique identifier. Nevertheless, even though the iMinds data warehouse includes some information regarding publications, it refers mainly to metadata, such as the title, authors publication date or category. There is no information regarding the actual content of publications. To enrich the information regarding publications, we considered integrating data from complementary repositories, namely universities' repositories, such as Ghent University Academic Bibliography digital repository[23] or the digital repository for KU Leuven Association research[24]. These repositories also provide the PDF file of open access publications which can be parsed and analyzed to derive more information.

Challenges. There were two challenges encountered with respect to publications' semantic annotation: (i) *aligning* publications as they appear in the iMinds data warehouse with corresponding publications in universities' repositories, and (ii) *enriching* the structured data annotation derived from the iMinds data warehouse with plain text enrichment derived from the publications' actual content.

To be more precise, in the former case, we needed to define the proper algorithms and heuristics which allowed us to identify the publications' content by comparing the titles of the publications, as they appear in the iMinds data warehouse, with the titles as extracted from the publications' PDF. In the latter case, once the PDF of a certain publication was identified, the extraction of meaningful keywords, the recognition of well-known entities among those keywords, and the enrichment of the publications with this additional knowledge was required.

---

[23] https://biblio.ugent.be/.
[24] https://lirias.kuleuven.be/.

4.3   Organizations

The iMinds research institute is a multi-part organization which consists of several labs which are also associated with different universities in Flanders. The information about each one of the labs was required to be semantically annotated. Persons, publications and projects are linked to the different iMinds labs.

4.4   Projects

Last, a preliminary effort was put on semantically annotating the information related to projects the different iMinds labs are involved in. The projects are associated with people who work on them, but only the information regarding the projects' research and project leads, as well as contact person was considered.

5   The iLastic Vocabulary

We considered the following commonly used vocabularies to semantically annotate the iMinds scholarly data: BIBO[25], bibTex[26], CERIF[27], DC[28] and FOAF[29]. An indicative list of the high level classes used for the iLastic dataset is available at Table 1 and the most frequently used properties is available at Table 2.

The Bibliographic Ontology (BIBO) provides basic concepts and properties to describe citations and bibliographic references. The bibTeX ontology is used to describe bibTeX entries. The Common European Research Information Format (CERIF) ontology provides basic concepts and properties for describing research information as semantic data. The DCMI Metadata Terms (DC) includes metadata terms maintained by the Dublin Core Metadata Initiative to describe general purpose high level information. Last, the Friend Of A Friend (FOAF) ontology is used to describe people.

Table 1. Classes used to semantically annotate the main iLastic entities

cerif:Person
cerif:OrganizationalUnit
cerif:Publication
cerif:Project

Different vocabularies were used for different concepts. In particular, we used CERIF, DC and FOAF vocabularies to annotate data regarding people. The

---

[25] http://purl.org/ontology/bibo/.
[26] http://purl.org/net/nknouf/ns/bibtex.
[27] http://spi-fm.uca.es/neologism/cerif.
[28] http://dublincore.org/documents/dcmi-terms/.
[29] http://xmlns.com/foaf/0.1/.

Table 2. Properties used to semantically annotate the iLastic data model

Bibo/bibTeX	CERIF	DCTerms/FoaF/iM
bibo:identifier	cerif:internalidentifier	dcterms:identifier
bibo:abstract	cerif:linksToOrganisationUnit	dcterms:issued
bibo:issn	cerif:linksToPublication	foaf:familyName
bibo:isbn13	cerif:name	foaf:givenName
bibo:uri	cerif:title	im:webOfScience
bibtex:howPublished	cerif:acronym	im:publicationCategory

more generic DC and FOAF vocabularies were used to annotate information regarding, for instance, the name and surname of the author, whereas CERIF was used to define and associate with its organization and publications.

BIBO, BibTex, CERIF and DC vocabularies were used to annotate publications, FOAF, CERIF and DC to annotate organizational units and CERIF to annotate projects. Note, to cover cases where the aforementioned or other vocabularies did not have properties to annotate particular internal concepts of the iMinds data, we used custom properties defined for our case. For instance, iMinds tracks if a certain publication is indexed by Web Of Science[30]. Therefore, a custom property (`im:webOfScience`) was introduced to represent this knowledge. Moreover, iMinds classifies publications in different categories. A custom property (`im:publicationCategory`) was introduced for this purpose.

6   The iLastic Dataset

The iLastic dataset contains information about 59,462 entities. In particular, it contains information about 12,472 researchers (both people affiliated with iMinds and externals), 22,728 publications, 81 organizational units, and 3,295 projects. It consists of 765,603 triples in total and is available for querying at http://explore.ilastic.be/sparql.

7   The iLastic Linked Data Publishing Workflow

In this section, we describe the complete workflow for the generation of Linked Data sets from scholarly data, as it was applied in the case of iMinds.

The workflow consists of two pipelines: (i) one enriching the research metadata derived from the iMinds data warehouse, and (ii) one enriching the publications' content. The two pipelines aim to deal with the peculiarities of the different nature that the original data has, namely the structured data and plain text data, while they merge when the final Linked Data set is generated and published. An interface is built on top of the iLastic dataset offering a uniform

---

[30] http://www.webofknowledge.com/.

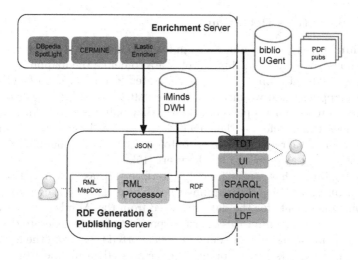

Fig. 1. Linked Data set generation and publishing workflow for the iLastic project.

interface to the users for searching and navigating within the iLastic dataset. The entire workflow consists of Open Source tools which are available for reuse.

The Linked Data publication workflow for iLastic is presented at Fig. 1. Data is derived from the iMinds data warehouse via the DataTank. For each publication whose authors are affiliated with Ghent University, its corresponding one is identified in the Ghent University repository. Its PDF is then processed by the *iLastic Enricher* and its RDF triples are generated in combination with the information residing in the iMinds data warehouse. The data is published via a Virtuoso SPARQL endpoint and SPARQL templates are published via the DataTank which are used by the iLastic User Interface. Organizations which desire to adopt our proposed Linked Data generation and publication workflow may follow the corresponding tutorial [9]. Moreover, it is possible to extend the range of data sources depending on the use case. For instance, publications may be e-prints, or might be derived from an open repository.

The workflow is described in more details in the following subsections. In the next section, we explain how the rules to generate Linked Data are defined in the case of the iLastic Linked Data publishing workflow (Sect. 7.1). Then, we describe how data is retrieved, both from the iMinds data warehouse and the Ghent University digital repository in our exemplary use case (Sect. 7.2). The aforementioned input data and rules are used to generate the Linked Data, the iLastic Linked Data set in our use case, using our proposed workflow, as specified in Sect. 7.3, which is then published, as specified in Sect. 7.4, and accessed via a dedicated user interface, as described in Sect. 8. Last, the installation of our use case is briefly mentioned at Sect. 7.5.

7.1 Mapping Rules Definition

Generation. Firstly, we obtained a sample of the data derived from the iMinds data warehouse. We relied on this sample data to define the mapping rules that specify how the iLastic Linked Data is generated in our case. To facilitate the editing of mapping rules, we incorporate the RMLEditor [16]. If other organizations desire to reuse our proposed workflow, they only need to define their own mapping rules which refer to their own data sources. Defining such mapping rules for certain data, relying on target ontologies or existing mapping rules may be automated, e.g., as proposed by Heyvaert [15].

The RMLEditor[31] has a user friendly interface [17], as shown in Fig. 2, that supports lay users to define the mapping rules. The RMLEditor is used to generate the mapping documents for the data retrieved from the iMinds data warehouse. A *mapping document* summarizes the rules specifying how to generate the Linked Data. After all mapping rules are defined, we exported them from the RMLEditor. The RMLEditor exports the mapping rules expressed using the RDF mapping language (RML) [12] in a single mapping document.

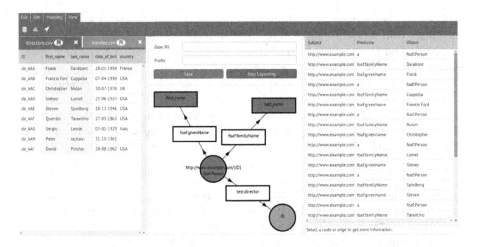

Fig. 2. The RMLEditor user interface for editing rules that define how iLastic Linked Data set is generated.

Validation. The exported mapping document is validated for its consistency using the RMLValidator [10]. At this step, we make sure that the semantic annotations defined are consistent and no violations occur because multiple vocabularies are (re)used and combined. Any violations are addressed and the final mapping document is produced to be used for generating the Linked Data set.

---

[31] http://rml.io/RMLeditor.

The mapping documents that were generated for the iLastic project are available at http://rml.io/data/iLastic/PubAuthGroup_Mapping.rml.ttl.

7.2   Data Access and Retrieval

The iLastic workflow consists of two input pipelines: (i) one for publishing structured data derived from the iMinds data warehouse, and (ii) one for publishing the results of the plain text enrichment. The two input pipelines are merged at the time of the Linked Data generation. Data originally residing at the iMinds data warehouse, as well as data derived from Ghent University digital repository, are considered to generate the iLastic Linked Data set.

Both input pipelines require accessing different parts of the data stored in the iMinds data warehouse. To achieve that, we published the corresponding SQL queries on a DataTank[32] instance that acts as the interface for accessing the underlying data for both pipelines. The DataTank offers a generic way to publish data sources and provides an HTTP API on top of them. The results of the SQL queries against the iMinds data warehouse and of the publications' enrichment are proxied by the DataTank and are returned in (paged) JSON format.

The original raw data as retrieved from the iMinds data warehouse and made available as Open Data can be found at http://explore.ilastic.be/iminds. The DataTank user interface is shown in Fig. 3.

Fig. 3. The DataTank interface for accessing the iMinds data as raw Open Data.

7.3   Linked Data Generation

Structured Data Pipeline. The *structured-data pipeline* aims to semantically annotate data derived from the iMinds data warehouse. It considers the input data as it is retrieved from the DataTank and aims to directly

---

[32] http://thedatatank.com/.

semantically annotate them with the aforementioned vocabularies and ontologies. The RMLProcessor relies on machine-interpretable descriptions of the data sources [13]. To access the iMinds data warehouse, the RMLProcessor relies on the API's description which is defined using the Hydra vocabulary[33].

Plain Text Enrichment Pipeline. The *plain-text-enrichment pipeline* aims to enrich the publications metadata with information derived from the publications' actual content. Thus, retrieving, extracting and processing each publication's text is required. This occurs in coordination with the university repositories. To be more precise, for each publication, the university affiliated with the authors which is also part of iMinds is considered to retrieve the publication from its repository. For our exemplary case, the Ghent University API is considered[34].

For each publication that appears at the iMinds data warehouse and its authors are affiliated with a Ghent University lab, the corresponding publication is identified in the set of publications retrieved from the Ghent University API. The same publications that appear both in the iMinds data warehouse and Ghent University repository are identified applying fuzzy matching over their title and author(s), if the latter is available.

The fuzzy matching is performed in different successive steps. (i) Firstly normalisation is applied to the titles. For instance, punctuation and redundant white spaces are removed. (ii) Once the normalization is completed, exact matching based on string comparison is performed. (iii) If exact match fails, matching based on individual words is performed and the words position is also taken into account. For instance, matching 'Linked Data' and 'Linked Open Data' scores well, whereas 'Linked Data' and 'Data Linked' scores worse. (iv) If the score is below a threshold, another matching algorithm is performed to avoid mismatching due to typos. The latter eliminates the same words from both titles (these get a high score) and compare the remaining words on a character basis. Dealing with typos, e.g., 'Lined' instead of 'Linked', acronyms, e.g., 'DQ' for 'Data Quality', and prefixes, such as 'Special issue on ... : <title>', were the most challenging cases we addressed.

As soon as a publication is retrieved, it is assessed whether it is required to be processed or not. It is checked if its PDF is open accessed and if it is, then it is checked if it is an old publication and it was already processed based on the last modified date of the PDF file. If it is open accessed and not processed before, the PDF is retrieved for further processing. Information extracted from the PDF, such as keywords or authors, may also be used to enrich the information derived from the data warehouse if such data is missing or is not complete.

The *iLastic Enricher* consists of two main components: CERMINE and DBpedia spotlight. Those two tools were chosen based on the 2015 Semantic Publishing Challenge results [8]. To be more precise, the former was the challenge's best performing tool, while the latter was broadly used by several solutions every year the challenge was organized [11] In the case of the iLastic Linked

---

[33] http://www.hydra-cg.com/spec/latest/core/.
[34] https://biblio.ugent.be/doc/api.

Data generation and publication workflow, each retrieved PDF file is fed to the *iLastic Enricher*. The *iLastic Enricher* uses the Content ExtRactor and MINEr (CERMINE[35]) [22] to extract the content of the corresponding PDF file. As soon as the publication's content is retrieved, its abstract and main body are fed to DBpedia spotlight[36] to identify and annotate entities that also appear in the DBpedia dataset. Besides the abstract and main body of the publication, the keywords assigned by the users are also extracted and annotated by DBpedia spotlight.

The output is summarized in a JSON file, where all identified terms are summarized. Such JSON files may be found at http://rml.io/data/iLastic/. The JSON file is passed to the RMLProcessor together with the rest of the data retrieved from the iMinds data warehouse, and the mapping document defined using the RMLEditor, to generate the resulting triples. This way, the corresponding publications information is enriched with data from its own text. Moreover, in cases where data derived from the iMinds data warehouse is missing, e.g., authors, the information is extracted from the publications. This way, not only the iLastic Linked Data set is enriched, but its completeness is also improved.

7.4 Linked Data Publication

Once the iLastic Linked Data set is generated, it is stored and published to a Virtuoso instance[37] which is installed on the same server for this purpose. Virtuoso is a cross-platform server that provides a triplestore and a SPARQL endpoint for querying the underlying Linked Data. This endpoint may be used by clients which desire to access the iLastic dataset, as it is used by the DataTank to provide data to the iLastic user interface –described in the next section (Sect. 8).

7.5 Current Installation

The iLastic Linked Data generation and publishing workflow consists of CERMINE which is available at https://github.com/CeON/CERMINE and DBpedia sportlight which is available at https://github.com/dbpedia-spotlight/dbpedia-spotlight for PDF extraction and annotation; the RMLProcessor which is available at https://github.com/RMLio/RML-Processor and RMLValidator which is available at https://github.com/RMLio/RML-Validator for the structured data annotation and alignment with non-structured data annotations; and the virtuoso endpoint which is available at https://github.com/openlink/virtuoso-opensource and DataTank which is available at https://github.com/tdt/ for data publishing.

The iLastic Linked Data publishing workflow runs on two servers. One accommodates the main part of the workflow. The data extraction and Linked Data

---

[35] http://cermine.ceon.pl/.

[36] https://github.com/dbpedia-spotlight/dbpedia-spotlight.

[37] https://github.com/openlink/virtuoso-opensource.

generation occurs there, namely the RMLProcessor runs there, as well as the publishing infrastructure are installed there, namely the Virtuoso instance, and the user interface. It runs on Ubuntu 14.04, with PHP 5.5.19, Java 1.7, MySQL 5.5, Virtuoso 7.20 and Nginx. Note the RMLEditor is used as a service residing on a different server, as it may be reused by other data owners too.

The publications enrichment, namely the *iLastic Enricher*, only takes place on a separate server, due to higher memory requirements. The server runs Debian GNU/Linux 7 with DBpedia Spotlight 0.7 and CERMINE installed.

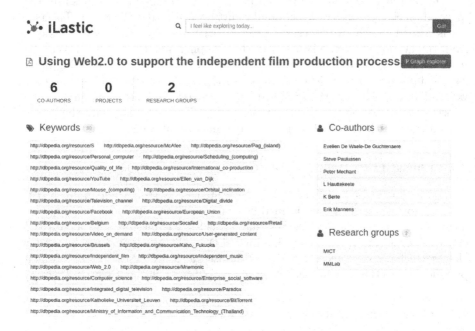

Fig. 4. A publication as presented at iLastic user interface with information derived both from iMinds data warehouse and the analyzed and enriched publication's content.

8   The iLastic User Interface

The iLastic user interface was included in the second phase of the project aiming to make the iLastic dataset accessible to non-Semantic Web experts who do not have the knowledge to query it via its endpoint and to showcase its potential.

Users of the iLastic interface may discover knowledge resulting of the combination of the two channels of information. Users may search for iMinds researchers, discover the group they belong to, the publications they co-authored, the research areas they are active in, other people they collaborate with and, thus, their network of collaborators. Moreover, users may look for publications and discover combined information derived from the publications metadata derived from the iMinds data warehouse, such are the publication's category, as well as the keywords and main entities derived from the publication's content.

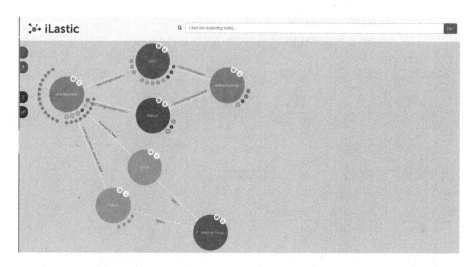

Fig. 5. The graph explorer view for Erik Mannens.

The iLastic user interface allows users to explore the different entities either using its regular interface or the graph explorer, or search within the Linked Data set. While the users explore the dataset via the user interface, their requests are translated in SPARQL queries which, on their own turn, are parameterized and published at the DataTank. Moreover, the search is supported by the iLastic sitemap. Both of them are explained in more details below.

The iLastic user interface relies on LodLive[38] [4], a demonstration of Linked Data standards' use to browse different resources of a dataset. The iLastic user interface can be accessed at http://explore.iLastic.be and a sreencast showcasing its functionality is available at https://youtu.be/ZxGrHnOuSvw.

Users may search for data in the iLastic Linked Data set. The iLastic sitemap was incorporated to support searching. It has a tree-like structure including the different entities handled in the iLastic project. This tree structure is indexed and serves as a search API, whose results are then used by the user interface's search application. The iLastic search application builds a front-end around the search API results where users can search for a person, publication or organization.

Moreover, a user may access the iLastic user interface to explore the integrated information on publications, as shown in Fig. 4. Besides the regular user interface, the users may take advantage of the incorporated graph explorer. For each one of the iLastic Linked Data set's entities, the user may switch from the regular interface to the graph explorer and vice versa. For instance, the graph explorer for 'Erik Mannens' is shown in Fig. 5. Last, a user may not only search for different entities within the iLastic Linked Data set, but also some preliminary analysis of the dataset's content is visualized, as shown in Fig. 6.

---

[38] http://en.lodlive.it/.

iMinds publications

A visualization that shows which organisations and which person have their share in publications.

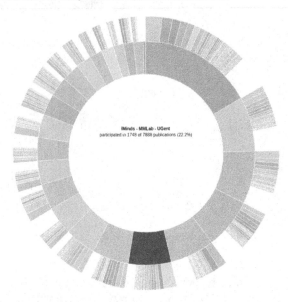

Fig. 6. The analyisis of iLastic Linked Data set.

9   Conclusions and Future Work

In this paper, we show how a general-purpose Linked Data generation workflow is adjusted to also generate Linked Data from raw scholarly data. Relying on such general-purpose workflows allows different data owners of scholarly data to reuse the same installations and re-purpose existing mapping rules to their own needs. This way, the implementation and maintenance costs are reduced.

In the future, we plan to extend the dataset with more data derived from both the iMinds research institute and the publications, such as references.

Acknowledgments. The described research activities were funded by Ghent University, imec, Flanders Innovation and Entrepreneurship (AIO), the Research Foundation – Flanders (FWO), and the European Union (EU).

References

1. Bagnacani, A., Ciancarini, P., Di Iorio, A., Nuzzolese, A.G., Peroni, S., Vitali, F.: The semantic lancet project: a linked open dataset for scholarly publishing. In: Lambrix, P. (ed.) EKAW 2014. LNCS (LNAI), vol. 8982, pp. 101–105. Springer, Cham (2015). https://doi.org/10.1007/978-3-319-17966-7_10
2. Bahar, S., Witte, R.: Semantic representation of scientific literature: bringing claims, contributions and named entities onto the linked open data cloud. PeerJ Comput. Sci. **1**, e37 (2015)

3. Bardi, A., Manghi, P.: Enhanced publication management systems: a systemic approach towards modern scientific communication. In: Proceedings of the 24th International Conference on World Wide Web, WWW 2015 Companion, pp. 1051–1052. ACM (2015)

4. Camarda, D.V., Mazzini, S., Antonuccio, A.: LodLive, exploring the web of data. In: Proceedings of the 8th International Conference on Semantic Systems, I-SEMANTICS 2012, pp. 197–200. ACM (2012)

5. Cyganiak, R., Bizer, C., Garbers, J., Maresch, O., Becker, C.: The D2RQ mapping language. Technical report, March 2012. http://d2rq.org/d2rq-language

6. Das, S., Sundara, S., Cyganiak, R.: R2RML: RDB to RDF mapping language. W3C Recommendation, W3C (2012). http://www.w3.org/TR/r2rml/

7. Dean, J., Ghemawat, S.: MapReduce: simplified data processing on large clusters. Commun. ACM **51**(1), 107–113 (2008)

8. Iorio, A.D., Lange, C., Dimou, A., Vahdati, S.: Semantic publishing challenge – assessing the quality of scientific output by information extraction and interlinking. In: Gandon, F., Cabrio, E., Stankovic, M., Zimmermann, A. (eds.) SemWebEval 2015. CCIS, vol. 548, pp. 65–80. Springer, Cham (2015). https://doi.org/10.1007/978-3-319-25518-7_6

9. Dimou, A., Heyvaert, P., Taelman, R., Verborgh, R.: Modeling, generating, and publishing knowledge as linked data. In: Ciancarini, P., et al. (eds.) EKAW 2016. LNCS (LNAI), vol. 10180, pp. 3–14. Springer, Cham (2017). https://doi.org/10.1007/978-3-319-58694-6_1

10. Dimou, A., et al.: Assessing and refining mappingsto RDF to improve dataset quality. In: Arenas, M., et al. (eds.) ISWC 2015. LNCS, vol. 9367, pp. 133–149. Springer, Cham (2015). https://doi.org/10.1007/978-3-319-25010-6_8

11. Dimou, A., Vahdati, S., Di Iorio, A., Lange, C., Verborgh, R., Mannens, E.: Challenges as enablers for high quality linked data: insights from the semantic publishing challenge. PeerJ Comput. Sci. **3**, e105 (2017)

12. Dimou, A., Vander Sande, M., Colpaert, P., Verborgh, R., Mannens, E., Van de Walle, R.: RML: a generic language for integrated RDF mappings of heterogeneous data. In: Proceedings of the 7th Workshop on Linked Data on the Web, CEUR Workshop Proceedings, vol. 1184 (2014)

13. Dimou, A., Verborgh, R., Sande, M.V., Mannens, E., Van de Walle, R.: Machine-interpretable dataset and service descriptions for heterogeneous data access and retrieval. In: Proceedings of the 11th International Conference on Semantic Systems, SEMANTICS 2015, pp. 145–152. ACM (2015)

14. Gentile, A.L., Nuzzolese, A.G.: cLODg - conference linked open data generator. In: Villata, S., Pan, J., Dragoni, M. (eds.) International Semantic Web Conference (Posters and Demos), CEUR Workshop Proceedings, vol. 1486. CEUR-WS.org (2015)

15. Heyvaert, P., Dimou, A., Verborgh, R., Mannens, E.: Ontology-based data access mapping generation using data, schema, query, and mapping knowledge. In: Blomqvist, E., Maynard, D., Gangemi, A., Hoekstra, R., Hitzler, P., Hartig, O. (eds.) ESWC 2017. LNCS, vol. 10250, pp. 205–215. Springer, Cham (2017). https://doi.org/10.1007/978-3-319-58451-5_15

16. Heyvaert, P., et al.: RMLEditor: a graph-based mapping editor for linked data mappings. In: Sack, H., Blomqvist, E., d'Aquin, M., Ghidini, C., Ponzetto, S.P., Lange, C. (eds.) ESWC 2016. LNCS, vol. 9678, pp. 709–723. Springer, Cham (2016). https://doi.org/10.1007/978-3-319-34129-3_43

17. Heyvaert, P., Dimou, A., Verborgh, R., Mannens, E., Van de Walle, R.: Towards a uniform user interface for editing mapping definitions. In: Workshop on Intelligent Exploration of Semantic Data (2015)
18. Möller, K., Heath, T., Handschuh, S., Domingue, J.: Recipes for semantic web dog food—the ESWC and ISWC metadata projects. In: Aberer, K. (ed.) ASWC/ISWC-2007. LNCS, vol. 4825, pp. 802–815. Springer, Heidelberg (2007). https://doi.org/10.1007/978-3-540-76298-0_58
19. Ronzano, F., Saggion, H.: Dr. Inventor framework: extracting structured information from scientific publications. In: Japkowicz, N., Matwin, S. (eds.) DS 2015. LNCS (LNAI), vol. 9356, pp. 209–220. Springer, Cham (2015). https://doi.org/10.1007/978-3-319-24282-8_18
20. Shotton, D.: Semantic publishing: the coming revolution in scientific journal publishing. Learn. Publ. **22**(2), 85–94 (2009)
21. Softic, S., De Vocht, L., Mannens, E., Ebner, M., Van de Walle, R.: COLINDA: modeling, representing and using scientific events in the web of data. In: Proceedings of the 4th International Workshop on Detection, Representation, and Exploitation of Events in the Semantic Web (DeRiVE 2015), CEUR Workshop Proceedings, vol. 1363 (2015)
22. Tkaczyk, D., Bolikowski, Ł.: Extracting contextual information from scientific literature using CERMINE system. In: Gandon, F., Cabrio, E., Stankovic, M., Zimmermann, A. (eds.) SemWebEval 2015. CCIS, vol. 548, pp. 93–104. Springer, Cham (2015). https://doi.org/10.1007/978-3-319-25518-7_8
23. Vahdati, S., Karim, F., Huang, J.-Y., Lange, C.: Mapping large scale research metadata to linked data: a performance comparison of HBase, CSV and XML. In: Garoufallou, E., Hartley, R.J., Gaitanou, P. (eds.) MTSR 2015. CCIS, vol. 544, pp. 261–273. Springer, Cham (2015). https://doi.org/10.1007/978-3-319-24129-6_23

About a BUOI: Joint Custody
of Persistent Universally Unique
Identifiers on the Web, or, Making PIDs
More FAIR

Joakim Philipson[(✉)]

Stockholm University, Stockholm, Sweden
joakim.philipson@su.se

Abstract. The findability and interoperability of some persistent identifiers (PIDs) in use on the internet and their compliance with the FAIR
data principles [12,35] are explored. It is suggested that the wide distribution and *findability* (e.g. by simple 'googling') on the internet may
be more important for the usefulness of identifiers, than the *resolvability* of links by one single authority, purportedly guaranteeing their permanence and authenticity. The prevalence of phenomena such as *link
rot* implies that the permanence of URLs, PURLs or URIs cannot be
trusted. By contrast, the well distributed, but seldom directly resolvable
ISBN identifier has proved remarkably resilient, with far-reaching per-
sistence, inherent structural meaning and good *validatability*, by means
of fixed string-length, pattern-recognition, restricted character set and
check digit. Adding *context* and meaning to identifiers through namespace prefixes and object types is also suggested. Arguing for a wide distribution of validatable identifiers, the conclusion resembles the experience
of the boy Marcus in the novel-based film *About a boy*, from living with
a suicidal mother: It's not sufficient to rely on one source only for sus-
tenance. You need more than that. You need backup, in case something
happens [20,32].

Keywords: FAIR data principles · PIDs · Findability · Identifiers
Interoperability · Metadata · Resolvability · Validation

1 Introduction: Identifiers in Science

Identifiers in science may refer to digital or physical objects, or concepts. They
may be general or domain-specific. Among the more prevalent general PID,
persistent identifier types are DOI, Handle and UUID. There are also 'old', bibliographic identifiers like ISBN. Created in the 1960's and -70's of the print era,
how come they survived into this digital age? Some reasons might be: they are
well distributed across the internet, and widely used by stake-holders (libraries,
publishers, readers). They have a semantic structure, identifying well-defined

© Springer Nature Switzerland AG 2018
A. González-Beltrán et al. (Eds.): SAVE-SD 2017/2018, LNCS 10959, pp. 33–48, 2018.
https://doi.org/10.1007/978-3-030-01379-0_3

objects, and a fairly precise validation mechanism through fixed string-lengths, limited character-set and check digits. Some of these properties of good identifiers are shared by DOIs, Handles and UUIDs, or other more domain specific identifiers used for scholarly data, but seldom all of them simultaneously. Among these characteristics the main focus here will be on validation, as seemingly somewhat neglected lately.

2   Identifiers - Why Do We Need Them?

The general purpose of identifiers is to serve as *references* to the objects that they are supposed to identify. This requires identifiers to indicate, preferably in and by themselves, what *type of objects* they are meant to identify. Now, far from all identifiers fulfil this requirement. Rather, it is often left to the *names* of things to *describe* the objects identified, thereby providing context and *meaning*. Scientific names may or may not be part of the metadata on the destination page of a PID-URI.

While scientific *names* are often useful for *describing* objects (or at least certain aspects or properties of 'things', organisms), they have other drawbacks compared to identifiers, some of which were identified by [26]. For example, homonymi and disambiguation should generally be a lesser problem for globally unique identifiers. And while concatenations or abbreviations may be problematic in the use of names for identification, string-length restrictions and pattern limits are useful for validation of identifiers, as is avoiding white space. Missing or added characters, all types of misspellings are easier to detect and validate in standardized identifiers of fixed string-length or well-defined character patterns. Inconsistent encoding should generally also not be a problem in good identifiers, for which the set of allowed characters may be limited. However, these assets of some identifiers may conflict with the legitimate interest in having also transparent, meaningful PIDs that at least in part "speak for themselves". The result of a compromise between these two interests may be seen in the *Handle* (hdl) system (below).

3   FAIR Principles

The FAIR guiding principles aim "to make data **Findable, Accessible, Interoperable, and Re-usable**" [12]. As such they concern also metadata in general and identifiers, PIDs, in particular, as is seen from some of the principles:

The FAIR principles clearly need interpretation to become fully operational, as several observers have noted, and such work is also in progress [7,9]. Further explications of some of the principles are also available from the originators [13]:

- 1. To be **Findable** any Data Object should be uniquely and persistently identifiable.
- 1.1. The same Data Object should be re-findable at any point in time, thus Data Objects should be persistent, with emphasis on their metadata...

To be Findable:

F1. (meta)data are assigned a globally unique and eternally persistent identifier.
F2. data are described with rich metadata.
F3. (meta)data are registered or indexed in a searchable resource.
F4. metadata specify the data identifier.

To be Accessible:

A1 (meta)data are retrievable by their identifier using a standardized communications protocol.
A1.1 the protocol is open, free, and universally implementable.
A1.2 the protocol allows for an authentication and authorization procedure, where necessary.
A2 metadata are accessible, even when the data are no longer available.

To be Interoperable:

I1. (meta)data use a formal, accessible, shared, and broadly applicable language for knowledge representation.
I2. (meta)data use vocabularies that follow FAIR principles.
I3. (meta)data include qualified references to other (meta)data.

To be Re-usable:

R1. meta(data) have a plurality of accurate and relevant attributes.
R1.1. (meta)data are released with a clear and accessible data usage license.
R1.2. (meta)data are associated with their provenance.
R1.3. (meta)data meet domain-relevant community standards.

Fig. 1. The FAIR data principles. [12]

- 1.2. A Data Object should minimally contain basic machine actionable meta-data that allows it to be distinguished from other Data Objects
- ...
- 2. Data is **Accessible** in that it can be always obtained by machines and humans
- ...
- 3. Data Objects can be **Interoperable** only if:
- 3.1. (Meta) data is machine-actionable [8. .... "Metadata being machine readable is a *conditio sine qua non* for FAIRness."] [11]
- ...
- 3.3 (Meta) data within the Data Object should thus be both syntactically parseable and semantically machine-accessible
- 4. For Data Objects to be **Re-usable** additional criteria are:
- 4.1 Data Objects should be compliant with principles 1–3
- 4.2 (Meta) data should be sufficiently well-described and rich that it can be automatically (or with minimal human effort) linked or integrated, like-with-like, with other data sources.

The FAIR principles have some resemblance with the Linked Data rules first fomulated by Tim Berners-Lee already back in 2006, updated in 2009 and 2010 [1]. There is, for example, the insistence on machine-readability and the linking of data sources with other data. But the FAIR principles do not necessarily require metadata to be expressed in RDF, as the Linked Data rules demand. It seems also that Berners-Lee is critical of identifier types using other schemes than simple HTTP URIs.

Neither the FAIR principles, nor the Linked Data rules say anything explicitly about *validation*. Still, particularly for the *Interoperability* and *Re-usability*, it is crucial that metadata can be properly validated against a schema, as adhering to an accepted metadata standard. And this includes also identifiers. We must be sure that they are of the type or format they claim to be, even if they cannot be resolved to a dedicated URI any longer. Failed validation, e.g. due to simple typos or wrong namespace, may even be one way of checking why an identifier or URI does not resolve as expected. It is also important for the possibility to export metadata to another format, thereby promoting the re-use of data, without exporting also potential errors. Although transformation or harvesting of metadata might be possible even without validation, the trust in the results and quality as well as the eventual findability of the data (and so again the re-usability) might be seriously affected. For enhanced findability, it is also important that standard, widely distributed identifiers are used.

Validation of an identifier means ensuring that it is true to its proclaimed type, for example, making sure that what is flagged as an ISBN is not in fact an ISSN (real use case), or that the string-length and check-sum is compliant with its type. A further advantage of promptly validatable identifiers, as against relying exclusively on resolvability, is that validation can be performed also off-line, by means of a more or less simple validation-algorithm and a piece of software such as a reasonably good XML-editor.

4   Resolvable or Findable?

In the present FAIR principles the focus is very much on resolvability of identifiers by an authority [13], despite the general awareness of phenomena like 'link rot' and 'reference rot' [14,21,33]. It has even been suggested to put up digital gravestones over disappeared resources, with metadata from their last known whereabouts serving as epitaphs [2]. A 2013 study in BMC Bioinformatics analyzed nearly 15,000 links in abstracts from Thomson Reuters' Web of Science citation index and found that the median lifespan of web pages was 9.3 years, and just 62% were archived [19]. This happens although there is an understanding that "[u]nique identifiers, and metadata describing the data, and its disposition, should persist – even beyond the lifespan of the data they describe" [5]. A recent study of some 40 research data repositories found that only one of these (3%) was compliant with the FAIR principle of Accessibility requiring "a clear policy statement (or various examples of data this has actually happened to) indicating that metadata is still available even if the data is removed" [9]. The argument here, though, is not that resolvable, persistent URIs should be avoided as identifiers; in fact, they often do serve their purpose of providing a more persistent metadata source than "ordinary", plain URLs. But, as has been eloquently remarked, "persistent URIs must be used to be persistent" [29]. Persistent, resolvable URIs as identifiers work by means of a decoupling of the location and the identification functions of URIs.

> The custodian of a web resource maintains the correspondence between the identifying URI and the locating URI in the resolver's look-up table as the resource's location changes over time. ... The solution comes at a price because it requires operating a resolver infrastructure and maintaining the look-up table that powers it [29].

This is true of DOIs, as well as Handles, PURLs and URNs. There are in fact numerous cases when the lookup-table is not maintained and updated as required. That is why it may be wise not to rely on a single 'custodian' for the resolution of identifiers and access to associated metadata. It is rather the *distribution* and use of identifiers - whether resolvable or not - that is important here. It seems not even the authors of [29] are true to their own principles, since three of their references that actually have DOIs are cited without them: [8, 22, 37]. So again, PIDs must be used and cited to remain persistent. Citations may also serve as a 'means of transportation' to achieve widest possible distribution. Further, it may be argued that wide distribution is *dependent* on good 'validatability', in order not to multiply errors and 'non-resolution' as a result.

One way to achieve wider distribution of identifiers might be the praiseworthy initiative of *signposting.org* (see also: [28]), using HTTP headers for retrieval of PIDs from simple URLs:

```
curl -I "https://doi.pangaea.de/10.1594/PANGAEA.867908"
HTTP/1.1 200 OK
Content-length: 8424
Content-type: text/html;charset=UTF-8
Link: <https://doi.org/10.1594/PANGAEA.867908> ; rel="identifier"
```

However, the signposting initiative, so far, only redirects the question of use from PIDs and DOIs to HTTP header links. Again, going back to the question of resolvability, the relationship between identifiers such as DOIs and URIs/IRIs is not always straightforward, and sometimes involves a chain of redirects ('303s'), before reaching eventually a destination holding also the appropriate metadata [30, 31]. Another reason resolvability may not be sufficient, even if the metadata is somehow in place, is that the file on the destination page resolved to is behind a paywall. This is a recent case, where apparently public domain content more than 100 years old was hidden behind a DOI-resolver charging 50$ for release of the content:

First, it is not true that every object only gets one and only one DOI. It is possible to mint several DOIs for the same resource by different agents, such as Dataverse, Figshare, ResearchGate etc. The DOI in question here is: 10.1080/00222930908692639[1]. Secondly, there are some remedies against these cases, notably the recently launched oaDOI at *oadoi.org*. [18] We try it out here:

---

[1] http://dx.doi.org/10.1080/00222930908692639.

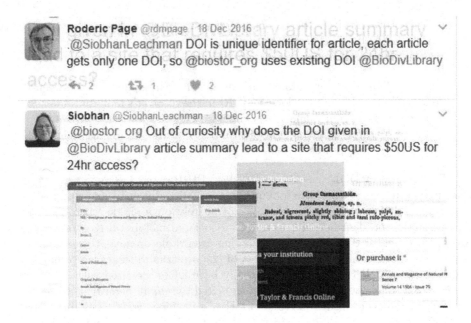

Fig. 2. Tweets about public domain resources behind DOI paywalls.

Fig. 3. Tweets about public domain resources behind DOI paywalls.

In several steps this eventually leads us via an API to an XML-file with a link to the freely accessible fulltext at http://www.biodiversitylibrary.org/part/ 60220. But, most often you are not so fortunate to find a free replacement copy of resources behind a paywall. What meets you when tested in those cases may be this telling message, when tried for the DOI of [25]:

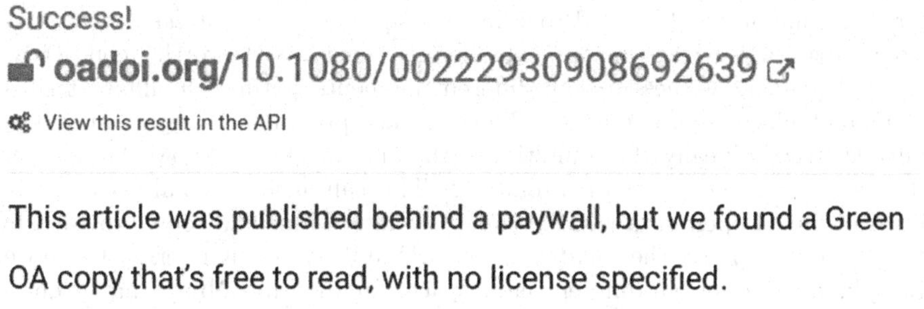

Success!

🔓 **oadoi.org**/10.1080/00222930908692639 ↗

⚙ View this result in the API

This article was published behind a paywall, but we found a Green

OA copy that's free to read, with no license specified.

Fig. 4. oadoi.org tool finding open access version of a resource referenced by a DOI behind a paywall.

No dice

🔒 **oadoi.org**/10.1109/5.771073 ↗

⚙ View this result in the API

Sorry, this article is behind a paywall, and we couldn't find a free

copy anywhere. Unfortunately, this is still true for around 80% of

scholarly articles..

↻ try another   ↩ report error

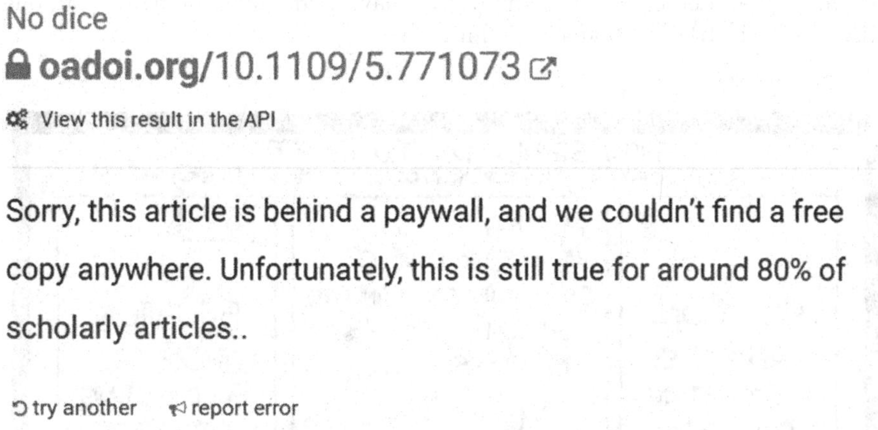

Fig. 5. oadoi.org tool not finding open access version of a resource referenced by a DOI behind a paywall.

And if *oadoi.org* (apparently just recently replaced by the browser add-on *unpaywall.org*) fails, identifiers.org SPARQL endpoint[2] might be useful [36]. But, it does not necessarily give us an open access URI in return. And it only works if the potential corresponding URIs have been assigned the property *owl:sameAs* just as the submitted subject URI. Unfortunately, in neither of our cases above these conditions are met.

Assuming we have finally found a single seemingly reliable custodian of our PIDs and URIs, promising 24/7 resolution and top quality metadata, should we rest content with that? Most serious lawyers and journalists probably would agree: it is wise not to judge by the testimony of a single witness, a single source alone. The evidence of at least two, mutually independent witnesses is generally preferred. Clark describes *multiple resolution* as representing a stage in the evolution of PIDs, that will eventually be surpassed by a more mature age when we supply also *data types* to come with the PIDs, in order to make them

---

[2] http://identifiers.org/services/sparql.

more machine actionable [2]. Providing multiple *access* to, or *identification* of resources through PIDs, that are capable of serving as trustworthy, competent, valid independent witnesses from different moments in time, at different sites, in different places is a good idea. Thus, we accept "that an object may have multiple PIDs". Ideally these multiple PIDs should get to "know about" each other as a way towards interoperability [2]. This can be achieved already, e.g. by means of linked open data (LOD), sameAs-relationships and tools provided by *n2t.net, oadoi.org* and the *identifiers.org* SPARQL endpoint referred to above. Multiple identifiers from different namespaces for the same object may even be desirable in order to ensure interoperability in different environments [25]. It is also in line with the principle of the semantic web known as the *NUNA, Non-Unique Naming Assumption*, implying that "things described in RDF data can have more than one name" and any object may be identified by more than one URI, serving in RDF as 'names' of things [3].

Fig. 6. Proliferating standards cartoon. Source: xkcd.com (https://xkcd.com/927/). CC BY-NC 2.5

However, the conclusion to be drawn from this cartoon and the website yapid.org[3] with regard to PIDs is not that any identifier is as good as the other. In fact, there are significant differences in quality between identifiers, particularly in terms of 'validatability' and 'meaningfulness', or 'semantic weight'. We are getting there a bit later.

But first, having referred to linked data and sameAs-relationships as a possible solution to achieving interoperability, what about long-term sustainability?

---

[3] http://yapid.org/.

Are LOD, relying heavily on URIs, fit for survival? Archival records for long-term preservation need to be self-sustained, carrying meaning within themselves, while the references may no longer be resolvable. In e-archives compliant with the OAIS-model and Trustworthy Digital Repositories standards for self-sustenance, this means that URIs lacking an inherently meaningful structure will often serve only as another set of dumb identifiers. Unless they can import some meaning from outside, through resolution or sameAs links, such opaque, non-resolvable URIs should henceforth rather be described as "non-semantic".

5   Which Identifiers are FAIR Enough?

We must ask about PIDs, "Persistent Identifiers", just how "persistent" they are really? Even if not always resolvable, are they in general still 'findable', well distributed over the internet in time and space? Are they 'validatable' (e.g. through fixed string-length, pattern-recognition, restricted character set, built-in checksum, built-in type?) Are they FAIR?

Findability: Beginning with the F for findability, for comparison we go back in time to 'old-fashioned' ISBNs, International Standard Book Numbers. Publicly declaring what type of objects they are meant to identify, ISBNs are rarely directly resolvable. But they are widely distributed, they have good *findability* in terms of *precision* hits, as seen by simple 'googling', with good survival rate, longer than the median age of web-pages 9.3 years. For example, look at ISBN 0-14-029161-X: *The Diversity of Life/Edward O. Wilson (2001)*. Simple googling of 014029161X, unprefixed and without hyphens results in 57/57 precision hits (date: 2017-01-30). ISBNs could also be searched in library catalogs, the most comprehensive of which is probably the Karlsruhe Virtual Catalog – KVK worldwide[4]. Result of the query '014029161X', with the same unprefixed ISBN without hyphens yields 123/123 precision hits, recall being difficult to compute since in 55 of 72 catalogs the search could not be successfully processed or no records were found. To counteract the possibly unfair bias with a modern classic like this, we try instead an even older, and presumably less well-known example: ISBN: 2130381030. *L'Identité : séminaire interdisciplinaire dirigé par Claude Lévi-Strauss, 1974–1975* (Paris: PUF, 1983). Googling without prefix (2130381030) the precision is between 14/39 and 22/50; with prefix (ISBN2130381030) it reaches as high as 17/18 (date: 2017-01-30).

These results could be compared to similar tests for identifiers of one of the most well studied organisms of all, the fruitfly *Drosophila melanogaster*. Starting with its GBIF ID 5073713[5], googling the unprefixed pure number gives the modest precision of 1/107 (date: 2017-01-30). Using instead the Global Names Resolver[6] to get a UUID v. 5 for *Drosophila melanogaster*, <gni-uuid>1bc2f359-47e4-5da6-a748-74676b7c8c5d</gni-uuid>, googling it either unprefixed or prefixed gives a zero result (0 recall, 0 precision, date: 2017-01-30). Trying instead

---

[4] https://kvk.bibliothek.kit.edu/.

[5] http://www.gbif.org/species/5073713.

[6] http://resolver.globalnames.org/.

the same UUID in a general search of all databases of NCBI, the US National Center for Biotechnology Information), we get 34 'hits' in 13 different databases, but all wrong (i.e. 0 precision) 1bc2f359-47e4-5da6-a748-74676b7c8c5d[7]. Apparently this is because the default search algorithm ignores the hyphens, or rather replaces them with a 'OR', so that we get chunks of the string interpreted as e.g. part of a gene locus or names of clones. Most notably, we get 0 hits in the NCBI Taxonomy database, that on the face of it would seem to be the most relevant to our search. Going back instead to the GBIF, using our gni-uuid for an overall search, restricting our search in several steps finally to only species we still get a result of 120613 'hits', simply too much to make precision all but negligible. So, while the UUID is imminently validatable, with fixed string-length and restricted character set, it is neither directly resolvable, nor findable in terms of search results. To earn significance and importance as identifiers gni-UUIDs must become more findable and re-usable, for example by ping-back and auto-update, assigning themselves to the records in the biodiversity database sources they were drawn from and make use of schema.org and similar to get incoming links and a better ranking in search engines.

Accessibility: Data and (digital) objects are accessible only in so far as identifiers are findable or resolvable preferably to open access landing pages with either direct availability of resources, or sufficient metadata to direct the user to such an access point. In this respect DOIs are often, but not always, as good as or sometimes better than ISBNs (for obvious reasons regarding print only material), while gni-UUIDs as described above are all but useless.

Interoperability and **Re-usability** are both intimately associated with 'validatability', as argued above. We will look more into detail at the performance of different PIDs regarding this below.

DOI: DOIs can look just like anything. Here are some real cases, all at the time of writing resolvable and with multiple findability also by simple googling, some of them pretty 'old', although they got their DOIs assigned fairly recently. One is even from 1977 (doi: 10.1177/030631277700700112), but it still produces an impressive precision score of 26/26 or 59/59 (date: 2017-01-30), mostly due to it quite high citation rate, yielding hits for all the citing sources.

- 10.1007/978-3-319-07443-6_39[8]
- 10.1002/asi.23256[9]
- 10.1177/030631277700700112[10]
- 10.1002/(SICI)1097-4571(199510)46:9<646::AID-ASI2>3.0.CO;2-1[11].
- 10.1007/s11192-007-1682-3[12]

---

[7] https://www.ncbi.nlm.nih.gov/gquery/?term=1bc2f359-47e4-5da6-a748-74676b7c8c5d.

[8] http://dx.doi.org/10.1007/978-3-319-07443-6_39.

[9] http://dx.doi.org/10.1002/asi.23256.

[10] http://dx.doi.org/10.1177/030631277700700112.

[11] http://dx.doi.org/10.1002/(SICI)1097-4571(199510)46:9¡H:646::AID-ASI2¿3.0.CO;2-1.

[12] http://dx.doi.org/10.1007/s11192-007-1682-3.

– 10.1023/B:SCIE.0000018543.82441.f1[13]

Now, following are two old DOIs from Wiley Online Library 1996 and Springer 2001 that do not seem to resolve properly (on 2017-01-31):

– 10.1002/(SICI)1520-6297(199601/02)12:1<67::AID-AGR6>3.3.CO;2-#[14]
– 10.1007/s00145-001-0001-x[15]

However, the two following old DOIs, again from Wiley Online 1996 and 1998, that were similarly unresolvable at the same date (2017-01-31), are proof that some PIDs might regain there resolvability later.

– 10.1002/(SICI)1520-6297(199601/02)12:1<67::AID-AGR6>3.3.CO;2-K[16]
– 10.1002/(SICI)1520-6297(199811/12)14:6<475::AID-AGR5>3.3.CO;2-6[17]

Obviously, all these DOIs, whether resolvable or not, vary substantially in string-length, from just 17 to over 60 characters, some involving abbreviations of journals or organisations, one an ISBN, and some containing characters in need of special XML-encoding, different from URI. Note that although the two last items in the first group are from the same journal, *Scientometrics*, they are quite in structure. Anyway, all the items in both groups are valid DOIs and all validate against the best we can offer as a schema, with only partial pattern recognition:

```
<sch:rule context="identifier[@type='doi']">
  <sch:let name="doi-pattern" value="'^(doi:10|10)[.][0-9]{4,}/\S+$'"/>
  <sch:assert test="matches(., $doi-pattern, 'i')">All DOI identifiers must start with
      10, followed by a minimum of 4 digits, a '/' and a suffix of any length
  </sch:assert>
</sch:rule>
```

But, so does this fake DOI equally:

```
http://dx.doi.org/10.1001/xxxxxxxxxxxxxxxxxxxxxxxxxxxxxxxxxxxxxxxxxxxxxxxx999999999
9999999999999999999999999999999999999999
```

To be sure, there are other schema rules and regular expressions suggested for DOIs, both those that are even more permissive (as DataCite 4.1 has it with the pattern value for doiType set to "10:+/.+") [6], and those that are more restrictive, but then obviously not catching all the now prevalent and permitted DOIs by one singular regular expression [10,15]. Thus, DOIs, as we have seen, unlike ISBNs are difficult to validate accurately. Or rather, it is difficult to find sufficiently discriminatory criteria to distinguish proper DOIs from fake ones. They have no fixed string-length, to start with, and very little of character set

---

[13] http://dx.doi.org/10.1023/B:SCIE.0000018543.82441.f1.

[14] http://dx.doi.org/10.1002/(SICI)1520-6297(199601/02)12:1¡67::AID-AGR6¿3.3.CO;2.

[15] http://dx.doi.org/10.1007/s00145-001-0001-x.

[16] http://dx.doi.org/10.1002/(SICI)1520-6297(199601/02)12:1¡105::AID-AGR10¿3.3.CO;2-K.

[17] http://dx.doi.org/10.1002/(SICI)1520-6297(199811/12)14:6¡475::AID-AGR5¿3.3.CO;2-6.

restrictions. All we can have is a partial pattern recognition such as the one in the schematron rule above.

Handle: The Handle identifier system seems fairly easy and handy at a first glance. Only, it comes in two different flavors. One is the semantically opaque, which has the structure: *Prefix/noid* (10079/sqv9sf1), where the NOID-part (for Nice Opaque Identifier [23]) is a 7-character long alphanumeric string from the restricted character set "0123456789bcdfghjkmnpqrstvwxz", with random minting order [4]. The other flavor is the semantically transparent, which could be of three different types: the URL handle: *Prefix/local-PID* (10079/bibid/123456), the user handle: *Prefix/netid/netid* (10079/netid/guoxinji) and the simpler group handle: *Prefix/group* (10079/ISPS). While being more instantly "meaningful", providing context, this kind of Handle, however, will prove less "validatable" in the sense that there is no longer any fixed string-length or restricted character-set.

UUID v5 has support within the field of biodiversity taxonomy, as an important complement to scientific names [26]. They were introduced to the field in 2015 by the Global Names Architecture - GNA [16]. The arguments for using them instead of name strings for certain functions are that they save space as index keys in databases, they have a fixed string length (36 characters, including the dashes) while scientific names are of different length. UUIDs do not suffer, as names sometimes do, from encoding problems that are difficult to detect and they are more easily distinguishable one from the other than name strings for closely related species variants. Specifically, it is argued that "UUIDs v5 ... can be generated independently by anybody and still be the same to the same name string... Same ID can be generated in any popular language following well-defined algorithm." The corresponding Ruby Gem app[18] is described thus: "Creates UUID version 5 out of scientific name string. It uses globalnames.org domain for DNS namespace. There is a 1:1 relationship between the string and the corresponding UUID, so it allows globally connect data about a name string originated from independent sources without a need to negotiate identifiers." Note, however, that it is actually the specific*name* string that is identified here, not the object, the organism, the 'thing itself'. Thus, the resulting UUID is completely dependent upon the particular name string (with its encoding), it cannot be used as a bridge between different name forms for the same organism, telling us that they are naming the same object. This is due to the fact that it is "generated by hashing a namespace identifier and name". [34] By contrast, the UUID v5 is easily validated, e.g. with an online validator[19].

6   Why Context?

Generally speaking, although it is preferable that identifiers be findable and identifiable also in their unprefixed, pure form, typed identifiers give context by

---

[18] http://globalnames.org/apps/gn-uuid/.
[19] http://www.freecodeformat.com/validate-uuid-guid.php.

means of namespace prefixes of a metadata standard, a vocabulary or ontology. They tell us what kind of identifier it is and sometimes what kind of objects it is used for (e.g. ISBN), but not always (cf. DOI, EAN, UUID). Most importantly they indicate what schema, which rules should be used for their validation.

Page [24] claimed that e.g. "dc:title" is adding "unnecessary complexity (why do we need to know that it's a "dc" title?)" in the JSON expression:

```
{"@context": { "dc:title": "http://purl.org/dc/terms/title" },
            "dc:title": "Darwin Core: An Evolving Community-Developed Biodiversity
                  Data
            Standard" }
```

A simple answer is that namespaces are important to retain meaning from context, serving as a key to interpretation for the future. Self-sustained long-term preservation should ideally mean in a case like this that the dc specification and schemas valid at the time be archived together with the records, or at least that there is provenance metadata including timestamps and namespace of terms used. Metadatafiles in XML usually have a xsi:schemaLocation indicating which schema to validate against, possibly also its @version. This information, together with timestamped metadata elements such as 'dateIssued' should be sufficient to provide context. For JSON metadata there are name/value pairs such as "protocol": "doi", ... "createTime": "2017-01-12T10:49:03Z", ... that could fill the same function. Secondly, context is just as important for validation of records also in the present.

7   A New Contextual, Integrated, Validatable DOI - A BUOI?

As we have seen in the case of Handle above, validatability sometimes comes at a cost: transparency lost. Are we forced to make a choice between the two, then, and let identifiers be fully validatable while we let associated, linked scientific names stand for transparency and meaning? Or, can we create identifiers that are both fully validatable and at the same time more meaningful, providing context? So, here we finally suggest such a 'yapid' model for a 'BUOI' (Best Unique Object Identifier):

```
Model: [namespace prefix].[object type].[object id: 10 positions]_[version]_.[issued date:
    YYYY-MM-DD].[registrant: org.id/ORCID]
```

```
Example (expression of this paper): fabio.Preprint.philipson1_v1-1_
    .2017-03-25.0000-0001-5699-994X
```

It is a model of a structured, contextual, modular, validatable identifier. To make it easier to implement, and more generalizable, there is no requirement of fixed string-length for the two first modules. This means already existing namespaces and object types could already be used to create a BUOI.

Each module/section may hold both letter characters and digits from a limited character set. The full stop (.) was chosen as module separator, since it works well in both xml- and http-environments, without encoding, and is not subject to confusion as sometimes hyphens and dashes (en-dash and em-dash) can be. It also works for tokenization of strings. The object type identified in the second module should belong to the initial namespace prefix. Every namespace can have as many object types as it likes. Namespace schemas could also define valid *data types* for their different object types, thus moving a step further towards supplying *data types* to come with the PIDs, in order to make them more machine actionable [2].

The scalability of the BUOI will mainly depend on the 10 character object id-module and how restricted the permitted character set is. A character set restricted to e.g. [A-Za-z0-9] will still have a potential 62^{10} unique permutations, within each namespace and object-type, still better than the 7 character Handle with NOID. But if this will not be sufficient, the permitted character set will have to be expanded. It is also conceivable, to allow for integration of already existing identifier schemes, that a namespace sets its own character set and string-length restrictions, as long as these are declared in the validation schemas of that namespace or they have otherwise well-known validation algorithms. Now there are also narrow identifier namespaces that do not have as yet different object types defined, possibly since they comprise basically only one type of object. Such is the case basically for e.g. ISBNs and ISSNs. To allow also for these in the BUOI model, we suggest as default second module *'NOT'* = No Object Type. So we could have BUOIs expressing e.g. an IGSN, *International Geo Sample Number* [27]:

Example: `IGSN.NOT.IECUR0002.2005-03-31.gswa-library`

The identifier should thus be fully validatable as a whole or in part (modules) in the corresponding namespace(s). Possibly the version and last two modules might be optional, but they are meant to offer built in data provenance. For organisation identifiers (org.ids), we are still awaiting a common standard like the ORCID for persons. Thus, the BUOI identifier should be right-truncatable so that the same object id from different dates and registrants could easily be searched for.

The resulting BUOIS should be minted within the corresponding namespaces, who would also be the 'custodians' and resolving authorities of their BUOIS, responsible for their uniqueness within their namespace. Another task would be to monitor and assign sameAs-properties to these BUOIs when identical twins of the same 'thing' are detected in other namespaces.

It has been suggested that in order "to build more connected, cross-linked and digitally accessible Internet content" it is necessary "to assign recognizable, persistent, globally unique, stable identifiers to . . . data objects" [17]. The model proposed here for a BUOI aims to make it fully recognizable, universally unique, stable, but always in a well-known context, seldom alone, and with great potential for backup.

References

1. Berners-Lee, T.: Linked Data (2009). https://www.w3.org/DesignIssues/ LinkedData.html
2. Clark, J.: PIDvasive: What's possible when everything has a persistent identifier? PIDapalooza, 10 November 2016 (2016). https://doi.org/10.6084/m9.figshare. 4233839.v1. Accessed 16 Jan 2017
3. Coyle, K., et al.: How semantic web differs from traditional data processing. RDF Validation in the Cultural Heritage Community. In: International Conference on Dublin Core and Metadata Applications, Austin, October 2014 (2014). http:// dcevents.dublincore.org/IntConf/dc-2014/paper/view/311. Accessed 24 Mar 2017
4. Guo, X.: Yale Persistent Linking Service PIDapalooza, 10 November 2016 (2016). https://doi.org/10.6084/m9.figshare.4235822.v1. Accessed 16 Jan 2017
5. Data Citation Synthesis Group, Martone, M. (ed.): Joint Declaration of Data Citation Principles. FORCE11, San Diego, CA (2014). https://www.force11.org/ group/joint-declaration-data-citation-principles-final
6. DataCite Metadata Working Group: DataCite Metadata Schema for the Publication and Citation of Research Data. Version 4.1. DataCite e.V. (2017). https://doi. org/10.5438/0015. Version 4.1 (2017). https://schema.datacite.org/meta/kernel-4. 1/
7. Doorn, P., Dillo, I.: Assessing the FAIRness of Datasets in Trustworthy Digital Repositories: A Proposal. IDCC Edinburgh, 22 Feb 2017 (2017). http://www.dcc. ac.uk/webfm_send/2481
8. Duerr, R.E., et al.: On the utility of identification schemes for digital earth science data: an assessment and recommendations. Earth Sci. Inform. 4, 139 (2011). ISSN 1865-0473 (Print) 1865-0481 (Online). https://doi.org/10.1007/s12145-011-0083-6
9. Dunning, A., de Smaele, M., Böhmer, J.: Are the FAIR data principles fair? Practice paper. In: 12th International Digital Curation Conference (IDCC 2017), Edinburgh, Scotland, 20–23 February 2017 (2017). https://doi.org/10.5281/zenodo. 321423
10. Fenner, M.: Cool DOI's. DataCite Blog (2016). https://doi.org/10.5438/55e5-t5c0
11. Force11: Guiding Principles for Findable, Accessible, Interoperable and Re-usable Data Publishing Version b1.0. FORCE11, San Diego, CA (2016). https://www. force11.org/node/6062/#Annex6-9
12. Force11: The FAIR Data Principles (2016a).https://www.force11.org/group/ fairgroup/fairprinciples
13. Force11: Guiding Principles for Findable, Accessible, Interoperable and Re-usable Data Publishing Version B1.0 (2016b). https://www.force11.org/fairprinciples
14. Gertler, A., Bullock, J.: Reference Rot: An Emerging Threat to Transparency in Political Science. The Profession (2017). https://doi.org/10.1017/ S1049096516002353
15. Gilmartin, A.: DOIs and matching regular expressions. Crossref Blog, 11 August 2015 (2015). https://www.crossref.org/blog/dois-and-matching-regular-expressions/
16. Global Names Architecture - GNA: New UUID v5 Generation Tool - gn_uuid v0.5.0 (2015).http://globalnames.org/news/2015/05/31/gn-uuid-0-5-0/
17. Guralnick, R., et al.: Community next steps for making globally unique identifiers work for biocollections data. ZooKeys 494, 133–154 (2015). https://doi.org/10. 3897/zookeys.494.9352

18. Hayes, C.: oaDOI: A New Tool for Discovering OA Content. Scholars Cooperative, Wayne State University (2016). http://blogs.wayne.edu/scholarscoop/2016/10/25/oadoi-a-new-tool-for-discovering-oa-content/

19. Hennessey, J., Ge, S.X.: A cross disciplinary study of link decay and the effectiveness of mitigation techniques. In: Proceedings of the Tenth Annual MCBIOS Conference, BMC Bioinform. **14**(Suppl. 14), S5 (2013). https://doi.org/10.1186/1471-2105-14-S14-S5

20. Hornby, N.: About a boy. Indigo (1999). ISBN 978-0-575-40229-4

21. Jones, S.M., Van de Sompel, H., Shankar, H., Klein, M̃., Tobin, R., Grover, C.: Scholarly context adrift: three out of four URI references lead to changed content. PLoS ONE **11**(12), e0167475 (2016). https://doi.org/10.1371/journal.pone.016747

22. Klein, M., et al.: Scholarly context not found: one in five articles suffers from reference rot. PLoS ONE **9**(12), e115253 (2014). https://doi.org/10.1371/journal.pone.0115253

23. Kunze, J., Russell, M.: Noid - search.cpan.org (2006). http://search.cpan.org/~jak/Noid/noid

24. Page, R.: Towards a biodiversity knowledge graph. Res. Ideas Outcomes **2**, e8767 (2016). https://doi.org/10.3897/rio.2.e8767

25. Paskin, N.: Toward unique identifiers. Proc. IEEE **87**(7), 1208–1227 (1999). https://doi.org/10.1109/5.771073

26. Patterson, D., et al.: Challenges with using names to link digital biodiversity information. Biodivers. Data J. **4**, e8080 (2016). https://doi.org/10.3897/BDJ.4.e8080

27. SESAR - System for Earth Sample Registration: What is the IGSN? (2017). http://www.geosamples.org/aboutigsn

28. Van de Sompel, H.: A Signposting Pattern for PIDs. PIDapalooza, Reykjavik, November 2016 (2016). https://doi.org/10.6084/m9.figshare.4249739.v1

29. Van de Sompel, H., Klein, M., Jones, S.M.: Persistent URIs Must Be Used To Be Persistent. In: WWW 2016 (2016). arXiv:1602.09102v1 [cs.DL]. Accessed 29 Feb 2016

30. Wass, J.: When PIDs aren't there. Tales from Crossref Event Data. PIDapalooza, Reykjavik, November 2016 (2016). GMT: https://doi.org/10.6084/m9.figshare.4220580.v1. Accessed 20 Mar 2017

31. Wass, J.: URLs and DOIs: a complicated relationship. CrossRef Blog, 31 January 2017 (2017). https://www.crossref.org/blog/urls-and-dois-a-complicated-relationship/

32. Weitz, C., Weitz, P.: About a boy (2002). http://www.imdb.com/title/tt0276751/, http://core.collectorz.com/movies/about-a-boy-2002. EAN: 3259190282520

33. Wikipedia: Link rot (2017a). https://en.wikipedia.org/wiki/Link_rot. Modified 13 Mar 2017, at 17:46. Retrieved 14 Mar 2017

34. Wikipedia: Universally unique identifier (2017b). https://en.wikipedia.org/wiki/Universally_unique_identifier. Modified 29 Jan 2017, at 15:28. Retrieved 30 Jan 2017

35. Wilkinson, M.D., et al.: The FAIR guiding principles for scientific data management and stewardship. Sci. Data **3**, 160018 (2016). https://doi.org/10.1038/sdata.2016.18

36. Wimalaratne, S., et al.: SPARQL-enabled identifier conversion with Identifiers.org. Bioinformatics **31**(11), 1875–1877 (2015). https://doi.org/10.1093/bioinformatics/btv064

37. Zhou, K., et al.: No more 404s: predicting referenced link rot in scholarly articles for pro-active archiving. In: Proceedings of the 15th ACM/IEEE-CE on Joint Conference on Digital Libraries, JCDL 2015, pp. 233–236 (2015). https://doi.org/10.1145/2756406.2756940

Extending ScholarlyData with Research Impact Indicators

Andrea Giovanni Nuzzolese[1][(✉)], Valentina Presutti[1], Aldo Gangemi[1,2], and Paolo Ciancarini[3]

[1] STLab, ISTC-CNR, Rome, Italy
{andrea.nuzzolese,valentina.presutti,aldo.gangemi}@cnr.it
[2] FICLIT, University of Bologna, Bologna, Italy
[3] DISI, University of Bologna, Bologna, Italy
paolo.ciancarini@unibo.it

Abstract. ScholarlyData is the reference linked dataset of the Semantic Web community about papers, people, organisations, and events related to its academic conferences. In this paper we present an extension of such a linked dataset and its associated ontology (i.e. the conference ontology) in order to represent research impact indicators. The latter includes both traditional (e.g. citation count) and alternative indicators (e.g. altmetrics).

1 Introduction

Citation-based metrics are the key tools used for evaluating the impact of research. As a matter of fact, scholars are ranked for a variety of reasons. For example, in many countries like Italy, France, or Germany there are governmental institutions that use citation count and h-index as the major indicators for carrying out national habilitation processess to the professorship. Nevertheless, non-citation-based metrics or alternative metrics (aka altmetrics) are gaining more and more interest in the scientometrics community as they are able to capture both the volume and nature of attention that research receives online. According to [7] altmetrics is the term that identifies both metrics and the study and use of scholarly impact measures based on activity in online tools and environments. Even though there is limited or none scientific evidence that altmetrics are valid proxies of either impact or utility, a few case studies [6,9,14] have reported moderate correlations between citation-based metrics and altmetrics. We believe that the semantic publishing [4] community might benefit from Linked Open Data that provide formal representation, querying, and reasoning capabilities for dealing with semantically enhanced indicators gathered both from citation-based metrics and altmetrics. Accordingly, we formalise an ontology, i.e. the *indicators-ontology* (I-Ont), designed as a modular extension of the conference-ontology. The latter is the ontology used in ScholaryData, which is the reference linked dataset of the Semantic Web community about papers, people, organisations, and events related to its academic conferences. For experimenting

A. González-Beltrán et al. (Eds.): SAVE-SD 2017/2018, LNCS 10959, pp. 49–60, 2018.
https://doi.org/10.1007/978-3-030-01379-0_4

with the ontology, we generate a linked dataset by adding indicators from Scopus[1] and PlumX[2] to a subset of articles from ScholarlyData and we publish such a dataset on the SPARQL endpoint of ScholarlyData. The rest of the paper is organised as follows. Section 2 presents the related work. Section 3 describes the ontology and provides its formal definition and examples. Section 4 presents the experimental extension of ScholarlyData by using the ontology. Finally, Sect. 5 concludes the paper.

2 Related Work

The knowledge management of scholarly products is an emerging research area in the Semantic Web field known as Semantic Publishing [4]. Semantic Publishing aims at providing access to semantic enhanced scholarly products with the aim of enabling a variety of semantically oriented tasks, such as knowledge discovery, knowledge exploration and data integration. In this context, ontologies for representing citations and scholarly artefacts are not novel. The Bibliographic Ontology[3] (BIBO) is an example of a widely adopted ontology for representing bibliographic things and citations on the Semantic Web. More recently, the Semantic Publishing and Referencing[4] (SPAR) Ontologies have been introduced as a suite of orthogonal and complementary ontologies that enable all aspects of the publishing process. Among the SPAR ontologies, there is a subset of them that is focused on representing bibliographic references and citations with different characterisations. This subsets includes: (i) the Bibliographic Reference Ontology[5] (BiRO) [3], which is an ontology meant to define bibliographic records, bibliographic references, and their compilation into bibliographic collections and bibliographic lists, respectively; (ii) the Citation Typing Ontology (See footnote 5) (CiTO) [12], which is an ontology that enables characterization of the nature or type of citations, both factually and rhetorically; and (iii) the Citation Counting and Context Characterization Ontology[6] (C4O) [3], which enables the representation of bibliographic citations in terms of their number and their context. All those ontological solutions focus on the representation of bibliographic entries and references. Among them, C4O is certainly the ontology that has more overlap with I-Ont. However, C4O is more focused in citation count only, while I-Ont is meant for dealing with a wider spectrum of quantitative indicators. To the best of our knowledge I-Ont is the first effort in providing formal representation to citation-based and alternative indicators in the Semantic Web.

---

[1] http://scopus.com/.
[2] https://plumanalytics.com/.
[3] http://purl.org/ontology/bibo/.
[4] https://w3id.org/spar.
[5] https://w3id.org/spar/biro.
[6] https://w3id.org/spar/c4o.

3   Extending the Conference Ontology with Indicators

ScholarlyData defines an ontology, named the conference-ontology[7], which formalises a subset of the scholarly domain focused on papers, people, organisations, and events related to academic conferences. In this paper we extend the conference-ontology by adding a new ontology module that defines concepts and properties in order to deal with the knowledge associated with research impact indicators and metrics. This module is named the indicators-ontology (I-Ont). In the following sub-sections we provide details about this extension in terms of the design methodology adopted, the description, the formalisation, and the usage example of the ontology.

3.1   Design Methodology

I-Ont is designed by following best design practices and pattern-based ontology engineering aimed at extensively re-using Ontology Design Patterns (ODPs) for modelling ontologies. The design methodology that we follow is based on an extension of the eXtreme Design, an agile design methodology developed in the context of the NeON project[8]. Such an extension mainly focuses on providing ontology engineer with clear strategies for ontology re-use. According to the guidelines provided by, we adopted the *indirect* re-use. This means that ODPs are used as templates. At the same time, the ontology guarantees interoperability by keeping the appropriate alignments with the external ODPs, and provides extensions that satisfy more specific requirements. reports the *competency questions* (CQs) [10] used at design time for modelling the ontology (Table 1).

Table 1. Competency questions used for modelling the ontology.

ID	Competency question
CQ1	What are the indicators a certain paper is associated with?
CQ2	What is the metric used for measuring a certain indicator?
CQ3	What is the value associated with a certain indicator?
CQ4	What is the source or provider of a certain indicator?
CQ5	Is any indicator composed of sub-indicators?

Those CQs are identified by analysing a basic scenario like the following:

According to Scopus, the article titled "Conference linked data: The scholarlydata project" is cited 4 times.

---

[7] https://w3id.org/scholarlydata/ontology/conference-ontology.owl.
[8] http://www.neon-project.org/nw/.

From the scenario we identify the following key points:

- there is a certain article (i.e. "Conference linked data: The scholarlydata project") that is associated with a specific indicator (i.e. the fact the article is cited 4 times by other articles). This point is addressed by CQ1;
- the indicator is measured with a certain metric (i.e. the citation coun). This point is addressed by CQ2;
- there is a certain value (i.e. 4) that the indicator tracks. This point is addressed by CQ3;
- the indicator comes from a certain source (i.e. Scopus). This point is addressed by CQ4.

Additionally, we analyse how article level indicators and metrics are typically represented in online scholarly platforms. Namely, we use PlumX (See footnote 2) for this purpose. We select PlumX as it is listed among the most prominent altmetrics providers [8] and it covers more than 52.6M[9] artefacts. PlumX aggregates different categories of metrics from different sources. This means that PlumX provide indicators at three different granularity level, ranging from the level of the category (i.e. the most general one) to the level of the source (i.e. the most specific one). For example, the article titled "Conference linked data: The scholarlydata project" is associated with 12 captures (i.e. the category in PlumX that indicates that someone wants to come back to a work). The number of captures is provided by PlumX by aggregating different metrics, which are the number of people who have added the article to their online library (i.e. 10 readers) and the number of times the article has been bookmarked (i.e. 2 bookmarks). Additionally, PlumX obtains the metrics by tracking different sources, which, in our example, are Mendeley and CiteULike with 8 and 2 readers, respectively, and Delicious with 2 bookmarks. This scenario is addressed by CQ5.

3.2 Ontology Description

Figure 1 shows the core classes and properties of the indicators-ontology. We use the prefixes : and sd: for the namespaces https://w3id.org/scholarlydata/ontology/indicators-ontology.owl# and https://w3id.org/scholarlydata/ontology/conference-ontology.owl#, respectively.

The class :Indicator represents an indicator. Examples of indicators are the citation count, social media mentions, reads on Mendeley, etc. An :Indicator is associated with a sd:Document by means of the object property :isIndicatorOf. A sd:Document is the class defined in the conference-ontology that represents a scholarly artefact. As the conference-ontology is focused on modelling conferences, the latter class may represent either in-proceedings or proceeding artefacts, i.e. sd:InProceedings and sd:Proceedings, respectively. This modelling solution addresses CQ1. Additionally, an :Indicator is linked to an :IndicatorSource, a :Metric, and an :IndicatorValue by the object properties :hasSource, :basedOnSource, and :hasIndicatorValue, respectively.

---

[9] M stands for millions.

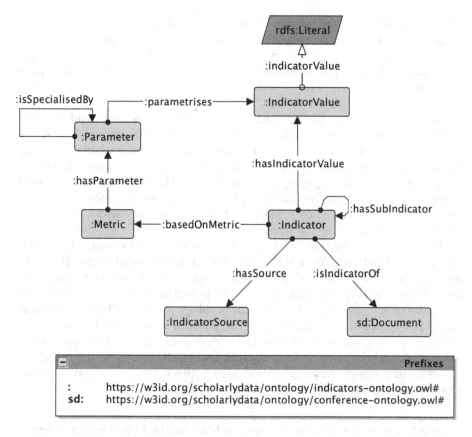

Fig. 1. Core classes and properties of the indicators-ontology.

An :IndicatorSource identifies the source a certain indicator is gathered from (i.e. CQ4). Instead, a :Metric represents the metric used for measuring an indicator. Examples of metrics are the citation count or the count of tweets on Twitter. Finally, an :IndicatorValue represents the actual value an indicator is associated with. The literal value is represented as an argument of an :IndicatorValue by using the datatype property :indicatorValue. The class :Metric is associated with the class :Parameter that represents a specific characteristic or parameter that is measured by using a specific metric. For modelling the classes and the relations among :Indicator, :IndicatorValue, and :Parameter we reuse the Parameter Region[10] ontology design pattern as template. For example, if we provide an indicator about the social media mentions of an article, then the :Parameter is represented by the social media mentions. The latter are measured by using a specific :Metric that can be the count of those mentions. The object property :parametrises is defined with :Parameter and :IndicatorValue as domain and range, respectively. This property is useful

---

[10] http://ontologydesignpatterns.org/cp/owl/parameterregion.owl.

when the possible values that can be associated with a parameter are within a certain range or region in a dimensional space. For example, if we have a parameter that represents the quality of an article in terms of *good* or *poor*, then the latters can be modelled as individuals of the class `:IndicatorValue` and linked to the individual of the class `:Parameter` that represents the quality by using the object property `:parametrises`.

The object property `:hasSubIndicator` is defined as transitive and allows to model hierarchies of indicators associated with an article. For example, it useful when the indicator provided by social media mentions is measured by using the number of tweets mentioning the article. The number of tweets identifies a narrower indicator of the paper, which is linked to the broader one represented by the social media mentions. Similarly, the object property `:hasSubParameter` allows to represent the same scenario but focused on parameters, e.g. twitter mentions narrow social media mentions.

The ontology is annotated with the OPLa ontology [11] for explicitly indicating the reused patterns. We use the property `opla:reusesPatternAsTemplate` to link I-Ont to the pattern we adopted as template i.e. Parameter Region. Similarly, we use the property `opla:isNativeTo` to indicate that certain classes and properties of are core elements of specific ontology patterns. These annotations enable the automatic identification of the patterns reused by I-Ont, e.g. with SPARQL queries, hence facilitating the correct reuse of the ontology. Finally, I-Ont is aligned, by means of an external file, to DOLCE+DnS UltraLight[11]. Tables 2 and 3 report the alignments axioms between the classes and the properties of the two ontologies, respectively.

Table 2. Alignments between the classes of I-Ont and DOLCE+DnS UltraLight.

I-Ont class	Align. axiom	DOLCE class
`:IndicatorValue`	`rdfs:subClassOf`	`dul:Region`
`:IndicatorValue`	`rdfs:subClassOf`	`dul:Amount`
`:Parameter`	`owl:equivalentClass`	`dul:Parameter`

Table 3. Alignments between the properties of I-Ont and DOLCE+DnS UltraLight.

I-Ont class	Align. axiom	DOLCE class
`:isSpecialisedBy`	`owl:equivalentProperty`	`dul:isSpecializedBy`
`:parametrises`	`owl:equivalentProperty`	`dul:parametrizes`
`:hasSubIndicator`	`rdfs:subPropertyOf`	`dul:isSpecializedBy`
`:indicatorValue`	`rdfs:subPropertyOf`	`dul:hasRegionDataValue`

---

[11] http://www.ontologydesignpatterns.org/ont/dul/DUL.owl.

Both I-Ont and the OWL file containing the alignments are available online[12].

3.3 Formalisation

The following is the formalisation of I-Ont described in Sect. 3.2. The formalisation is expressed in Description Logics.

$$
\begin{aligned}
\text{IndicatorValue} &\sqsubseteq = 1value.\text{Literal} \\
\text{Parameter} &\sqsubseteq \forall parametrizes.\text{IndicatorValue} \\
&\sqcap \forall isSpecializedBy.\text{Parameter} \\
\text{Metric} &\sqsubseteq \exists hasParameter.\text{Parameter} \\
\text{Indicator} &\sqsubseteq = 1basedOnMetric.\text{Metric} \\
&\sqcap = 1hasIndictorValue.\text{IndicatorValue} \\
&\sqcap = 1isIndictorOf.\text{Document} \\
&\sqcap \exists hasSource.\text{IndicatorSource} \\
&\sqcap \forall hasSubIndicator.\text{Indicator}
\end{aligned}
\tag{1}
$$

3.4 Usage Example

As a usage example of I-Ont, we show the RDF representation of the scenario we introduce in Sect. 3.1. We remind that such a scenario is about the indicators associated with the papers titled "Conference linked data: The scholarlydata project". The data we present below are expressed as RDF serialised in TURTLE[13]. We use the namespaces available from ScholarlyData.

```
1.  @prefix : <https://w3id.org/scholarlydata/examples/save-sd/>
2.  @prefix sd: <https://w3id.org/scholarlydata/ontology/conference-ontology.
       owl#>
3.  @prefix sd-ind: <https://w3id.org/scholarlydata/ontology/indicators-
       ontology.owl#>
4.  @prefix sd-inpro: <https://w3id.org/scholarlydata/inproceedings/iswc2016/
       paper/resource/>
5.  @prefix rdf: <http://www.w3.org/1999/02/22-rdf-syntax-ns#>
6.
7.  :resource-25-citation-count a sd-ind:Indicator;
8.    sd-ind:isIndicatorOf sd-inpro:resource-25;
9.    sd-ind:hasSource :scopus;
10.   sd-ind:basedOnMetric :scopus-citation-count;
11.   sd-ind:hasIndicatorValue :resource-25-citation-count-value .
12.
13. sd-inpro:resource-25 a sd:InProceedings;
14.      sd:title "Conference Linked Data: the ScholarlyData project" .
15.
16. :scopus-citation-count a :Metric;
17.      sd-ind:hasParameter :citation-count .
18.
19. :resource-25-citation-count-value a :IndicatorValue
20.      sd-ind:indicatorValue 4 .
```

---

[12] I-Ont is available at https://w3id.org/scholarlydata/ontology/indicators-ontology.owl. The alignments are available at https://w3id.org/scholarlydata/ontology/indicators-ontology-aligns.owl.

[13] https://www.w3.org/TR/turtle/.

The example describes an indicator, i.e. `:resource-25-citation-count` associated with:

- a document (cf. line 8). The relation is expressed by the predicate-object `sd-ind:isIndicatorOf sd-inpro:resource-25`, where the object identifies the in-proceedings article (cf. line 13) titled "Conference Linked Data: the ScholarlyData project" (cf. line 14);
- a source (cf. line 9), which is, namely Scopus (i.e. `:scopus`);
- a metric (cf. line 10), which is the Scopus-based citation count `:scopus-citation-count`. This metric has the citation count (i.e. `:citation-count`) as the parameter being measured (cf. line 17);
- an indicator value metric (cf. line 11), which represents the number of citations tracked by Scopus for the specific article.

Instead, the RDF below provides different indicators based on altmetrics tracked by PlumX for the same article of the example above.

```
1.  :resource-25-captures a sd-ind:Indicator;
2.  sd-ind:isIndicatorOf sd-inpro:resource-25;
3.  sd-ind:hasSource :plumx;
4.  sd-ind:basedOnMetric :plumx-captures;
5.  sd-ind:hasIndicatorValue :resource-25-captures-value ;
6.      sd-ind:hasSubIndicator :resource-25-readers, :resource-25-bookmarks .
7.
8.  :resource-25-readers a sd-ind:Indicator;
9.  sd-ind:isIndicatorOf sd-inpro:resource-25;
10. sd-ind:hasSource :plumx;
11. sd-ind:basedOnMetric :plumx-readers;
12. sd-ind:hasIndicatorValue :resource-25-readers-value ;
13. sd-ind:hasSubIndicator :resource-25-mendeley-readers, :resource-25-citeulike-readers .
14.
15. :resource-25-bookmarks a sd-ind:Indicator;
16. sd-ind:isIndicatorOf sd-inpro:resource-25;
17. sd-ind:hasSource :plumx;
18. sd-ind:basedOnMetric :plumx-bookmarks;
19. sd-ind:hasIndicatorValue :resource-25-bookmarks-value ;
20.     sd-ind:hasSubIndicator :resource-25-delicious-bookmarks .
21.
22. :resource-25-mendeley-readers a sd-ind:Indicator;
23. sd-ind:isIndicatorOf sd-inpro:resource-25;
24. sd-ind:hasSource :mendeley;
25. sd-ind:basedOnMetric :mendeley-readers;
26. sd-ind:hasIndicatorValue :resource-25-mendeley-readers-value .
27.
28. :resource-25-citeulike-readers a sd-ind:Indicator;
29. sd-ind:isIndicatorOf sd-inpro:resource-25;
30. sd-ind:hasSource :citeulike;
31. sd-ind:basedOnMetric :citeulike-readers;
32. sd-ind:hasIndicatorValue :resource-25-citeulike-readers-value .
33.
28. :resource-25-delicious-bookmarks a sd-ind:Indicator;
29. sd-ind:isIndicatorOf sd-inpro:resource-25;
30. sd-ind:hasSource :delicious;
31. sd-ind:basedOnMetric :delicious-bookmarks;
32. sd-ind:hasIndicatorValue :resource-25-delicious-bookmarks-value .
33.
34. :plumx-captures a sd-ind:Metric;
35.     sd-ind:hasParameter :captures .
36.
37. :plumx-readers a sd-ind:Metric;
38.     sd-ind:hasParameter :readers .
39.
```

```
40. :plumx-bookmarks a sd-ind:Metric;
41.     sd-ind:hasParameter :captures .
42.
43. :menedely-readers a sd-ind:Metric;
44.     sd-ind:hasParameter :readers .
45.
46. :citeulike-readers a sd-ind:Metric;
47.     sd-ind:hasParameter :readers .
48.
49. :delicious-bookmarks a sd-ind:Metric;
50.     sd-ind:hasParameter :bookmarks .
51.
52. :captures a sd-ind:Parameter;
53.     sd-ind:isSpecialisedBy :readers , :bookmarks .
54.
55. :readers a sd-ind:Parameter .
56.
57. :bookmarks a sd-ind:Parameter
58.
59. :resource-25-captures-value a :IndicatorValue
60.     sd-ind:indicatorValue 12 .
61.
62. :resource-25-readers-value a :IndicatorValue
63.     sd-ind:indicatorValue 10 .
64.
65. :resource-25-bookmarks-value a :IndicatorValue
66.     sd-ind:indicatorValue 2 .
67.
68. :resource-25-mendeley-readers-value a :IndicatorValue
69.     sd-ind:indicatorValue 8 .
70.
71. :resource-25-citeulike-readers-value a :IndicatorValue
72.     sd-ind:indicatorValue 2 .
73.
74. :resource-25-delicious-bookmarks-value a :IndicatorValue
75.     sd-ind:indicatorValue 2 .
```

In the example above the article sd-inpro:resource-25 is associated with different indicators, i.e. :resource-25-captures, :resource-25-readers, :resource-25-bookmarks, :resource-25-mendeley-readers, :resource-25-citeulike-readers, and :resource-25-delicious-bookmarks. Those indicators, are organised hierarchically. In fact, :resource-25-captures is the top-level indicator, which has two sub-indicators consisting of :resource-25-readers and :resource-25-bookmarks, respectively (cf. line 6). In turn, :resource-25-readers has two sub-indicators, i.e. :resource-25-mendeley-readers and :resource-25-citeulike-readers (cf. line 13), and :resource-25-bookmarks has one sub-indicator only, i.e. :resource-25-delicious-bookmarks. The indicators are described by the same properties as in the previous example.

4   Extending the Linked Dataset

I-Ont is used for modelling an extension of ScholarlyData that exposes a linked open dataset with research impact indicators based both on citation count metrics and altmetrics. The extension is performed by taking into account only the in-proceedings articles that are associated with a DOI in ScholarlyData. As at February 2018 ScholarlyData contains 828 out of 5,185 (~6%) in-proceedings articles with a DOI. Accordingly, we generate an RDF graph for those articles that counts 25,400 triples. The RDF graph is available for download on the portal[14] as N-TRIPLES and is accessible from the page about data dumps[15]. We plan to release periodic updates of the indicators in ScholarlyData, thus the naming convention adopted for RDF dumps uses the date when a certain update has been performed (e.g. 03-02-2018-indicators.nt). Additionally, the latest version of the dump is available for querying on the SPARQL endpoint[16]. The following example shows a SPARQL query that retrieves all the articles with their associated indicator values (i.e. ?source) tracked by a source (i.e. ?source) for a certain parameter (i.e. ?parameter).

```
PREFIX iont: <https://w3id.org/scholarlydata/ontology/indicators-ontology.owl#>
SELECT ?article ?parameter ?source ?value
WHERE{
   ?indicator iont:isIndicatorOf ?article;
       iont:basedOnMetric/iont:hasParameter ?parameter;
       iont:hasSource ?source;
       iont:hasIndicatorValue/iont:indicatorValue ?value
}
```

Table 4 reports the number of individuals in ScholarlyData modelled with the classes of I-Ont. The figures reported in Table 4 can be obtained via SPARQL[17].

Table 4. Number of individual by class of I-Ont in ScholarlyData.

I-Ont class	# of individuals
:IndicatorValue	2,511
:Indicator	2,511
:Metric	31
:Parameter	16
:IndicatorSource	12

Table 5 reports the average values we record on the dataset for the parameters measured on different sources with specific metrics. We use the hierarchy of indicators enabled by the property :hasSubIndicator (cf. Section 3.2) in order to get those value via the SPARQL endpoint of ScholarlyData[18].

---

[14] https://w3id.org/scholarlydata/dumps/indicators/03-02-2018-indicators.nt.
[15] https://w3id.org/scholarlydata/dumps.
[16] https://w3id.org/scholarlydata/sparql.
[17] https://goo.gl/t88H9c.
[18] https://goo.gl/jxSRSx.

Table 5. Average values for parameters used as indicators.

Provider	Top-level parameter	Parameter	Source	Avg value
Scopus	Citations	Citation count	Scopus	23.75
PlumX	Captures	Exports-saves	Ebsco	3.5
PlumX	Captures	Readers	CiteULike	3.64
PlumX	Captures	Readers	Mendeley	34.92
PlumX	Captures	Readers	SSRN	2
PlumX	Mentions	Blog mentions	Blogs	1
PlumX	Mentions	References	Wikipedia	1
PlumX	Social media	Shares, like & comments	Facebook	1.5
PlumX	Social media	+1s	Google+	10
PlumX	Social media	Tweets	Twitter	1.5
PlumX	Usage	Downloads	SSRN	469
PlumX	Usage	Abstract view	DSpace	16
PlumX	Usage	Abstract view	EBSCO	21.33
PlumX	Usage	Abstract view	SSRN	2.106
PlumX	Usage	Full-text view	EBSCO	3
PlumX	Usage	Links out	EBSCO	10

5   Conclusions

This work presents the indicator-ontology (I-Ont), which is designed as a modular extension of the conference-ontology used by ScholarlyData. Such an extension is obtained by using well established ontology engineering methods based on the reuse and interlink of ontology design patterns. We showcase I-Ont by using the ontology for representing indicators for a subset of articles in ScholarlyData. The result of the showcase is an RDF graph that is published in the public SPARQL endpoint of ScholarlyData and can be downloaded as a separate dump. As a future work we aim at aligning I-Ont with SPAR ontologies, i.e. c4o, and covering the whole ScholarlyData linked dataset with indicator.

Acknowledgements. This work has been part-funded by the Italian National Agency for the Evaluation of Universities and Research Institutes (ANVUR) under grant agreement "Measuring the Impact of Research: Alterative Indicators" (MIRA).

References

1. Gangemi, A., Presutti, V.: Ontology design patterns. In: Staab, S., Studer, R. (eds.) Handbook on Ontologies. IHIS, pp. 221–243. Springer, Heidelberg (2009). https://doi.org/10.1007/978-3-540-92673-3_10

2. Nuzzolese, A.G., Gentile, A.L., Presutti, V., Gangemi, A.: Conference linked data: the ScholarlyData project. In: Groth, P., et al. (eds.) ISWC 2016. LNCS, vol. 9982, pp. 150–158. Springer, Cham (2016). https://doi.org/10.1007/978-3-319-46547-0_16

3. Di Iorio, A., et al.: Describing bibliographic references in RDF. In: Proceedings of 4th Workshop on Semantic Publishing, SePublica 2014, CEUR Workshop Proceedings 1155. CEUR-WS.org (2014)

4. Shotton, D.: Semantic publishing: the coming revolution in scientific journal publishing. Learn. Publ. **22**(2), 85–94 (2009)

5. Blomqvist, E., Presutti, V., Daga, E., Gangemi, A.: Experimenting with eXtreme design. In: Cimiano, P., Pinto, H.S. (eds.) EKAW 2010. LNCS (LNAI), vol. 6317, pp. 120–134. Springer, Heidelberg (2010). https://doi.org/10.1007/978-3-642-16438-5_9

6. Shema, H., et al.: Do blog citations correlate with a higher number of future citations? Research blogs as a potential source for alternative metrics. J. Assoc. Inf. Sci. Technol. **65**(5), 1018–1027 (2014)

7. Priem, J., et al.: The altmetrics collection. PloS one **7**(11), e48753 (2012)

8. Ortega, J.L.: Reliability and accuracy of altmetric providers: a comparison among Altmetric, PlumX and Crossref Event Data (2018)

9. Bar-Ilan, J.: JASIST 2001–2010. Bull. Assoc. Inf. Sci. Technol. **38**(6), 24–28 (2012)

10. Grüninger, M., Fox, M.S.: The role of competency questions in enterprise engineering. In: Rolstadås, A. (ed.) Benchmarking—Theory and Practice. IAICT, pp. 22–31. Springer, Boston (1995). https://doi.org/10.1007/978-0-387-34847-6_3

11. Hitzler, P., et al.: Towards a simple but useful ontology design pattern representation language. In: WOP 2017. CEUR-ws (2017)

12. Peroni, S., Shotton, D.: FaBiO and CiTO: ontologies for describing bibliographic resources and citations. J. Web Semant.: Sci. Serv. Agents World Wide Web **17**, 33–43 (2012)

13. Presutti, V., Lodi, G., Nuzzolese, A., Gangemi, A., Peroni, S., Asprino, L.: The role of ontology design patterns in linked data projects. In: Comyn-Wattiau, I., Tanaka, K., Song, I.-Y., Yamamoto, S., Saeki, M. (eds.) ER 2016. LNCS, vol. 9974, pp. 113–121. Springer, Cham (2016). https://doi.org/10.1007/978-3-319-46397-1_9

14. Li, X., et al.: Validating online reference managers for scholarly impact measurement. Scientometrics **91**(2), 461–471 (2012)

Geographical Trends in Research: A Preliminary Analysis on Authors' Affiliations

Andrea Mannocci[✉], Francesco Osborne, and Enrico Motta

Knowledge Media Institute, The Open University, Milton Keynes, UK
{andrea.mannocci,francesco.osborne,enrico.motta}@open.ac.uk

Abstract. In the last decade, research literature reached an enormous volume with an unprecedented current annual increase of 1.5 million new publications. As research gets ever more global and new countries and institutions, either from academia or corporate environment, start to contribute with their share, it is important to monitor this complex scenario and understand its dynamics.

We present a study on a conference proceedings dataset extracted from Springer Nature Scigraph that illustrates insightful geographical trends and highlights the unbalanced growth of competitive research institutions worldwide. Results emerged from our micro and macro analysis show that the distributions among countries of institutions and papers follow a power law, and thus very few countries keep producing most of the papers accepted by high-tier conferences. In addition, we found that the annual and overall turnover rate of the top 5, 10 and 25 countries is extremely low, suggesting a very static landscape in which new entries struggle to emerge. Finally, we highlight the presence of an increasing gap between the number of institutions initiating and overseeing research endeavours (i.e. first and last authors' affiliations) and the total number of institutions participating in research. As a consequence of our analysis, the paper also discusses our experience in working with affiliations: an utterly simple matter at first glance, that is instead revealed to be a complex research and technical challenge yet far from being solved.

Keywords: Scholarly knowledge · Affiliations · Conferences
Scientometrics · Research · SciGraph

1 Introduction

Over the last decade, research started to scale up in terms of produced volume of papers, authors and contributing institutions. Nowadays, research literature is estimated to round up 100–150 million publications with an annual increase rate around 1.5 million new publications [2]. Such a complex, global-scale system is worth studying in order to understand its dynamics and internal equilibria. In particular, the study of authors' affiliations [7,15] has concrete impact on

© Springer Nature Switzerland AG 2018
A. González-Beltrán et al. (Eds.): SAVE-SD 2017/2018, LNCS 10959, pp. 61–77, 2018.
https://doi.org/10.1007/978-3-030-01379-0_5

the interpretation of research as a complex phenomenon inserted in a delicate socioeconomic and geopolitical scenario.

In this study, we present an analysis on a dataset of conference proceedings metadata covering the 1996–2017 period, which was distilled from SciGraph[1], a free linked open data (LOD) dataset about scholarly knowledge published and curated by Springer Nature. In particular, we first present a *macro analysis* on the full dataset, including conference proceedings across several scientific disciplines (e.g. computer science, life sciences, chemistry, engineering) and then a *micro analysis*, which focuses on three high-tier conferences close to our area of expertise: the International Semantic Web Conference (ISWC), the Extended Semantic Web Conference (ESWC), and the International Conference on Theory and Practice of Digital Libraries (TPDL).

The main contribution of this work is threefold. Firstly, we found that, over the observed period, the distributions of institutions and papers among countries follow a power law, consistently to what previously demonstrated in the literature across the 1981–2010 period [4,10,12,15]. Therefore, very few subjects keep producing most of the papers accepted by scientific conferences. Secondly, we show how the annual and overall turnover rate of the top 5, 10 and 25 countries is extremely low, suggesting a very static landscape in which new entries struggle to emerge. Finally, we highlight an increasing gap between the number of institutions initiating and overseeing research endeavours (i.e. first and last authors' affiliations) and the total number of institutions participating in research.

2   Literature Review

A variety of bibliometrics studies in the last 30 years highlighted the importance of different factors (or *proxies*) of the presumed quality of research produced by researchers, institutions, and countries. In particular, they showed how researchers' performance can be affected by factors such as gender [9], location [7], reputation [18], centrality in the co-authorship network [19], online presence [20], and so on. For instance, Jadidi et al. [9] investigated gender-specific differences on about 1 million computer scientists over the course of 47 years and observed that women are on average less likely to adopt the collaboration patterns associated with a strong research impact. Petersen et al. [18] introduced an approach for quantifying the influence of an author reputation on their future research impact and found that reputation is associated with the citation count of articles, but only during the early phase of the citation lifecycle. Sarigol et al. [19] demonstrated that a classifier based only on co-authorship network centrality metrics can predict with high precision whether an article will be highly cited within five years after the publication. Thelwall et al. [20] showed that there is a significant association between eleven tested altmetrics and citations in the Web of Science dataset.

---

[1] Springer   Nature   SciGraph,   https://www.springernature.com/gp/researchers/scigraph.

Some groundbreaking work focused in particular on the role of countries, cities, and organisations (e.g. university, research institutes) and highlighted the great discrepancy in quality and quality of the research produced by different nations. For instance, May [12] analysed the numbers of publications and citations of different countries in the 1981–1994 period using the Institute for Scientific Information database (Ed. then Thomson ISI and finally Clarivate Analytics), which included more than 8,4 million papers and 72 million citations. In accordance with our results, the authors found that the countries that produced the highest share of research papers more than 20 years ago were USA, United Kingdom, Japan, Germany, France, Canada, Italy, India, Australia, and Netherlands. King [10] built on this work and analysed the 1993–2002 period adopting again the Thomson ISI dataset. Ten years after May's study, the most important countries regarding research were essentially the same. In particular, King found that the countries that produced most of the top 1% highly cited publications were USA, United Kingdom, Germany, Japan, France, Canada, Italy, Switzerland, Netherlands, and Australia. Pan et al. [15] continued this line of work by performing a systematic analysis of citation networks between cities and countries in the 2003–2010 period. In accordance to our findings, they found that the citation distribution of countries and cities follows a power law. According to their citation rank, the main producer of research in the period under analysis were USA, United Kingdom, Germany, Japan, France, Canada, China, Italy, Netherlands, and Australia. Interestingly, they also argued that a necessary (but not sufficient) condition for a country to reach an impact larger than the world average is to invest more than about 100,000 USD per researcher annually.

Other studies are more restricted in scope and focus either on specific locations [1,3,13] or on specific research areas, such as tropical medicine [5], nanomedicine [23], biomedicine [6], and e-learning [8]. A good review of bibliometrics studies that explicitly take into account the spatial factor can be found in Frenken et al. [7]. Unlike the aforementioned analyses, in this preliminary study we (i) focused on the temporal evolution of countries and institutions in conference papers, (ii) performed an analysis on the first and last authors' affiliations, and (iii) addressed specific high-tier conferences in the domain of semantic web and digital libraries during the 2003–2017 period.

3 Data

A main premise for our study is the availability of a scholarly knowledge dataset containing information about authors' affiliations sufficiently detailed and structured, i.e. including both institution name and country, possibly disambiguated through a persistent identifier.

For the time being, given the preliminary character of this analysis, we kept intentionally out of consideration pay-walled data sources such as Scopus[2], Web

---

[2] Scopus, https://www.scopus.com.

of Science[3], and Microsoft Academic[4], and we focused on what can be freely retrieved on the Web, in the spirit of open and reproducible science [22].

Some top-quality scholarly datasets such as DBLP [11] and Semantic Scholar[5] are not apt to our study as they miss essential information about authors' affiliations. Other datasets technically provide authors' affiliations, but the relevant metadata are often incomplete. For example, Crossref[6], despite declaring a field devised for affiliations in their metadata API JSON format[7], provides in a minority of cases a simple array of affiliation strings. Besides, affiliation strings often exhibit several well-known ambiguity issues due to (i) alternate forms (e.g., "Open University" and "The Open University"), (ii) different languages (e.g., "Università di Pisa" and "University of Pisa"), (iii) different granularity and missing information (e.g., "Knowledge Media Institute, Milton Keynes").

After an analysis of current solutions for selecting a dataset curated at the source with regards to these aspects, our choice fell onto SciGraph[8], a LOD dataset published and curated by Springer Nature. To the best of our knowledge, SciGraph is the only large-scale dataset providing reconciliation of authors' affiliations by disambiguating and linking them to an external authoritative datasets in terms of institutions (in this case GRID, the Global Research Identifier Database[9]). In its entirety, SciGraph consists of 78 distinct datasets and includes about 2 billion triples describing research literature objects such as journal articles, conference papers, books, and monographs published by Springer Nature and spanning over a broad set of topics such as computer science, medicine, life sciences, chemistry, engineering, astronomy, and more.

For our analysis we focused on conferences proceedings as conferences are the focal point of networking and knowledge exchange among practitioners. To this end, we downloaded from SciGraph the *books* and *book chapters* datasets spanning from 1996 to 2017 and the *conferences* dataset linking together all the books related to the same conference series. Additionally, we downloaded the ancillary GRID dataset[10] providing a high-quality and curated database of institutions and organisations participating in research. These datasets were loaded in a graph database[11] resulting in a graph of 313,035,870 triples. Then we extracted via a SPARQL query[12] a TSV (tab-separated values) dump describing all the authors' contributions[13] to papers published in conference proceedings.

---

[3] Web of Science, https://clarivate.com/products/web-of-science.
[4] Microsoft Academic, https://academic.microsoft.com.
[5] Semantic Scholar, https://www.semanticscholar.org.
[6] Crossref, https://www.crossref.org.
[7] https://github.com/Crossref/rest-api-doc/blob/master/api_format.md.
[8] SciGraph datasets, http://scigraph.springernature.com/explorer/downloads/.
[9] GRID, https://www.grid.ac.
[10] GRID dataset, https://www.grid.ac/downloads.
[11] GraphDB, http://graphdb.ontotext.com.
[12] https://github.com/andremann/SAVE-SD-2018/blob/master/extract.sparql.
[13] For the sake of clarity, if paper p is authored by authors a_1 and a_2, two distinct *contributions* (i.e. two distinct rows) are present in our dataset, one for each author.

This raw dataset counts 1,770,091 contributions for a total of 506,049 unique papers, accepted in 1,028 conferences.

4   Methodology

Since we intended to address both general and specific trends, we performed a *macro analysis*, on the full dataset, and a *micro analysis*, on three high-tier conferences.

In the *macro analysis* we considered all conferences in the 1996–2016 period. We did not consider 2017, since in this year we observed a fairly lower number of contributions and a large amount of unresolved affiliations. The resulting dataset includes 1,664,733 contributions (477,921 unique papers), of which 946,165 contributions are attributed to 1,016 unique conference series.

For the *micro analysis* we focused instead on three high-tier conferences in the fields of semantic web and digital libraries: the International Semantic Web Conference (ISWC), the Extended Semantic Web Conference (ESWC), and the International Conference on Theory and Practice of Digital Libraries (TPDL). We selected them for two main reasons. First, we want to perform this preliminary analysis on familiar venues near to our field of expertise. In the second instance, we were interested in comparing ISWC and ESWC, which are considered the two top conference in the semantic web domain and they traditionally tend to attract quite different demographics. The first is more international, while the second (previously called "European Semantic Web Conference") is more grounded in Europe. Focusing the analysis on three conferences enabled us to manually curate and enrich their data and therefore produce a very comprehensive representation of the involved institution and countries.

The datasets of these conferences were extracted from the raw dataset by selecting the contributions with the relevant DBLP conference series identifier (respectively *semweb*, *esws* and *ercimdl*). In some cases we deliberately chose to manually integrate some conference editions that we found missing (e.g., ISWC 2007 and 2015) and drop contributions that had been mistakenly attributed to the wrong conference (e.g., the First International Workshop of Semantic Web Services and Web Process Composition). For reasons beyond our knowledge, a conference edition appears to be missing from SciGraph (i.e., ESWC 2007) and a couple of others count less contributions than expected (i.e., TPDL 2014 and 2015). However, these few missing and circumscribed data points should not affect the overall validity of our analysis.

The manual curation phase principally aimed at resolving missing affiliations and linking them to correct institutions in the GRID database. In particular, for each contribution whose affiliation details (i.e. gridId, organisation name, city, and country) were empty, we used its affiliation string (a plain "catch-all" text field) to infer the missing pieces of information. Often, for lack of clarity of such a string, we availed of information accessible in the Springer web page about the paper and from institutional websites in order to resolve the affiliation correctly. Whenever GRID provided no entry for the institution in question, yet we were able to narrow down at least its country (e.g. aCompany GmbH), we opted for "minting" a fictional identifier. When even this was not possible, we had no other option but to leave the affiliation unresolved. Fortunately, our enrichment procedure left our datasets with a minority of unresolved contributions, as we discuss later. We argue that this process, even if time consuming, enabled us to analyse affiliations with a good granularity and to take into account also institutions involved in a small number of research outputs. Table 1 summarises the key features about the datasets used in our analysis.

For each dataset, we took in consideration the author order and hypothesise that the first author indicates the *initiator* of a research effort, while the last author indicates the professor or the research line manager acting as an *overseer* of the work; a hypothesis that seems reasonable in many disciplines, and especially computer science. We validated this intuition by analysing the name of the researchers that appeared most as last author in the datasets under analysis. In the macro analysis dataset, we found as overseers a number of very influential scientists that lead significant research groups, such as Dinggang Shen, director of several units at UNC-Chapel Hill, Jason H. Moore, director of the Institute for Biomedical Informatics at the School of Medicine of the University of Pennsylvania, Zhang Mengjie, and so on. Similarly, in the semantic web field we encountered influential professors and scientists such as Ian Horrocks, Mark A. Musen, Stefan Decker and Sören Auer. Of course this hypothesis does not hold in all the cases (e.g. papers in which the order is alphabetical) and does not reflect a common custom for all academic disciplines (e.g. in Humanities & Social Sciences); however, we believe that this can be a good approximation that works well for this study.

We also analysed trends about papers (identified by unique Digital Object Identifiers, *DOIs*), countries, and institutions (identified by unique *gridIDs*) over time, as well as their distributions across the entire observed period. Besides, we tried to assess to what extent the research landscape is open (or closed) to changes by measuring the variability of country rankings over the years. To this end, we defined as rate of change r_{change} the percentage of new entries (not considering permutations) entering in a top-n rankings from one year to the following. For example, if in year x the top-3 ranking is $\{a, b, c\}$ and in year $x + 1$ is $\{a, c, d\}$ then $r_{change} = 0.33$.

The result shown in the following are obtained by analysing the datasets within a Python notebook[14] availing of Pandas library[15]. For reproducibility purposes, the curated datasets and the Python notebook are accessible on Github[16]. Due to Github limitations on files size, the dataset used for the macro analysis has not been uploaded (851 MB); however, it can be easily reconstructed following the methodology we just described. All the plots here included, and many

---

[14] Jupiter notebook, https://ipython.org/notebook.html.

[15] Pandas library, https://pandas.pydata.org.

[16] Code and datasets, https://github.com/andremann/SAVE-SD-2018.

Table 1. Features of the datasets used for our analysis

	Macro analysis	Micro analysis		
		ISWC	ESWC	TPDL
Observation period	1996–2016	2003–2016	2004–2017 (excl. 2007)	2003–2017
Contributions	1,664,733	3,924	4,224	3,271
Unique papers (DOIs)	477,921	1,028	1,141	919
Countries	163	44	54	52
Institutions (gridIDs)	14,773	3,739	4,076	3,208
Conference series	1,016	-	-	-

others not reported for the sake of space, are available online[17] as well. As the plots are rich in content, the images reported here cannot adequately render all the information available. Therefore, we strongly suggest the reader to consult also the online resources.

5 Results

In this Section, we report the results emerged from our macro and micro analysis. The discussion of such results can be found in Sect. 6.

5.1 Macro Analysis

The number of contributions for each year, either with or without resolved affiliations, is reported in Fig. 1a. We can notice how information about authors' affiliation is present in the majority of contributions in our dataset. Figure 1b shows the number of unique papers ($DOIs$) and the number of unique institutions ($gridIDs$) over the years. Despite a scale factor, the two trends are correlated with a Pearson correlation coefficient [17] of 0.987, suggesting that not only the volume of research literature has increased, but also that the number of institutions contributing to research has gone through the same trend.

Figure 2a presents the number of institutions involved in research over time and highlights in two dedicated series the number of institutions appearing as affiliations of the first (in yellow) and last authors (in green) respectively. For the sake of clarity, we included also the differential trend (in red) between first/last authors' affiliations and all the others, by computing $gridIDs_{total} - mean(gridIDs_{first}, gridIDs_{last})$. The figure suggests that there is a substantial gap between the number of institutions that initiate (first author) and overseer (last author) a research endeavour versus the total number of institutions involved in research. Also, this gap appears to grow over time despite the fact that the average number of authors per paper does not exhibit the same growth,

---

[17] http://nbviewer.jupyter.org/github/andremann/SAVE-SD-2018/blob/master/Analysis.ipynb?flush_cache=true.

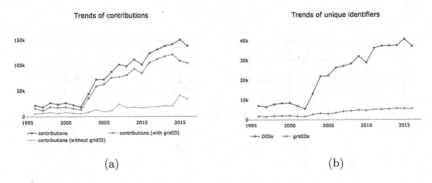

Fig. 1. Trends of contributions (with and without resolved affiliations), papers and institutions

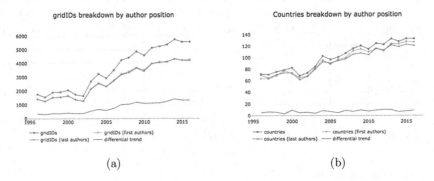

Fig. 2. Institutions and countries breakdown according to author position (Color figure online)

oscillating steadily between 2.6 and 3.3 in the same time interval (not reported here for space reasons, but available online). We will investigate this phenomenon further in the micro analysis.

Similarly, Fig. 2b highlights the trend of countries in function of author position. Also in this case, we see a gap between the number of first/last authors' countries of affiliation and the total number of countries involved in research. The differential trend oscillate from 5 to 9 over the observed period, despite being not remarkably growing as in the case of institutions. We believe that this is due to the naturally limited number of countries, as opposed to the virtually unbounded number of new institutions that keep appearing each year.

Figure 3a reports the distribution of papers among countries over the observed period without taking initiators and overseers into account. The distribution is heavily skewed in favour of USA, China, and Germany, highlighting a potential bias in the dataset. Indeed, a manual inspection of the dataset revealed the presence of many local Asian, Chinese, German, and American conferences. Despite the potential bias, the power law characteristic of the distribution is evident. In the figure inset, we report the best fit power law obtained by fitting

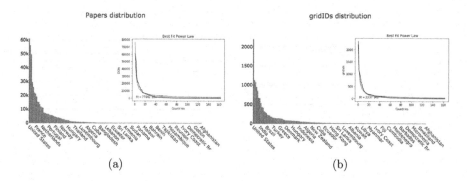

Fig. 3. Papers and institutions distributions across countries and their power law approximation

the data points with the least squares method to a power law function of the type $y = ax^s$, with $s < 0$. Interestingly, the power law characteristic of the paper distribution over countries is also valid in each year across the period. We verified this by checking Pareto rule [16] for every year, and discovered that invariably 20% of the countries produces more than 80% of the papers.

The distribution of institutions over countries (i.e. the number of institutions present in a given country) follows as well a power law, as shown by Fig. 3b. For the sake of space, we omitted the details about the distributions of papers for first and last authors, which the reader can consult online.

We also noticed that the average r_{change} for the top-5, top-10 and top-25 across the observed period yielded 0.13, 0.09, and 0.08 respectively. This suggests that (i) year by year it is fairly hard for outsiders to break in a top-n, and (ii) that it gets harder and harder as the top-n set broadens. In addition, over the 21 year span of our observation, the top-5 has been visited by 10 countries, the top-10 by 16 and the top-25 by 36. For example, the top-10 has been visited by USA (21), Germany (21), Japan (21), United Kingdom (21), Italy (21), France (21), Spain (19), Canada (16), China(13), Netherlands (9), South Korea (6), India (6), Poland (5), Russia (4), Australia (3), Switzerland (3); further details are available online.

5.2 Micro Analysis

Here we summarise the results obtained by analysing the three high-tier conferences (i.e., ISWC, ESWC and TPDL).

Figures 4 and 5 show respectively the number of contributions, and the number of papers and institutions contributing to the conferences over the years. Since we manually curated the three datasets, the percentage of unresolved affiliations is much lower than the one of the macro analysis. Again we can observe a high correlation between the number of papers accepted and the number of contributing institutions. As opposed to what we observed in the macro analysis, this time the number of papers and institutions are within the same order

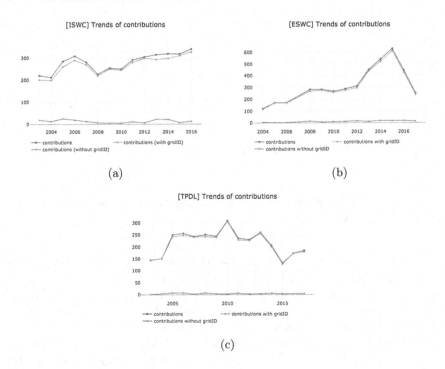

Fig. 4. Trends of contributions with and without resolved affiliations

of magnitude. This can be explained considering that the number of papers accepted each year by a conference is naturally limited, whereas there is not limitation to the number of institutions that can apply.

Similar to what was observed in the macro analysis, Fig. 6 shows the number of institutions contributing to the conferences and highlights the trends of the ones appearing as first and last authors' affiliations. As in the previous analysis, the growing gap between the institutions associated with first/last authors and the total number of affiliations is present for all the three conferences as suggested by the differential trend.

We investigated further and retrieved the sets of institutions never appearing as either first or last authors' affiliations throughout the entire observed periods (available online). Here it can be noted how prestigious universities and research centres appear side by side with smaller firms and less well-known universities or institutions. This result indicates that the gap is "populated" by institutions that at some point collaborated in semantic web research (or digital libraries) making it through, whereas they never stand out on their own (for reasons beyond our knowledge) in the communities of the respective conferences. Institutions like national libraries, the European Bioinformatics Institute, the British Geological Survey, the National Institute of Standards and Technology, and so on, provided interesting research case studies or support that eventually culminated in a publication, but apparently never happened to author a paper

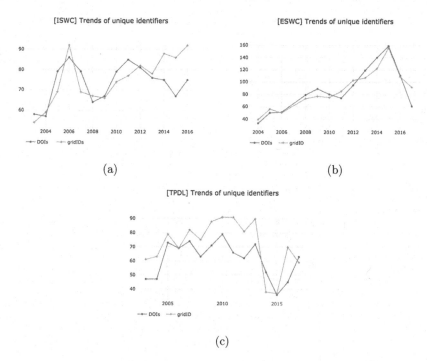

Fig. 5. Trends of papers and institutions

on their own. We also verified that the intersection between these sets across different conferences is not empty, suggesting that a few institutions struggled to surface as key contributors, despite being present in either community.

It is important to stress that the sets of institutions appearing as first/last authors' affiliation in different years are very likely to differ; it is not the intention of this study to suggest that institutions initiating or overseeing research are essentially unaltered throughout time.

Figure 7 shows the trend of countries contributing to the conferences, highlighting country affiliations of first and last authors. Consistently to what we observed in the macro analysis a gap is present and growing.

Figures 8 and 9 again confirm the results shown in previous section even at micro level: the distribution of papers and institutions across countries indeed follows a power law. However, the power law characteristic surfaces only across the entire observed period as, in general, in a single year the Pareto rule might not be verified mainly because of insufficient data points (i.e. in a single conference edition the number of papers is limited). In this case, evaluating a top-n stratified rate of change for single conferences gets difficult as the set of countries participating in a single year can be quite limited. However, as can be seen in the results online, the situation in the top-10 achieves an average $r_{change} \approx 0.23$. Moreover, it appears that the top-10 is regularly visited by a small number of countries. In particular, in ISWC only 13 countries enter the top-10 more then

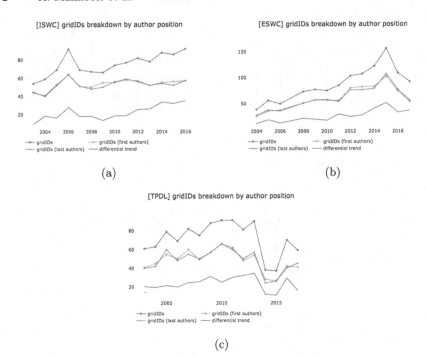

Fig. 6. Institutions breakdown according to author position

3 times in the 14 year period. Similarly, only 14 countries enter the top-10 in ESWC and TPDL.

Finally, we noticed a stronger presence of European countries in ESWC than in the other two conferences; this is probably due to the initial local target of the conference. China is quite involved in the semantic web community, but, perhaps surprising, is less active in the TPDL conference and never appears in the top-10.

6   Discussion

The study of authors' affiliations in research literature has been performed for decades as it can provide answers to socioeconomic questions and frame academic research on a geopolitical canvas rather than studying it as an isolated complex system. In this work we analysed four datasets distilled from Springer Nature Scigraph and provided results on both a macro and a micro scale, focusing on three different high-tier conferences.

The results, in accordance with previous studies [10,12,15], showed that distributions of papers and institutions across countries still exhibit a power law characteristic in the period 1996–2016. In addition, our analysis of the turnover rate highlights that not only top ranks in research are limited to a handful of countries and institutions, but that the situation appears also to be stagnant

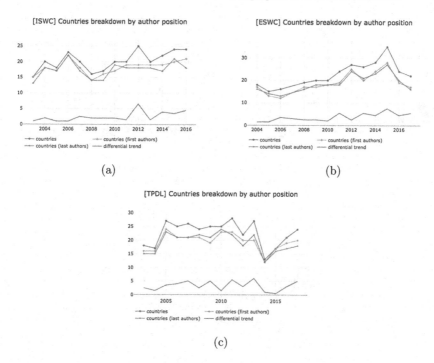

Fig. 7. Countries breakdown according to author position

towards the lower ranks. In general, this reflects the intuition that well-formed research communities exhibit a sort of resistance towards the permeation of outsiders not always sharing knowledge and best practices consolidated over the years. Therefore, we believe that this phenomenon is worth studying further. Besides, the papers eventually accepted in conferences is a minimal fraction of the whole amount of submissions; a much clearer view about openness/closeness of conferences and research communities could be achieved by having access to data about rejected papers held in conference management systems such as EasyChair[18] or ConfTool[19].

The results from our study on first and last authors' affiliations show that, in principle, weighting authors' contributions is an intuition that can provide different keys to interpret data. Other studies dealing with researchers' seniority, for example, take into account the volume of publications produced by a single author throughout a sliding window of W years [21], or the number of consecutive years of publishing activity [9]. We intend to further investigate these techniques and test further our intuition in order to understand its applicability in other disciplines and extend the approach by including other metrics (e.g., seniority); nonetheless, the preliminary results are indeed interesting.

---

[18] EasyChair conference management system, http://easychair.org.

[19] ConfTool conference & event management software, http://www.conftool.net.

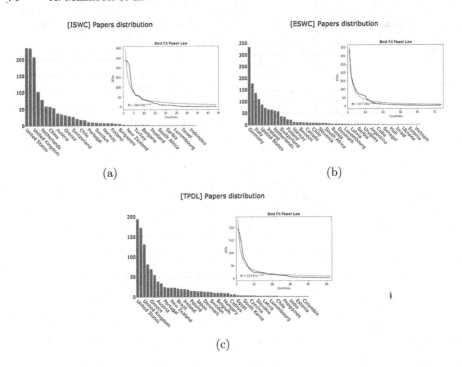

Fig. 8. Paper distributions across countries and power law approximations

Furthermore, a final remark has to be spent about the very peculiar nature of the data here considered: conference papers; usually not covered by traditional scientometrics and bibliometrics studies that instead mainly focus on journals. Unlike journal papers, having a publication accepted in conference proceedings often requires that at least an author is registered to the event and presents the work at the venue. This aspect has major implications that need to be studied further. For example, scientists' mobility is subject to economic and geopolitical factors such as geographic distance, budget availability for travels, and travel bans. In some cases, being physically present at the conference venue means taking long-haul flights; for some countries, such as Australia and similarly rather isolated countries, the chances of being poorly connected to the conference venues are high. In other cases, despite feasible connections are available, the physical attendance might be hindered by economic factors, that in turn can depend on strategic and political decisions within the single country. Finally, factors driven by international politics can play a major role too. In several occasions, travel bans disrupted scientists' mobility; in 2013, for example, NASA prevented Chinese nationals to set foot in the space agency's Ames research centre in California[20].

---

[20] https://www.theguardian.com/science/2013/oct/05/us-scientists-boycott-nasa-china-ban.

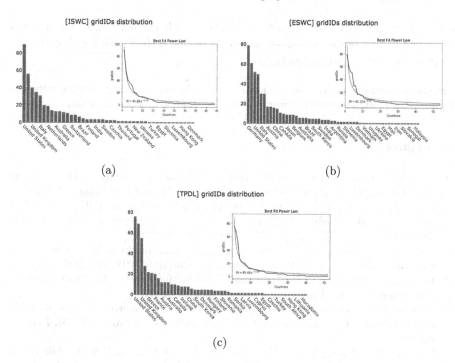

Fig. 9. gridIDs distributions across countries and power law approximations

Furthermore, citizens of countries with an important Muslim background always have encountered more difficulties for getting travel visas to European or USA countries. In addition, recent USA's international policies and travel restrictions, possibly have made this even worse [14]. However, it has to be noted that these concerns about researchers' freedom of movement affect only conference papers in which all the authors are subject to the same kind of restrictions; in the case of papers whose authors have heterogeneous affiliations, for example, the author with less restrictive constraints is, in principle, free to reach the venue and present the findings on behalf of the colleagues. All these implications are worth studying. To this end, a future extension of this work could include the comparison of country rankings among high-tier conferences and journals from a controlled set of academic fields in order to analyse whether the freedom of mobility has an impact or not on how countries perform.

In conclusion, we advocate openness and transparency for research literature metadata. It is detrimental to research itself to relinquish information about venues, papers, authorship and much more in data silos hard (or almost impossible) to access. Datasets like SciGraph are a bless for researchers working on scholarly analytics and such initiatives should be fostered. Moreover, new best practices for declaring unambiguous authors' affiliations should be devised in order to facilitate the work of researcher working with scholarly knowledge. Being able to access high quality research literature metadata is key for enabling large-scale analytics and cross-correlate scholarly knowledge with external datasets and hopefully get better and more thorough insight on the existing global dynamics prevailing in academic research.

Acknowledgements. We would like to thank the SciGraph team, especially Dr. Michele Pasin, whose work and prompt response made this study possible.

References

1. Börner, K., Penumarthy, S.: Spatio-temporal information production and consumption of major US research institutions. In: Proceedings of ISSI Volume 1 (2005)
2. Bornmann, L., Mutz, R.: Growth rates of modern science: a bibliometric analysis based on the number of publications and cited references. J. Assoc. Inf. Sci. Technol. **66**(11), 2215–2222 (2015)
3. Carvalho, R., Batty, M.: The geography of scientific productivity: scaling in US computer science. J. Stat. Mech.: Theor. Exp. **2006**(10), P10012 (2006)
4. Egghe, L.: Power Laws in the Information Production Process: Lotkaian Informetrics. Emerald Group Publishing Limited, Bingley (2005)
5. Falagas, M.E., Karavasiou, A.I., Bliziotis, I.A.: A bibliometric analysis of global trends of research productivity in tropical medicine. Acta Trop. **99**(2–3), 155–159 (2006)
6. Falagas, M.E., Michalopoulos, A.S., Bliziotis, I.A., Soteriades, E.S.: A bibliometric analysis by geographic area of published research in several biomedical fields, 1995–2003. Can. Med. Assoc. J. **175**(11), 1389–1390 (2006)
7. Frenken, K., Hardeman, S., Hoekman, J.: Spatial scientometrics: towards a cumulative research program. J. Inf. **3**(3), 222–232 (2009)
8. Hung, J.L.: Trends of e-learning research from 2000 to 2008: use of text mining and bibliometrics. Br. J. Educ. Technol. **43**(1), 5–16 (2012)
9. Jadidi, M., Karimi, F., Lietz, H., Wagner, C.: Gender disparities in science? Dropout, productivity, collaborations and success of male and female computer scientists. Adv. Complex Syst. **21**(03n04), 1750011 (2018)
10. King, D.A.: The scientific impact of nations. Nature **430**, 311 (2004)
11. Ley, M.: DBLP: some lessons learned. Proc. VLDB Endow. **2**(2), 1493–1500 (2009)
12. May, R.M.: The scientific wealth of nations. Science **275**(5301), 793–796 (1997)
13. Monroe-White, T., Woodson, T.S.: Inequalities in scholarly knowledge: public value failures and their impact on global science. Afr. J. Sci. Technol. Innov. Dev. **8**(2), 178–186 (2016)
14. Morello, L., Reardon, S.: Others: scientists struggle with Trump immigration ban. Nature **542**(7639), 13–14 (2017)
15. Pan, R.K., Kaski, K., Fortunato, S.: World citation and collaboration networks: uncovering the role of geography in science. Sci. Rep. **2**, 902 (2012)
16. Pareto, V., Page, A.N.: Translation of Manuale di economia politica (Manual of Political Economy). AM Kelley, New York (1971)
17. Pearson, K.: Mathematical contributions to the theory of evolution. III. Regression, heredity, and panmixia. Philos. Trans. R. Soc. Lond. Ser. A Contain. Pap. Math. Phys. Charact. **187**, 253–318 (1896)
18. Petersen, A.M., et al.: Reputation and impact in academic careers. Proc. Natl. Acad. Sci. **111**(43), 15316–15321 (2014)

19. Sarigöl, E., Pfitzner, R., Scholtes, I., Garas, A., Schweitzer, F.: Predicting scientific success based on coauthorship networks. EPJ Data Sci. **3**(1), 9 (2014)
20. Thelwall, M., Haustein, S., Larivière, V., Sugimoto, C.R.: Do altmetrics work? Twitter and ten other social web services. PloS One **8**(5), e64841 (2013)
21. Verleysen, F.T., Weeren, A.: Clustering by publication patterns of senior authors in the social sciences and humanities. J. Inf. **10**(1), 254–272 (2016)
22. Wilkinson, M.D., et al.: The FAIR guiding principles for scientific data management and stewardship. Sci. Data **3** (2016). https://www.nature.com/articles/sdata201618.pdf
23. Woodson, T.S.: Research inequality in nanomedicine. J. Bus. Chem. **9**(3), 133–146 (2012)

A Web Application for Creating and Sharing Visual Bibliographies

Marco Corbatto and Antonina Dattolo[✉]

SASWEB Lab, DMIF, University of Udine, Gorizia, Italy
{marco.corbatto,antonina.dattolo}@uniud.it

Abstract. The amount of information provided by peer-reviewed scientific literature citation indexes such as Scopus, Web of Science (WOS), CrossRef and OpenCitations is huge: it offers users a lot of metadata about publications, such as the list of papers written by a specific author, the editorial and content details of a paper, the list of references and citations. But, for a researcher it could also be interesting to: extract these data in real time in order to create bibliographies, for example, by starting with a small set of significant papers or a restricted number of authors, progressively enriching them by exploring cited/citing references; dispose them in a graphical and aggregate representation; be able to easily share them with other interested researchers.

With these main intents, we modelled and realized VisualBib, a Web application prototype, which enables the user to select sets of papers and/or authors in order to create customized bibliographies, and visualize them in real time, aggregating data from different sources in a comprehensive, holistic graphical view.

The bibliographies are displayed using time-based visualizations, called narrative views, which contain explicit representations of the authorship and citing relations. These views may help users to: describe a research area; disseminate research on a specific topic and share personal opinions; present or evaluate the entire production of a researcher or research groups in a fresh way.

Keywords: Graphic organizer · Holistic view
Human computer interaction (HCI) · Information visualization
Visual bibliography · Visualization design and evaluation methods

1 Introduction

A search in scientific literature is traditionally carried out by specifying a set of words in specialized search engines. Generally a massive volume of documents are returned at every search and this involves considerable effort for the researcher in trying to map the results inside of a general vision of the topic. The results are generally presented in a long list that provides users with a poor understanding of the relationships between the documents, forcing them to play out complex heuristic strategies in order to rank the items and to build up a consistent

© Springer Nature Switzerland AG 2018
A. González-Beltrán et al. (Eds.): SAVE-SD 2017/2018, LNCS 10959, pp. 78–94, 2018.
https://doi.org/10.1007/978-3-030-01379-0_6

mental vision of the research topic. Using citation indexes, such as Scopus, Web of Science (WOS), CrossRef or OpenCitations, makes it difficult to follow a paper over time, and identify the relations between papers of different authors, or have a quick overall idea of the production of an author.

In this paper we introduce VisualBib, a Web application prototype which interacts with external data providers in order to retrieve bibliographic metadata, offering researchers an interactive visual representation of the set of retrieved documents. The visual representation we have adopted is a time-based chart that shows the authors and citation relationships between papers, giving users the opportunity to manage a bibliography by deleting documents or adding new ones, starting with an author, a document id and subsequently exploring the cited/citing references for every paper.

We have called the proposed visual representations narrative view since the paths which link the papers and their authors, together with the explicit connections between citing and cited papers, illustrate the history of the authors' production in a specific area; delineate the collaborations between them; say something about the influence that a paper has had on subsequent works.

The idea is to give users the opportunity to progressively build up a customized and shareable bibliography. In VisualBib, significant documents can be discovered by starting from the publications of given key authors or from a restricted set of well known papers, then analyzing and expanding the cited references; alternatively, the user may explore citing references for discovering relevant documents, understanding the direction of the research and drawing inspiration for new projects.

VisualBib shows a bibliography inside of a holistic view which highlights the collaborations between authors and help to get answers to questions such as the following: who worked with whom in a certain period of time and on what; what are the sources of inspiration behind a specific paper or what subsequent papers have followed a specific work.

This paper is organized as follows: Sect. 2 discusses related work, emphasizing open issues and challenges in graphical representation of bibliographies; Sect. 3 presents our prototype, VisualBib, introducing its basic functionalities and user interface; Sect. 4 proposes its architecture and some implementation details; the evaluation carried out as a comparative study between VisualBib and Scopus follows in Sect. 5. The final section discusses conclusions and future work.

2   Related Work

In recent years, several tools have been proposed to graphically represent bibliographic data and to support researchers in analyzing and exploring data and relationships.

Two recent surveys can be found in [1], where 109 different approaches, which emerged between 1991 and 2016, are analyzed using two dimensions for the classification, data types and analysis tasks; and in [12], where authors present an interactive visual survey of text visualization techniques, which displays a total of 400 different techniques.

Some projects and tools emerged from the InfoVis2004 contest [8]: for example, BiblioViz [21] which integrates table and network 2D/3D views of bibliographic data; PaperLens [3] where tightly coupled views across papers, authors, and references are presented in order to understand the popularity of a topic, the degree of separation of authors and the most cited papers/authors.

Other visual interfaces for bibliographic visualization tools have been more recently proposed: among them, CitNetExplorer [14] provides the visualization of citation networks offering expansion and reduction operations and clustering of the publications in groups; PivotPaths [13] uses a node-link representation of authors, publications, and keywords, all integrated in an attractive interface with smooth animations; JigSaw [4] is a visual analytic system which provides multiple coordinated views of document entities with visual connections across the documents; PaperCube [18] offers a suite of alternative visualizations based on graph, hierarchy, and timeline integrated into an analysis framework, although the project appears to have stopped in 2009. The genealogy of citation patterns, Citeology [10], connects titles of papers which are organized in a chronological layout, controlling the number of generations to display and the shortest path between two selected papers.

In spite of the great number of existing tools, we would like to highlight some open challenges and weaknesses in the apps which are currently available, and relative to the importance of:

- creating a personal view of a bibliography, selecting authors and papers;
- saving personal views and sharing them in write or only-read mode;
- providing a holistic narrative view of papers, authors and cited/citing relationships;
- retrieving metadata from multiple online repositories and not from static datasets;
- using an online, real-time Web app.

Our contribution focuses on these objectives and proposes an online Web application that distinguishes itself from the existing ones, for these primary features.

3   Basic Functionalities and User Interface of VisualBib

VisualBib is an online app prototype conceived for supporting researchers in the creation of bibliographies, starting from papers or authors of their interest; it is freely available for non commercial research and teaching purposes at http://visualbib.uniud.it/. In the current version VisualBib retrieves data in real-time from the Scopus and OpenCitations platforms. For Scopus, being a commercial service, it is necessary to navigate in VisualBib from a subscriber's domain in order to get the required data from the Scopus Application Programming Interface (API).

The data providers available in the current prototype were chosen after evaluating the eligibility of the metadata provided by various data sources; we are planning, however, to integrate new citation indexes in future releases.

Figure 1 shows a typical visual representation of a bibliography, generated by VisualBib, when searching for an author by their last name. In order to disambiguate between homonyms, the list of authors is enriched with their name, affiliation (if present and only in Scopus), subject areas (if present and only in Scopus), id, and ORCID (if present). Once the author is chosen, the user will see a temporally ordered list of his/her publications. The selection by the user of all (or part of) the publications, will allow him/her to visualize a narrative diagram, as shown at the bottom of Fig. 1.

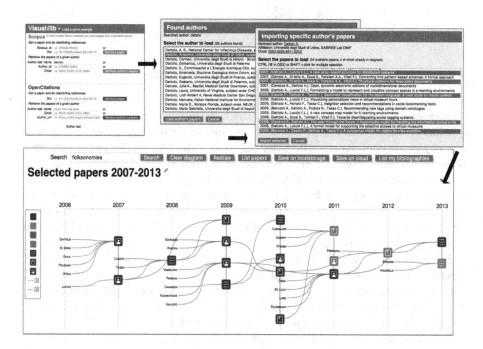

Fig. 1. A look of VisualBib interface: search of an author given the last name. (Color figure online)

The narrative diagram is a 2-dimensional space: one dimension is time, arranged horizontally and discretized by years; the vertical dimension is spatial and is used to properly organize authors, papers and their relationships. The coloured, round-cornered square items (in blue and green in Fig. 1) represent the publications retrieved from data providers.

The diagram includes the last names of the authors involved in at least one paper of the current set: each author is associated with a goldenrod line that connects all his/her papers, from the oldest to the newest, giving an indication of his/her professional path (clearly limited to the current set of imported publications) over the years.

The cited/citing relationships between papers are not automatically retrieved, but must be explicitly requested for the single paper: clicking over

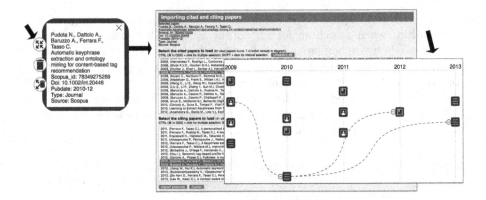

Fig. 2. Adding citing/cited relationships.

a paper icon (in the example in Fig. 1, the last (bottom) paper of 2010), a pop-up window opens (see Fig. 2, top left) to show some bibliographic data, where each of the authors' names, the title, the id and the DOI of the paper are links to dedicated Web pages. A click on the four-arrowed icon (see Fig. 2 top left) loads, in a separate form, the list of cited /citing papers (Fig. 2, center). Inside each selection list, all the cited/citing papers matching any paper already in the diagram, appear highlighted in blue. The users may select, from the two lists (cited/citing papers), the documents of their interest and import them (with the relative relations) in the diagram.

In the example of Fig. 2, the user chooses to import the three preloaded papers and, as shown on the right of the same Fig. 2, right, the cited/citing relations become visible as blue dashed lines. Due to the potentially high number of citations, the system offers the possibility to recursively hide all the citations of each paper through a "minus" icon situated near its left side.

Following the legend of Fig. 1, expanded in Fig. 3:

- the three different icons associated to publications enable users to distinguish between *three typologies of papers*: journal papers; books or book chapters; conference or workshop proceedings. If the type is different or unknown, no specific icon is associated to the items;
- the colour of the icons indicates the paper's state: blue is associated to a completely loaded paper (all the available data and metadata have been loaded); gray indicates a partially loaded paper, which has been retrieved during a cited/citing search (this operation returns only a subset of paper's metadata); red is used to emphasize semantic relationships during user interaction, as described later; and, finally, green marks the found papers of a textual search (in Fig. 1, they are the papers found looking for "folksonomies");
- the two toggle switches allow user to hide/show respectively the connections between cited/citing papers and those joining an author with his/her papers.

Finally, by moving the cursor over an *author name* the application will emphasize, in red, all the relative papers in the current view (Fig. 4 - top: the

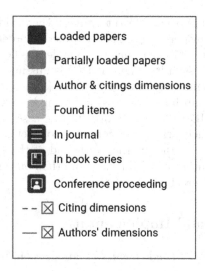

Fig. 3. The legend.

author Vassileva); moving the cursor over a *paper* the application will emphasize in red all of its authors' last names (Fig. 4 - bottom left) and/or citing/cited connections (Fig. 4 - bottom right).

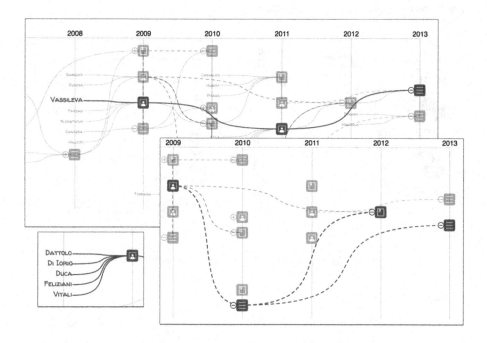

Fig. 4. Focus on author(s) and citing/cited relations between papers.

VisualBib merges data from different sources: when loading a new paper or a citation from a data provider, a check is performed in order to verify whether it was already present in the bibliography. If available, the DOI code is used for the univocal match, regardless of its origin. If DOI is missing, a check is performed using the paper id specific to each data provider (for example the Scopus id or an url for OC). For the authors, the cross matching between the data providers is possible if the ORCID code is provided: in this case, all the papers of that author, regardless of their origin, are correctly connected together by a single path. In the opposite case, the internal author id of the specific data provider is used and the same author could appear more than once in the diagram, since an automatic univocal matching is not possible.

4   Architecture and Implementation

VisualBib is organized as a single page Web application, based on:

- HTML5, CSS3 and SVG W3C standard languages;
- D3js [5], an efficient framework for data and DOM manipulation, and visual element management;
- AJAX techniques to perform Cross Origin Resource Sharing (CORS) calls and client-server interactions.

Figure 5 shows the architecture of VisualBib, and its main modules, described in next Subsect. 4.1, 4.2, 4.3, 4.4 and 4.5.

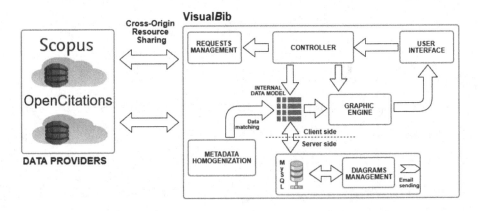

Fig. 5. The architecture of the VisualBib application.

4.1   Data Providers

VisualBib retrieves data from two repositories, the well-known Scopus and the open access OpenCitations (OC) [17]; other repositories will be considered in future releases.

Scopus [19] is the world's largest abstract and citation database of peer-reviewed research literature. It currently indexes more than 70 million items of bibliographic data, and is accessible programmatically via dedicated API, which offers 11 different query types [6], aggregated in four groups: data search, data retrieval, other metadata retrieval, author feedback. Furthermore, each query returns data in various forms, called views, organized in levels with each level providing a superset of the data exposed by the previous level; the access to the views is subject to restrictions due to service entitlements. To avoid misuse of data, the platform imposes some limitations [7] including selective weekly limits in the number of API calls, in the number of results returned in the response and in the number of calls per minute. To access the service, it is firstly necessary to require a personal API Key which permits the app to overcome the imposed restriction of user agents in performing cross-origin HTTP requests. The platform manages both simple requests based on API key and preflighted requests which generate a secured auth-token for the subsequent main request.

The OpenCitations (OC) platform [17] is the expansion of the Open Citations Corpus (OCC) [16], an open repository of scholarly citation data made available under a Creative Commons public domain. OCC is an ontology currently explorable through the use of SPARQL query language [20] and provides accurate bibliographic references harvested from scholarly literature, that others may freely build upon, enhance and reuse for any purpose, without restriction under copyright or database law. OC aggregates different open access data sources and on December 25, 2017, it published 298,797 citing bibliographic resources, 6,488,914 cited bibliographic resources and 12,652,601 citation links. The data can be freely downloaded but we chose to harvest the repository using specific SPARQL queries through the API service made available by the platform [15].

4.2   Internal Data Model

For each bibliography, VisualBib manages an internal representation of significant metadata:

- for papers: authors (with links), title (with link), publication year, abstract, subject areas, Scopus or OC ids (with links), DOI (as link), issn, references list. The links connect the metadata to the corresponding resource on the used repository (Scopus or OC);
- for authors: first, middle and last name (with link), preferred name, affiliation, ORCID, Scopus or OC id, and the list of his/her papers loaded into the narrative view.

A suitable data structure [22,23], represented by two multiple lists, contains cross-references in order to replicate the many-to-many relations given by citations and authorships. The consistency of the structure is preserved during deletions of a single paper or groups of papers, the loadings of a new author's papers and cited/citing references.

4.3 Requests Management, Metadata Homogenization and Controller

The data retrieval procedures from the two repositories differ substantially: although the availability of a common format for the data interchange (JSON), the typologies and the numbers of queries needed to get the same piece of information (for example the list of publications of an author or the paper metadata including cited/citing references) are not comparable.

The *request management module* prepares the correct sequence of queries and manages the responses and the error conditions.

Due to the asynchronous nature of the AJAX calls, each query must be executed from the listen function of the previous call. Furthermore, in case of fragmented responses, due to the existing limits on the number of results per single request, the internal retrieve loop must be managed through recursive functions to assure that the next fragment is requested after receiving the previous one. The actions to be taken at the end of the process can be triggered only in the inner execution of the function, when the complete data transfer condition is observed.

The *metadata homogenization* module:

- handles the data received from each repository;
- carries out the necessary conversions of format to make the data compatible with the internal data model;
- performs the match of the incoming data, in order to map new papers and authors to those already present in the internal data model;
- builds and shows suitable forms to let the users choose the set of papers and citations to import into the current bibliography;
- merges the new items into the internal data model and creates new data connections according to the detected authorship and citing relations.

The AJAX requests are triggered by the following user actions, managed by the controller module:

- *search of an author given the last name*. After sending the query, each fragment, received from the chosen data provider, is merged in the ordered list of authors with the same last names; after user disambiguation, the list of author publications is retrieved and visualized following the steps shown in Fig. 1;
- *search of an author given the ORCID, Scopus id or a specific url of the OC ontology*. In this case, the system will query the data provider to retrieve the list of all the papers of a specific author. The list is compared with the internal data model in order to recognize which papers are already loaded in the current bibliography and which are new; a selection form, where existing

papers are properly highlighted, is then presented to the user (Fig. 1, top right);

- *search of a paper given its DOI or Scopus id.* In this case, the system verifies the existence of the requested paper in the selected data provider and subsequently retrieves all the available metadata, including the information about cited/citing papers. Each cited/citing paper is compared with the current set in order to recognize possible matching papers. Then a selection form is presented to the users to allow them the selection of the papers to import (Fig. 2 - center).

4.4   Graphic Engine and User Interface

The *graphic engine* maps the internal data model into an interactive visual representation, called *narrative view*, examples are visible in previous Figs. 1, 2 and 4. The scale of the axes is dynamically computed at every change in the bibliography in order to cover, respectively, the entire temporal span and the maximum number of items per column.

The positioning of the items along the vertical dimension is critical for a proper interpretation of the information in the diagram; and a specific algorithm has been designed in order to achieve:

- no overlapping of the items in the same column;
- a balanced distribution of the paper icons along the vertical dimension;
- the correct positioning of the authors' labels on the immediate left of their older paper, in correspondence to the previous year;
- a regular space distribution between papers and authors' labels in every year column.

4.5   Server Side Management

In order to store and retrieve user generated bibliographies, VisualBib includes a server side module, *the diagram management*, equipped with a MySql database server and a Php interpreter. User diagrams are described by title, content represented in JSON format, email address relative to the owner and two unique urls: every time a new bibliography is saved (clicking on "Save on cloud" button in Fig. 1), the user is asked to specify an email address; the system generates a couple of unique urls for future accesses and/or for sharing with other users in both read-write and read-only mode. The users may request to receive by email the list of their saved bibliographies, clicking on the 'List my bibliographies' button in Fig. 1. VisualBib also has a simpler mechanism (activatable by clicking on 'Save on localstorage' button in Fig. 1) to save a bibliography on client-side, into the localstorage of the browser: it is a permanent (but erasable) space which is not shareable, both fast and useful for frequent savings.

5   Evaluation

The evaluation was conducted as a comparative study between VisualBib and Scopus, with the aim of collecting user opinions and feelings after experiencing the platform by means of some search activities described later. For the comparative evaluation, Scopus was chosen in order to evaluate two different search approaches to exactly the same data source. It is important to clarify that the activities performed by the participants involved a subset of the functionalities of the two platforms; for this reason, the SUS values referred only to the considered aspects.

In particular, we intended to evaluate:

- the perceived usability level of the application using the well-known SUS (System Usability Scale) questionnaire [9];
- the feelings about the aesthetic and the innovative solution of the user interface, using 5-likert scales.

5.1   Study Design and Procedures

The participants were recruited on a voluntary basis among undergraduate students, researchers and professors of the University of Udine and other universities. In total 67 participants were recruited (37 F, 30 M): 31 of them (21 F, 10 M) evaluated the Scopus platform and the remaining 36 (16 F, 20 M) our application VisualBib.

We prepared two short presentations (about 15 slides each) of the two platforms and distributed them to each participant in order to illustrate the interfaces and the basic features available in each application.

For the undergraduate students, with no significant experience in bibliographic search, we organized a live presentation to illustrate both platforms, to clarify technical terms and to familiarize them with the interfaces.

Before taking the survey, we asked the participants to perform 12 activities consisting of specific bibliographic searches in order to guide them in interacting with the platform under test. The activities were the same for the two platforms, took about 20–30 min to be carried out and consisted in searching for the publications of some authors, counting the papers written in collaboration during a time interval, individuating the type of each publication, performing textual search in the metadata, searching for specific citing and cited papers and the relative authors. To be sure that all the activities were executed correctly by all the participants, we asked them to fill in the answers of each activity on an online form which provided the users with negative feedback in case of wrong answers, forcing them in a loop until the right answer was acquired.

For the SUS evaluation, we adopted an Italian version of the standard SUS questionnaire, leaving out the first question: "I think that I would like to use this system frequently" [11]. This choice comes from observing that the systems under study would probably be used infrequently by the participants and the presence of that question would distort the score and probably confuse the participants.

We will refer to this questionnaire as SUS-01: like the SUS, it is a mixed-tone questionnaire but, having dropped the first question, the odd-numbered items now have a negative tone and the even-numbered items have a positive tone.

Finally, we asked the user to evaluate on a likert scale from 1 (not at all) to 5 (very much):

- the presence of innovative solutions in the application;
- the level of appreciation of the user interface and its aesthetic.

5.2 Data Analysis and Results

Lewis and Sauro [11] studied the effects of dropping an item from the standard SUS questionnaire: specifically, when leaving out the first question, they measured a mean difference from the score the full SUS survey of -0.66 points, considering a 95% confidence interval.

Furthermore, we were interested in estimating the difference between the SUS score of the two platforms more than in absolute values.

The value of SUS-01 was computed for each participant with the formula:

$$SUS_{-01} = \left(\sum\nolimits_{k=0}^{4} (5 - A_{2k+1}) + \sum\nolimits_{k=1}^{4} (A_{2k} - 1) \right) * \frac{100}{36}$$

The distribution of SUS-01 is summarized, for the two samples, in Table 1 and in the graph of Fig. 6.

Table 1. The distributions' parameters of the two samples.

Platform	Sample size	Min	1st qu.	Median	Mean	Std. dev.	3rd qu.	Max
Scopus	31	31.00	43.00	53.00	52.39	12.76	58.00	86.00
VisualBib	36	36.00	53.00	72.00	68.53	17.20	78.00	100.00

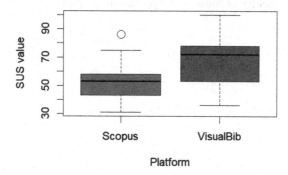

Fig. 6. The evaluated SUS-01 distributions for the two platforms.

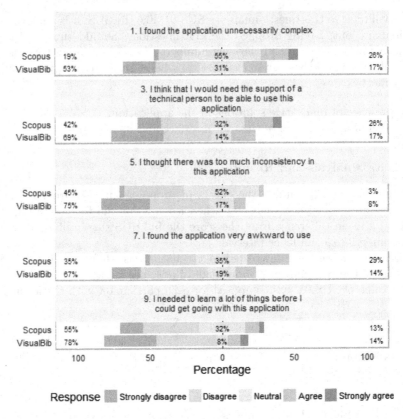

Fig. 7. SUS-01: the comparative distributions of answers to the odd questions (negative tone questions) for the two platforms.

We noted that the VisualBib's SUS-01 results present a mean value which is significantly higher in comparison with Scopus and a wider distribution. The absolute values of SUS for both platforms are relatively low and this fact probably reflects the difficulty of some of the participants in dealing with bibliographic search tasks.

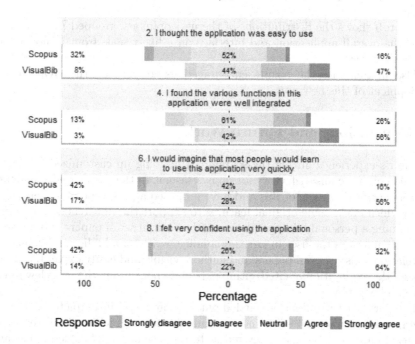

Fig. 8. SUS-01: the comparative distributions of answers to the even questions (positive tone questions) for the two platforms.

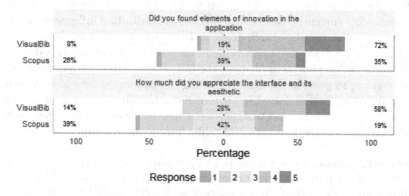

Fig. 9. The evaluation of the overall application.

The distributions of the single SUS-01 answers, grouped per platform, are visible in the following Figs. 7 and 8; for an easier data reading, in Fig. 7, we reported the odd questions (negative tone questions), while in Fig. 8 the even questions (positive tone ones).

Analyzing the answers to the single questions, we always observed a positive difference in scores in favor of VisualBib, more pronounced in questions 1, 2, 6, 7, 8. This seems to underline the intuitiveness of the simpler interface of VisualBib which presents a smaller number of data and details on the page.

Figure 9 shows the distributions of the user opinions, grouped per platform, about the overall application and interface on a likert scale from 1 (not at all) to 5 (very much).

Also in this case the results encouraged us to work on the creation and development of this new app.

6   Conclusions and Future Work

The user's experience during the search and building up customized bibliographies can often be unsatisfactory for many reasons. In this paper we have identified some critical aspects of this and have proposed a prototype of a Web application which offers some original features to support the researchers in creating and refining a personal bibliography around an initial set of papers and authors. The system assists the user in creating a holistic view of a bibliography, making the relationships between papers and authors visible and easily expanding them through the exploration of cited/citing papers without losing the overview of the entire bibliography.

The partial user evaluation carried out, although still incomplete, highlights some interest on the part of the user community for interactive visual representations of data, which has encouraged us to propose new applicable models and investigate how they may help the users in reducing the cognitive overload and gathering, at a glance, significant relationships.

An extension of the user evaluation to further aspects besides usability is described in [2]; currently, we are studying how visualization influences the user's effort to carry out specific search goals and the time to perform them.

Future work will involve improvements on VisualBib and the introduction of new features i.e. we plan to implement the import and export of papers using the Bibtex format, to provide the data regarding the papers' editing history so as to manage publications not found in current data providers, to expand the list of the repositories to query, and to experiment new forms of visual representations in order to improve the harvesting of bibliographic information.

Acknowledgements. We would like to thank Meshna Koren for confirming the Elsevier interest in our project and for having enabled us to use the Scopus API, applying specific settings; Silvio Peroni, for having enthusiastically supported us on many occasions during the implementation of the remote access procedures relative to OpenCitations repository.

References

1. Federico, P., Heimerl, F., Koch, S., Miksch, S.: A survey on visual approaches for analyzing scientific literature and patents. IEEE Trans. Vis. Comput. Graph. **23**(9), 2179–2198 (2017). https://doi.org/10.1109/TVCG.2016.2610422
2. Dattolo, A., Corbatto, M.: VisualBib: narrative views for customized bibliographies. In: Proceedings of the 22nd International Conference on Information Visualisation, IV 2018, Salerno, Italy, 10–13 July 2018, pp. 133–138. IEEE Press (2018). https://doi.org/10.1109/iV.2018.00033
3. Lee, B., Czerwinski, M., Robertson, G., Bederson, B.B.: Understanding research trends in conferences using paperlens. In: Proceedings of the International Conference on Human Factors in Computing Systems, CHI 2005 Extended Abstracts, Portland, Oregon, USA, 2–7 April 2005, pp. 1969–1972 (2005). https://doi.org/10.1145/1056808.1057069
4. Görg, C., Liu, Z., Kihm, J., Choo, J., Park, H., Stasko, J.: Combining computational analyses and interactive visualization for document exploration and sensemaking in jigsaw. IEEE Trans. Vis. Comput. Graph. **19**(10), 1646–1663 (2013). https://doi.org/10.1109/TVCG.2012.324
5. D3: Data Driven Documents. https://d3js.org/. Accessed 23 October 2017
6. Elsevier Developers: API interface specification. https://dev.elsevier.com/api_docs.html. Accessed 26 January 2018
7. Elsevier Developers: API key settings. https://dev.elsevier.com/api_key_settings.html. Accessed 26 January 2018
8. Infovis 2004 contest: dataset and tasks (2004). http://www.cs.umd.edu/hcil/iv04contest/info.html. Accessed 1 February 2018
9. Brooke, J.: SUS: a retrospective. J. Usability Stud. **8**(2), 29–40 (2013)
10. Matejka, J., Grossman, T., Fitzmaurice, G.: Citeology: visualizing paper genealogy. In: Proceedings of the International Conference on the Human Factors in Computing Systems, CHI 2012, Austin, TX, United States, 5–10 May 2012, pp. 181–189. https://doi.org/10.1145/2212776.2212796
11. Lewis, J.R., Sauro, J.: Can i leave this one out? The effect of dropping an item from the SUS. J. Usability Stud. **13**(1), 38–46 (2017)
12. Kucher, K., Kerren, A.: Text visualization techniques: taxonomy, visual survey, and community insights. In: Proceedings of the 2015 8th IEEE Pacific Visualization Symposium, PacificVis 2015, Hangzhou, China, 14–15 April 2015, vol. 2015, pp. 117–121, July 2015. https://doi.org/10.1109/PACIFICVIS.2015.7156366
13. Dork, M., Henry Riche, N., Ramos, G., Dumais, S.: PivotPaths: strolling through faceted information spaces. IEEE Trans. Vis. Comput. Graph. **18**(12), 2709–2718 (2012)
14. van Eck, N., Waltman, L.: Citnetexplorer: a new software tool for analyzing and visualizing citation networks. J. Inf. **8**(4), 802–823 (2014). https://doi.org/10.1016/j.joi.2014.07.006
15. OCC SPARQL endpoint GUI. http://opencitations.net/sparql. Accessed 26 January 2018
16. OpenCitations corpus. http://opencitations.net/corpus. Accessed 26 January 2018
17. OpenCitations. http://opencitations.net/. Accessed 26 January 2018
18. Bergström, P., Atkinson, D.C.: Augmenting the exploration of digital libraries with web-based visualizations. In: Proceedings of the Fourth International Conference on Digital Information Management, ICDIM 2009, Ann Arbor, Michigan, USA, 1–9 November 2009, pp. 1–7 (2009). https://doi.org/10.1109/ICDIM.2009.5356798

19. Scopus. https://scopus.com. Accessed 26 January 2018
20. SPARQL Query Language for RDF. https://www.w3.org/TR/rdf-sparql-query/. Accessed 26 January 2018
21. Shen, Z., Ogawa, M., Teoh, S.T., Ma, K.L.: BiblioViz: a system for visualizing bibliography information. In: Proceedings of the 2006 Asia-Pacific Symposium on Information Visualisation, APVis 2006, Tokyo, Japan, 1–3 February 2006, vol. 60, pp. 93–102.35. Australian Computer Society, Inc. (2006). http://dl.acm.org/citation.cfm?id=1151903.1151918
22. Dattolo, A., Luccio, F.L.: A formal description of zz-structures. In: Proceedings of 1st Workshop on New Forms of Xanalogical Storage and Function, Held as Part of the ACM Hypertext 2009, Turin, Italy, 29 June 2009. CEUR Workshop Proceedings, vol. 508, pp. 7–11 (2009)
23. Dattolo, A., Luccio, F.L.: A state of art survey on zz-structures. In: Proceedings of 1st Workshop on New Forms of Xanalogical Storage and Function, Held as Part of the ACM Hypertext 2009, Turin, Italy, 29 June 2009. CEUR Workshop Proceedings, vol. 508, pp. 1–6 (2009)

Optimized Machine Learning Methods Predict Discourse Segment Type in Biological Research Articles

Jessica Cox, Corey A. Harper$^{(\boxtimes)}$, and Anita de Waard

Elsevier, Amsterdam, Netherlands
{j.cox, c.harper}@elsevier.com

Abstract. To define salient rhetorical elements in scholarly text, we have earlier defined a set of Discourse Segment Types: semantically defined spans of discourse at the level of a clause with a single rhetorical purpose, such as Hypothesis, Method or Result. In this paper, we use machine learning methods to predict these Discourse Segment Types in a corpus of biomedical research papers. The initial experiment used features related to verb type and form, obtaining F-scores ranging from 0.41–0.65. To improve our results, we explored a variety of methods for balancing classes, before applying classification algorithms. We also performed an ablation study and stepwise approach for feature selection. Through these feature selection processes, we were able to reduce our 37 features to the 9 most informative ones, while maintaining F1 scores in the range of 0.63–0.65. Next, we performed an experiment with a reduced set of target classes. Using only verb tense features, logistic regression, a decision tree classifier and a random forest classifier, we predicted that a segment type was either a Result/Method or a Fact/Implication, with F1 scores above 0.8. Interestingly, findings from this machine learning approach are in line with a reader experiment, which found a correlation between verb tense and a biomedical reader's interpretation of discourse segment type. This suggests that experimental and concept-centric discourse in biology texts can be distinguished by humans or machines, using verb tense as a key feature.

Keywords: Discourse segments · Machine learning · Sentence structure
Linguistics

1 Introduction

To make sense of the overwhelming flood of scientific literature, a wealth of research has been done to support the development of online reasoning systems by analysing linear scholarly narratives and identifying salient components (see e.g. [1] for an overview of related work). As a first step in this analysis, the text needs to be parsed to identify the level of textual granularity that most closely defines what a 'salient component' is. Various different schemes for annotating discourse elements in scientific texts have been proposed (see e.g. [9] for an overview of other models of analysis).

To motivate our own choice of granularity, see sentences (1)–(3), taken from Voorhoeve et al. [13]:

© Springer Nature Switzerland AG 2018
A. González-Beltrán et al. (Eds.): SAVE-SD 2017/2018, LNCS 10959, pp. 95–109, 2018.
https://doi.org/10.1007/978-3-030-01379-0_7

(1) [An] escape from oncogene-induced senescence is a prerequisite for full transformation into tumor cells. (FACT)

(2) a. To identify miRNAs that can interfere with this process (GOAL)
   b. and thus might contribute to the development of tumor cells, (HYPOTHESIS)
   c. we transduced BJ/ET fibroblasts with miR-Lib (METHOD)
   d. and subsequently transduced them with either RASV12 or a control vector. (METHOD)

(3) After 2 or 3 weeks in culture, senescence-induced differences in abundance of all miR-Vecs were determined with the miR-Array. (RESULT)

Clearly, several distinct meanings are stated within these three single sentences: for example, in (2), the goal of the (sub)-experiment is first stated, followed by a hypothesis. After the comma, this is followed by a description of methods used. Given these definitions, it is clear that sentences are not the right level of granularity to qualify as Discourse Segments. Given this, we decided to identify Discourse Segments at approximately the level of a clause (i.e. a coherent sentence fragment containing a single verb). Next, we defined a small taxonomy of semantic (or pragmatic) segment types, with which to classify these Discourse Segments (see Table 1 for a definition of these types, taken from [4]). For further details on our segmentation and motivation for these Discourse Segment Types or DSTs, see [4].

Table 1. Discourse segment type classification (DST)

Discourse segment type	Definition	Example
Goal	Research goal	*To examine the role of endogenous TGF-β signaling in restraining cell transformation*
Fact	A known fact, a statement taken to be true by the author	*Sustained proliferation of cells in the presence of oncogenic signals is a major leap toward tumorigenicity*
Result	The outcome of an experiment	*Two largely overlapping constructs encoded both miRNA-371 and 372 (miR-Vec-371&2)*
Hypothesis	A claim proposed by the author	*These miRNAs could act on a factor upstream of p53 as a cellular suppressor to oncogenic RAS*
Method	Experimental method	*We examined p53 mutations in exons five to eight in the primary tumors*
Problem	An unresolved or contradictory issue	*The mechanism underlying this effect and its conservation to other tissues is not known*
Implication	An interpretation of the results	*[This indicates that] miR-372/3 acts as a molecular switch*

In earlier work, we identified three types of lexicogrammatical features that identify the various 'discourse realms' which these segments occupy, in particular: is the

Discourse Segment related to *experimental* text (as in the case of Goals, Methods and Results), or *conceptual* text (as in the case of Hypotheses, Problems, Implications and Facts) (see [6] for a further definition of these ideas). The features we explored were

i. verb tense and form: Tense (i.e., Past/Present/Future tense), Verb Form (Perfective, Progressive, or unmarked) for each tense, and two nonfinite verb forms (To-infinitive or Gerund or '-ing' form) [6];
ii. a taxonomy of semantic verb classes [7], and
iii. a series of modality markers [12].

Our previous research established that there was a clear correlation between, in particular, verb tense and form, and discourse realm. In particular, Methods and Results were correlated with Past Tense, Hypotheses with Modal Auxiliary Verbs, and Goals with To-Infinitives. We found a correlation in both our corpus study as well as in a reader experiment showing that changing the verb tense changed the reader's interpretation of the discourse segment [4].

We saw that this work could be applied, for instance, to identify salient segment types, such as Implications (i.e., a conclusion drawn from an experimental Result), from large corpora of text. This means there might be applications from this work to support, for instance, automated summarization efforts. A first effort to scale up the identification of DSTs with text processing tools was done quite early on, with some promising results [5], but this was not done at scale. In later work, we developed a CRF-based classifier for these seven DSTs and trained this on sentences in the Results sections of biology papers, achieving an overall F-score of 0.63 [1]. We also developed a neural network-based classifier, SciDT, which was trained on these same results sections, and achieved an overall F-score of 0.74 [2]. The current work is motivated by wanting to improve on these scores and enable large-scale text processing and identification of DSTs. In particular, we were interested to know if the verb features that were so significant for the reader studies could be used to identify discourse segments and help build tools that identify key conclusions or experimental segments from papers.

In this study, we present an approach to automatically identifying discourse segment types using supervised machine learning methods. We work on the full text of a manually curated set of biomedical research papers, using a set of features derived from the corpus studies. This dataset presents a challenge in employing classification algorithms, due to the severe class imbalance of our predicted classes. We attempted to improve model fitting and accuracy by first balancing the classes before subjecting them to classifiers, using several different under- and over-sampling methods [10]. This resulted in a set of 36 models that all used a different combination of class balancers and classification algorithms to predict segment discourse type. After finding that class balancers did not substantively improve our accuracy, we culled these models to select only those that include the most important features and produce the highest F1 scores. We also investigated a simplified version of our classification problem that limited our reduced our target classes from 7 to 2.

2 Methods and Results

In exploring this data, we first ran some pre-processing and filtering on our dataset and tackled some preliminary feature selection. We then ran 3 baseline classification algorithms on this preprocessed data, before proceeding with 4 experiments. Experiment 1 was a test of Class Balancing tools, experiments 2 and 3 were ablation studies to further limit our features, and experiment 4 was a separate and simplified classification problem prompted by our findings in the initial three experiments. After discussing the data preparation, we will discuss each of these experiments and their outcomes. A summary of all 4 experiments is presented in Fig. 1 at the end of the section.

2.1 Dataset Curation

The dataset we used was based on a set of 10 full-text papers in cell biology and electrophysiology, which was manually split into discourse segments and marked up with Discourse Segment Types described above, and in [4]. The full, manually curated dataset can be found on Mendeley Data at https://data.mendeley.com/datasets/4bh33fdx4v/3 [3].

The corpus started as a set of 3,239 Type-identified Discourse Segments, which were loaded into a Jupyter notebook. (See Supplementary Material, below.) Our predicted class is "Discourse Segment Type", as outlined in Table 1. Data points with the segment type "blank" (316), "header" (134), or "null" (1) were eliminated from the dataset, as were entries containing an empty verb type or verb form field (8). The missing verb data points were most likely due to an inability of the curators to identify the target class or feature, while blank discourse segment types represent paragraph breaks and headers are section headers. We determined *Header* to not be a useful discourse segment type for prediction in this case. We also eliminated those that were labeled "Intratextual" or "Intertextual" (taken from our earlier taxonomy, but not included in the current set of DST's, as their classes were particularly small relative to the size of the dataset, (71 and 14, respectively)). Our final dataset contained 2,695 points.

2.2 Feature Selection

We created a set of 32 features. These features were based on the three earlier linguistic explorations and can be grouped in three distinct classes: Verb form/tense, Verb Class, and Modality markers. Next to these, we created a new feature that reflects whether the verb used in the segment was in the top 10 most frequently used verbs: "show", "indicate", "demonstrate", "suggest", "use", "identify", "reduce", "suppress", "express", and "examine", as well as a separate feature, 'Show'. All of our categorical features were converted to dummy variables so that they could be appropriately included within the model. These are described in Appendix 5.1.

2.3   Model Construction

Given that many of the predicted classes are severely unbalanced, as shown in Table 2, we began by employing a variety of methods to account for these differences, by either under-sampling the majority class or over-sampling the minority classes. These methods were imported from the scikit-learn imblearn library [10]. We used 6 under-samplers, 4 over-samplers and 2 that used a combination of under- and over-sampling. The list and brief description of the 12 class balancers used are described in Appendix 5.2.

Table 2. Number of segments per DST

Segment type	Number
Result	851
Implication	657
Method	351
Hypothesis	315
Fact	262
Goal	149
Problem	110

The data was split into a test and training set, using a test size equivalent to 30% of the total data. It was first fed through one of the 12 class balancers, and then to one of three classifiers (experiment 1): logistic regression (LR), decision tree classifier (DTC) or random forest classifier (RFC). Logistic regression was performed using an LBFGS solver to handle multinomial loss. In addition to our experiment with class balancers, we also ran a baseline set of all 3 classifiers with no Class Balancer included. The accuracy, precision, recall and F1 scores were generated for each of these models and then compared, shown in Appendix 5.3.

The results in Appendix 5.3 show models ran with TomekLinks, SMOTE, SMOTEborderline, SMOTEborderline2 and SMOTETomek to have the highest performance. Highest accuracy was achieved by a decision tree and random forest classifier, using TomekLinks, with a score of 0.64. Highest precision was scattered across a few class balancers that used logistic regression with a score of 0.68. The highest recall score was 0.64, achieved by decision tree and random forest with TomekLinks. The highest F1 score was 0.65, also scattered across models that used a few class balancers and logistic regression.

Because these scores showed no improvement over our baseline model, we next sought to reduce model complexity and identify the most significant features. An ablation study (experiment 2) was performed using a random forest classifier. We looped through the model, and on each iteration removed the least informative feature in the dataset. During this process, our F1 Score stayed between .62–.64 until we'd removed more than half of our features. We ranked the features based on their significance to the model and then trimmed the features to the 9 most significant ('Past',

'Present', 'To-infinitive', 'Interpretation', 'Investigation', 'Procedure', 'Modal', 'Verb_ Class_Interpretaion', 'Ruled_by_VC_Interpretation'). These features were determined to be most significant by building a feature ranking list for each model, dropping the least significant and stopping when we'd reached a significant drop in F1 score.

We then reran these features through a smaller set of class balancers, (TomekLinks, SMOTE, SMOTEborderline, SMOTEborderline2, SMOTETomek) followed by logistic regression, decision tree or random forest, reported in Table 3. These class balancers were chosen because they produced models with the highest overall metrics in the outcomes of experiment 1. We did not observe a vast improvement in performance in these models compared to those containing all of the features outlined in Appendix 5.3. However, it is worth noting that we did not experience a drop-off in results either. This indicates that the majority of predictive power is coming a smaller number of features. In fact, if you look at the feature importance on this 9-feature model, nearly 45% of the descriptive confidence is coming from the first two features alone, past vs present tense verb.

Table 3. Ablation study model performance metrics

Classifier	Class balancer	Accuracy	Precision	Recall	F1
LR	TomekLinks	0.64	0.67	0.64	0.65
DTC	TomekLinks	0.65	0.66	0.65	0.64
RFC	TomeLinks	0.65	0.66	0.65	0.64
LR	SMOTE	0.64	0.67	0.64	0.65
DTC	SMOTE	0.63	0.66	0.63	0.64
RFC	SMOTE	0.63	0.66	0.63	0.63
LR	SMOTEborderline	0.60	0.66	0.60	0.62
DTC	SMOTEborderline	0.57	0.65	0.57	0.59
RFC	SMOTEborderline	0.57	0.65	0.57	0.59
LR	SMOTEborderline2	0.61	0.66	0.61	0.62
DTC	SMOTEborderline2	0.63	0.66	0.63	0.64
RFC	SMOTEborderline2	0.63	0.66	0.63	0.63
LR	SMOTETomek	0.64	0.67	0.64	0.65
DTC	SMOTETomek	0.63	0.66	0.63	0.64
RFC	SMOTETomek	0.63	0.65	0.63	0.64

We then performed a third experiment, using another manual approach to feature reduction, in which we used forward feature selection, incorporating each feature in turn into a random forest model, and comparing metrics (experiment 3). This resulted in 13 features to be included ('Past', 'Procedure', 'To-infinitive', 'Modal', 'Properties', 'Investigation', 'Future', 'show_verb', 'Observation', 'Verb_Class_Interpretation', 'Interpretation', 'Ruled_by_VC_Interpretation', and 'Past Progressive'). Of note, this list has a fairly consistent overlap with the features appeared in our initial ablation study. Again, we reran these features through a same smaller set of class balancers and through logistic regression, decision tree and random forest classifiers. Metrics are reported in Table 4.

Table 4. Forward selection study model performance metrics

Classifier	Class balancer	Accuracy	Precision	Recall	F1
LR	TomekLinks	0.65	0.68	0.65	0.65
DTC	TomekLinks	0.66	0.68	0.66	0.66
RFC	TomekLinks	0.66	0.68	0.66	0.66
LR	SMOTE	0.65	0.68	0.65	0.65
DTC	SMOTE	0.62	0.69	0.62	0.64
RFC	SMOTE	0.62	0.69	0.62	0.64
LR	SMOTEborderline	0.57	0.65	0.57	0.59
DTC	SMOTEborderline	0.57	0.64	0.57	0.59
RFC	SMOTEborderline	0.57	0.64	0.57	0.59
LR	SMOTEborderline2	0.56	0.65	0.56	0.56
DTC	SMOTEborderline2	0.65	0.67	0.65	0.65
RFC	SMOTEborderline2	0.65	0.67	0.65	0.65
LR	SMOTETomek	0.65	0.68	0.65	0.65
DTC	SMOTETomek	0.62	0.69	0.62	0.64
RFC	SMOTETomek	0.62	0.69	0.62	0.64

Again, we did not observe a vast improvement in performance in this subset of features. However, these scores do mirror and slightly improve those presented in Appendix 5.3 and Table 3, reinforcing the significance of these specific features. A confusion matrix was generated for each model presented in these tables. This provides a more nuanced view of the breakdown of class prediction. These matrices are available in our supplemental dataset in Mendeley: http://dx.doi.org/10.17632/ tds3k5kyvg.1.

2.4   Verb Tense Experiment

Due to concerns regarding dataset size and predicted class distribution, we designed a fourth experiment that diverged from the others in two ways. First, we subsampled from the larger dataset, specifically data labeled with a segment type of "Result", "Method", "Fact" or "Implication". The second difference is that we limited our feature set to verb tense features ("Future", "Gerund", "Past", "Past participle", "Past perfect", "Past progressive", "Present", "Present perfect", "Present progressive", "To-infinitive"). In earlier manual corpus work [6] we established that Present was the predominant tense for Fact and Implication statements, and Method and Result were predominantly described with a Past tense. We interpreted these results from a cognitive linguistics standpoint as tense markings being specific for a specific 'discourse realm', where experimental segments (such as Method and Result) are predominantly described in a (narrative) past, which lies within the author's personal experience, whereas factual or conceptual statements are presented in the 'gnomic', eternal Present, also used to describe faculties of statements of fact in other forms of discourse, such as mythological text.

For this experiment, we ended up with a "Result/Method" class with 1205 data points, and "Fact/Implication" class with 922 data points. Because these classes are more balanced, we did not need to first subject them to a class balancer. We again ran the data through three classifiers: logistic regression, decision tree and random forest, shown in Table 5. Tables 6, 7 and 8 present the confusion matrices generated for each of the three models represented in Table 5. The results presented in Tables 5, 6, 7 and 8 show that these models perform remarkably similarly and all achieved an F1 score of 0.80–0.81.

Table 5. Performance metrics of 3 models to evaluate segment type based on verb tense.

Classifier	Accuracy	Precision	Recall	F1 score
Logistic regression	0.80	0.81	0.80	0.80
Decision tree classifier	0.81	0.82	0.81	0.81
Random forest	0.81	0.82	0.81	0.81

Table 6. Logistic regression model confusion matrix

True label	Result/Method	238	37
	Fact/Implication	91	271
		Result/Method	Fact/Implication
		Predicted label	

Table 7. Decision tree classifier model confusion matrix

True label	Result/Method	238	37
	Fact/Implication	86	276
		Result/Method	Fact/Implication
		Predicted label	

Table 8. Random forest classifier model confusion matrix

True label	Result/Method	236	39
	Fact/Implication	84	278
		Result/Method	Fact/Implication
		Predicted label	

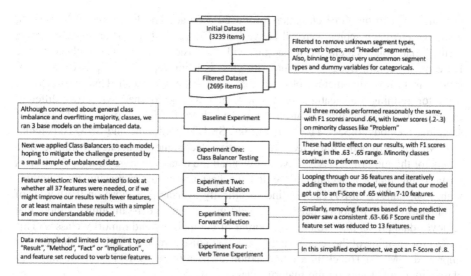

Although concerned about general class imbalance and overfitting majority, classes, we ran 3 base models on the imbalanced data.

Next we applied Class Balancers to each model, hoping to mitigate the challenge presented by a small sample of unbalanced data.

Feature selection: Next we wanted to look at whether all 37 features were needed, or if we might improve our results with fewer features, or at least maintain these results with a simpler and more understandable model.

Data resampled and limited to segment type of "Result", "Method", "Fact" or "Implication", and feature set reduced to verb tense features.

Initial Dataset (3239 items)

Filtered to remove unknown segment types, empty verb types, and "Header" segments. Also, binning to group very uncommon segment types and dummy variables for categoricals.

Filtered Dataset (2695 items)

Baseline Experiment

All three models performed reasonably the same, with F1 scores around .64, with lower scores (.2-.3) on minority classes like "Problem"

Experiment One: Class Balancer Testing

These had little effect on our results, with F1 scores staying in the .63 - .65 range. Minority classes continue to perform worse.

Experiment Two: Backward Ablation

Looping through our 36 features and iteratively adding them to the model, we found that our model got up to an F-Score of .65 within 7-10 features.

Experiment Three: Forward Selection

Similarly, removing features based on the predictive power saw a consistent .63-.66 F Score until the feature set was reduced to 13 features.

Experiment Four: Verb Tense Experiment

In this simplified experiment, we got an F-Score of .8.

Fig. 1. A summary of the 4 separate experiments undertaken for this research

3 Discussion

The current work presents a methodical machine learning approach to classifying segment discourse type, using verb tense features of the segment. We approached this problem using a variety of machine learning methods. The first challenge we encountered was the severe class imbalance amongst the predicted segment types. The Result and Implication classes both had greater than 650 data points each, while the five remaining classes had less than 351 each. The smallest class, Problem, only had 110. While this is reflective of the breakdown of segment discourse within a biomedical research paper, it makes for an obstacle when using machine learning algorithms that rely on relatively balanced classes.

We turned to the imblearn package in scikit-learn [10] to aid in balancing the classes before running our classifiers. This package provides a suite of sampling methods that can be used to either over-sample the minority class by synthetically generating these data points, or under-sample the majority class by throwing some points out. If the classes remained unbalanced, we would observe bias towards the majority classes. To avoid this, we decided to try a combination of all of these methods in conjunction with our classifiers and to evaluate the differences between them. This approach is similar to what [8] used in their paper, where they compared performance metrics of different combinations of sampling methods and classifiers on two different datasets.

In our first experiment, we observed that models that performed more poorly than our baseline all used the same balance method, and there didn't appear to be large differences in what classifier was used. While the remaining balancers didn't seem to have a huge impact on results. Specifically, these poorly performing balancers appeared to boost precision over recall. For example, we observed use of ClusterCentroids in conjunction with the three classifiers produced accuracy and F1 scores of 0.35–0.55, while the precision scores were all above 0.55. ClusterCentroids is an undersampling method that replaces a cluster of samples with its cluster centroid, as calculated by the KMeans algorithm. Because the majority class is being replaced with its cluster centroid, it is unsurprising that we observe higher precision than recall. This illustrated the need for refining our feature selection, which we approached with two different experiments. Additionally, we used the metrics from the first experiment to limit or sampling methods to SMOTE, TomekLinks, SMOTEborderline and SMOTETomek.

SMOTE (synthetic minority over-sampling technique) generates synthetic data points for the minority classes. Given how small the dataset is in general (~ 2600) it is unsurprising that this technique yielded the best results by increasing the numbers within our dataset. SMOTEborderline specifically oversamples those on the border of the majority and minority classes. TomekLinks is an under-sampling method that removes data points that are near the border of the majority and minority classes. This allows for cleaning of the data in such a way that noise is reduced and the training set is improved. SMOTETomek is a combination of performing SMOTE on the minority class and TomkeLinks on the majority class.

After identifying the top performing models in Appendix 5.3, we designed two additional experiments to refine our feature selection and reduce model complexity. Our ablation study identified 9 significant features: 'Past', 'Present', 'To-infinitive', 'Interpretation', 'Investigation', 'Procedure', Modal, 'Verb_Class_Interpretation', 'Ruled_by_VC_Interpretation'. Our forward selection experiment identified 13 significant features: 'Past', 'Procedure', 'To-infinitive', 'Modal', 'Properties', 'Investigation', 'Future', 'show_verb', 'Observation', 'Verb_Class_Interpretaion', 'Interpretation', 'Ruled_by_VC_Interpretation', and 'Past Progressive'.

We did not observe a remarkable improvement in model performance, largely due to the limitation of our sample size, though our overall F1 Scores seemed to improve slightly from an average of 63–64 to an average of 65–66. Some of the class sizes in our test set classes had less than 50 data points. This is comparable to the 0.63 F-score reported using Conditional Random Fields (CRF) [1].

We also wanted to compare these results to SciDT, the Neural Network Based Discourse Segment Tagger discussed previously. The authors provided us a pre-trained model, trained on their corpus of Results sections from 75 intercellular cancer pathways papers. [2] We ran our sentences through this model resulting in an F-score of 0.49. While this is substantively lower than the .74 score previously achieved with this model, there are a number of factors that may account for the difference. Most notably, the pre-trained model was developed on Results sections, and we ran it on entire papers. Additionally, SciDT is able to take into account paragraph breaks in predicting classes, while we had stripped the paragraph breaks out of our dataset.

Interestingly, these experimental results suggest that indeed, verb class and verb form are key markers for Discourse Segment Type: Past, Present, Modal and To-infinitive are important markers for identifying the realm of the Discourse, as found in the reader study described above. Of the Verb Classes, again, these were predominant markers, and therefore match reader experiments [4]. This implies in any event that verb tense should not be discarded or ignored in text mining experiments, as is often done.

Given the small sample size and average model results, we took on a second approach in which we subsetted the data. We grouped together the Result and Method classes and the Fact and Implication classes and dropped all other points to explore correlations between the two most frequent experimental Discourse Segment Types and the two predominant conceptual Discourse Segment Types. We also limited our features to those that were related to verb tense. Table 5 lists the performance metrics of the three models, in which the scores were very similar to one another, and significantly higher than what we observed in the first few experiments. This was in line with our expectations, given the tighter classes and the selected features. The confusion matrices also illustrate how the classes are predicted in our test set, and all three models tend to classify them the same.

In earlier discourse work, we investigated whether these tense correlations were perceived to be defining of discourse realm for a reader. In [4] we conducted a reader experiment, where 21 subjects with a biology background were asked to identify Discourse Segment Type for a set of segments which presented either in unmodified form, of with a modified tense. We found that significantly, verb tense was strongly correlated with segment type, especially for Implications and Results. This bears a striking similarity with the machine learning results found in this study.

We are exploring a number of future directions for this research. One line of research is to experiment with other corpora, e.g. in other domains, or other document types. Our data set is hand-coded and it remains to be seen how these results apply to unknown data. The challenge here is getting labels of discourse type assigned to test data. The features themselves likely don't need to be hand-curated and can be generated with standard natural language processing (NLP) techniques. However, labeling segment types correctly requires more work. Initial explorations look fruitful, and we are exploring the use of "Snorkel" [11] to produce noise aware generative models to help bootstrap additional training data in other domains. Additional future work involves applying the segment types on the sentences of citations to other papers. In combination with graph and network analysis and other term frequency analysis, this would support the classification of reason and type of citation.

In summary, our main objective was to predict segment discourse types based on lexicogrammatical features, and in doing so, we have found a good correlation with corpus studies. In the process of doing this, we contribute to the development of methods used to examine an unbalanced dataset in linguistic discourse analysis. Future work includes applying our models on additional datasets and combining with other research, such as citing sentence and citation graph analyses.

4   Supplemental Material

Full manually curated dataset can be found here: de Waard (2017), "Discourse Segment Type vs. Linguistic Features", Mendeley Data, v3 http://dx.doi.org/10.17632/4bh33fdx4v.3.

Jupyter notebooks containing steps to reproduce, analyze and view output are available here: Cox (2017), "Optimised Machine Learning Methods Predict Discourse Segment Type in Biological Research Articles", Mendeley Data http://dx.doi.org/10.17632/tds3k5kyvg.1.

Appendices

Appendix 5.1. Starting Feature List and Descriptions

Feature class	Feature	Included in experiment #
Frequently Used Verb	Top 10 Verb	1
Frequently Used Verb	'Show' Verb	1, 3
Verb Tense	Future	1, 3, 4
Verb Tense	Gerund	1, 4
Verb Tense	Past	1, 2, 3, 4
Verb Tense	Past participle	1, 4
Verb Tense	Past perfect	1, 4
Verb Tense	Past progressive	1, 3, 4
Verb Tense	Present	1, 2, 4
Verb Tense	Present perfect	1, 4
Verb Tense	Present progressive	1, 4
Verb Tense	To-infinitive	1, 2, 3, 4
Verb Class	Cause and effect	1
Verb Class	Change and growth	1
Verb Class	Discourse verb	1
Verb Class	Interpretation	1, 2, 3
Verb Class	Investigation	1, 2, 3
Verb Class	None	1
Verb Class	Observation	1, 3
Verb Class	Prediction	1
Verb Class	Procedure	1, 2, 3
Verb Class	Properties	1, 3
Modality Marker	Modal	1, 2, 3
Modality Marker	Verb class interpretation	1, 2, 3
Modality Marker	Ruled by verb class interpretation	1, 2, 3
Modality Marker	Reference internal	1
Modality Marker	Reference external	1
Modality Marker	First person	1
Modality Marker	Modal significant_ly	1
Modality Marker	Possible_ility_ly	1
Modality Marker	Potential_ly	1

(continued)

(*continued*)

Feature class	Feature	Included in experiment #
Modality Marker	UN_Likely	1
Modality Marker	Sum_Adverbs_YesNO	1

Appendix 5.2. Description of Sampling Methods Used

Sampling method	Description	Method
RandomUnderSampler	Undersamples the majority classes by randomly picking samples	Undersampler
Tomeklinks	Undersamples the majority classes by removing Tomek's links	Undersampler
ClusterCentroids	Under samples the majority classes by replacing a cluster of the majority samples by the cluster centroid of a KMeans algorithm	Undersampler
CondensedNearestNeighbor	Under samples the majority classes using the condensed nearest neighbor method	Undersampler
OneSidedSelection	Uses one-sided selection method on majority classes	Undersampler
InstanceHardnessThreshold	Samples with lower probabilities are removed from the majority class	Undersampler
RandomOverSampler	Randomly generates new samples from the minority classes	Oversampler
SMOTE	Synthetic Minority Oversampling Technique; generates new samples of minority class by interpolation	Oversampler
SMOTEborderline	Generates new samples of minority class specific to the borders between two classes	Oversampler
SMOTEborderline2	Generates new samples of minority class specific to the borders between two classes	Oversampler
SMOTETomek	Combines use of SMOTE on minority class and Tomek Links on majority class	Over and undersampler
SMOTEENN	Combines use of SMOTE on minority class and Edited Nearest Neighbors on majority class	Over and undersampler

Appendix 5.3. Accuracy, Precision, Recall and F1 Scores of All 36 Models Tested

Classifier	Class balancer	Accuracy	Precision	Recall	F1
LR	No Class Balancer	0.62	0.68	0.63	0.64
DTC	No Class Balancer	0.64	0.64	0.64	0.64
RFC	No Class Balancer	0.64	0.65	0.65	0.64
LR	RandomUnderSampler	0.58	0.64	0.58	0.59
DTC	RandomUnderSampler	0.55	0.64	0.55	0.56
RFC	RandomUnderSampler	0.57	0.63	0.56	0.57
LR	Tomeklinks	0.63	**0.68**	0.63	0.64
DTC	Tomeklinks	**0.64**	0.64	**0.64**	0.64
RFC	Tomeklinks	**0.64**	0.64	**0.64**	0.64
LR	ClusterCentroids	0.55	0.64	0.55	0.55
DTC	ClusterCentroids	0.35	0.48	0.35	0.32
RFC	ClusterCentroids	0.38	0.47	0.38	0.35
LR	CondensedNearestNeighbor	0.62	0.67	0.62	0.62
DTC	CondensedNearestNeighbor	0.53	0.59	0.53	0.53
RFC	CondensedNearestNeighbor	0.55	0.60	0.55	0.55
LR	OneSidedSelection	0.60	0.65	0.6	0.61
DTC	OneSidedSelection	0.47	0.47	0.47	0.46
RFC	OneSidedSelection	0.48	0.43	0.48	0.45
LR	InstanceHarnessThreshold	0.46	0.58	0.46	0.5
DTC	InstanceHarnessThreshold	0.37	0.61	0.37	0.41
RFC	InstanceHarnessThreshold	0.40	0.61	0.4	0.44
LR	RandomOverSampler	0.63	**0.68**	0.63	0.64
DTC	RandomOverSampler	0.60	0.64	0.6	0.61
RFC	RandomOverSampler	0.61	0.64	0.61	0.61
LR	SMOTE	0.63	**0.68**	0.63	0.64
DTC	SMOTE	0.62	0.64	0.63	0.63
RFC	SMOTE	0.63	0.64	0.63	0.63
LR	SMOTEborderline	0.63	**0.68**	0.63	**0.65**
DTC	SMOTEborderline	0.63	0.64	0.63	0.63
RFC	SMOTEborderline	0.62	0.63	0.62	0.62
LR	SMOTEborderline2	0.63	**0.68**	0.63	0.64
DTC	SMOTEborderline3	0.63	0.64	0.63	0.63
RFC	SMOTEborderline4	0.62	0.64	0.62	0.62
LR	SMOTETomek	0.63	**0.68**	0.63	**0.65**
DTC	SMOTETomek	0.63	0.64	0.63	0.63
RFC	SMOTETomek	0.63	0.65	0.63	0.63
LR	SMOTEENN	0.50	0.63	0.50	0.52
DTC	SMOTEENN	0.42	0.65	0.42	0.45
RFC	SMOTEENN	0.44	0.63	0.44	0.46

References

1. Burns, G.A.P.C., Dasigi, P., de Waard, A., Hovy, E.H.: Automated detection of discourse segment and experimental types from the text of cancer pathway results sections. Database **2016** (2016). baw122. https://doi.org/10.1093/database/baw122
2. Dasigi, P., Burns, G.A.P.C., Hovy, E.H., de Waard, A.: Experiment segmentation in scientific discourse as clause-level structured prediction using recurrent neural networks. arXiv preprint arXiv:1702.05398. https://arxiv.org/abs/1702.05398 (2017)
3. de Waard, A.: Manually curated dataset of papers into segments and DSTs: "Discourse Segment Type vs. Linguistic Features". Mendeley Data, vol. 3 (2017). http://dx.doi.org/10.17632/4bh33fdx4v.3
4. de Waard, A., Pander Maat, H.: Verb form indicates discourse segment type in biological research papers: experimental evidence. J. Engl. Acad. Purp. **11**(4), 357–366 (2012)
5. de Waard, A., Buitelaar, P., Eigner, T.: Identifying the epistemic value of discourse segments in biology texts. In: Bunt, H., Petukhova, V., Wubben, S. (eds.) Proceedings of the Eighth International Conference on Computational Semantics (IWCS-8 2009), pp. 351–354. Association for Computational Linguistics, Stroudsburg (2009)
6. de Waard, A.: Realm traversal in biological discourse: from model to experiment and back again. In: Multidisciplinary Perspectives on Signalling Text Organisation, MAD 2010, Moissac, 17–20 March 2010, p. 136 (2010). https://hal.archives-ouvertes.fr/hal-01391515/document#page=139
7. de Waard, A., Pander Maat, H.: A classification of research verbs to facilitate discourse segment identification in biological text. In: Proceedings from the Interdisciplinary Workshop on Verbs. The Identification and Representation of Verb Features, Pisa, Italy (2010). http://linguistica.sns.it/Workshop_verb/papers/de%20Waard_verb2010_submission_69.pdf
8. Elhassan, T., Aljurf, M., Al-Mohanna, F., Shoukri, M.: Classification of imbalance data using tomek link (T-Link) combined with random under-sampling (RUS) as a data reduction Method. J. Informat. Data Min. **1**(2), 1–12 (2016). http://datamining.imedpub.com/classification-of-imbalance-data-using-tomek-linktlink-combined-with-random-undersampling-rus-as-a-data-reduction-method.pdf
9. Liakata, M., Thomson, P., de Waard, A., et al.: A three-way perspective on scientific discourse annotation for knowledge extraction. In: Proceedings of the 50th Annual Meeting of the Association for Computational Linguistics, pp. 37–46, Jeju, Republic of Korea, 12 July 2012 (2012). http://www.aclweb.org/anthology/W12–4305
10. Lemaitre, G., Nogueira, F., Aridas, C.K.: Imbalanced-learn: a python toolbox to tackle the curse of imbalanced datasets in machine learning. J. Mach. Learn. Res. **18**(17), 1–5 (2017). http://jmlr.org/papers/v18/16-365
11. Ratner, A., Bach, S.H., Ehrenberg, H., Fries, J., Wu, S., Ré, C.: Snorkel: rapid training data creation with weak supervision. Proc. VLDB Endow. **11**(3), 269–282 (2017)
12. de Waard, A., Pander Maat, H.: Epistemic modality and knowledge attribution in scientific discourse: a taxonomy of types and overview of features. In Proceedings of the Workshop on Detecting Structure in Scholarly Discourse (ACL 2012), pp. 47–55. Association for Computational Linguistics, Stroudsburg, PA, USA (2012). https://dl.acm.org/citation.cfm?id=2391180
13. Voorhoeve, P.M., et al.: A genetic screen implicates miRNA-372 and miRNA-373 as oncogenes in testicular germ cell tumors. Cell **124**(6), 1169–1181 (2006). https://www.ncbi.nlm.nih.gov/pubmed/16564011

EVENTS: A Dataset on the History of Top-Prestigious Events in Five Computer Science Communities

Said Fathalla[1,2]([✉]) and Christoph Lange[1,3]

[1] Smart Data Analytics (SDA), University of Bonn, Bonn, Germany
{fathalla,langec}@cs.uni-bonn.de
[2] Faculty of Science, University of Alexandria, Alexandria, Egypt
[3] Fraunhofer IAIS, Sankt Augustin, Germany

Abstract. Information emanating from scientific events, journal, organizations, institutions as well as scholars become increasingly available online. Therefore, there is a great demand to assess, analyze and organize this huge amount of data produced every day, or even every hour. In this paper, we present a dataset (EVENTS) of scientific events, containing historical data about the publications, submissions, start date, end date, location and homepage for 25 top-prestigious event series (718 editions in total) in five computer science communities. The dataset is publicly available online in three different formats (i.e., CSV, XML, and RDF). It is of primary interest to the steering committees or program chairs of the events to assess the progress of their event over time and compare it to competing events in the same field, and to potential authors looking for events to publish their work. In addition, we shed light on these events by analyzing their metadata over the last 50 years. Our transferable analysis is based on exploratory data analysis.

Keywords: Scientific events dataset · Scholarly communication
Digitization · Metadata analysis

1 Introduction

Digitization is of crucial importance to all areas of scholarly communication. Therefore, over the last two decades, many organizations and institutes have begun to organize and establish new scientific events. This paper discusses some facts and figures representing 50 years[1] of history of computer science events, where conferences, symposia, and workshops are of paramount importance and a major means of scholarly communication. A key question is: How does digitization affect scholarly communication in computer science? In particular, we address the following questions:

---

[1] The oldest data points.

© Springer Nature Switzerland AG 2018
A. González-Beltrán et al. (Eds.): SAVE-SD 2017/2018, LNCS 10959, pp. 110–120, 2018.
https://doi.org/10.1007/978-3-030-01379-0_8

(a) What is the trend of submissions and acceptance rates?
(b) How did the number of publications change?
(c) Is there an augmentation of publications of a computer science sub-community?
(d) Has the geographical distribution of events changed across various regions of the world?
(e) Which events are more geographically diverse than others?

We target some of these questions by analyzing comprehensive scholarly communication metadata from computer science events in the last 50 years. Our analysis methodology is based on exploratory data analysis, which aims at analyzing data to explore the main characteristics, oftentimes with visual methods. We analyze the key characteristics of scientific events over time, including their CORE[2], Qualis (Q)[3] and GII rankings[4], geographic distribution, average acceptance rate, time distribution over the year, submissions and accepted papers. We selected five top-prestigious events in five CS communities derived from analyzing the topics covered by each event series, then mapping the event series to the ACM Computing Classification System (CCS)[5]: Information systems (IS), Security and privacy (SEC), Artificial intelligence (AI), Computer systems organization (CSO) and Software and its engineering (SE). Events will only be referred to using their acronym. We believe that EVENTS dataset will have a great impact on scholarly communication community, particularly for the following stakeholders (cf. [6]):

(a) *Event organizers:* to trace their events' progress/impact,
(b) *Authors:* to identify prestigious events to submit their research results to,
(c) *Proceedings publishers:* to know the impact of the events whose proceedings they are publishing.

This article is organized as follows: Sect. 2 gives an overview of related work. Section 3 presents the main characteristics of the dataset. Section 4 explains the curation process of creating and evolving the dataset. Section 5 discusses the results of our analysis of the dataset. Section 6 concludes and outlines our future work.

2   Related Work

In our recent review of the literature [1,4,5,8–10], we found that most studies tended to focus on grabbing information about scholarly communication from bibliographic metadata. Ameloot et al. [2] presented a comprehensive analysis of the Principles of Database Systems (PODS) conference series including word clouds of most PODS researchers and newcomers, longest streaks and locations of

---

[2] http://www.core.edu.au/.
[3] http://qualis.ic.ufmt.br/.
[4] http://valutazione.unibas.it/gii-grin-scie-rating/.
[5] https://dl.acm.org/ccs/ccs.cfm.

PODS in the period 2002–2011. Similarly, Aumüller and Rahm [3] analyzed affiliations of database publications using author information from DBLP. Fathalla et al. [7] provided an analysis of 40 computer science conference series in terms of continuity, time and geographic distribution, submissions and publications. Barbosa et al. [4] analyzed the metadata of 340 full papers published in 14 editions of the Brazilian Symposium on Human Factors in Computing Systems (IHC). Vasilescu et al. [11] presented a dataset of eleven software engineering conferences, containing historical data about publications and program committees in the period 1994–2012. Agarwal et al. [1] presented a bibliometric analysis of the metadata of seven ACM conferences covering different CS fields, such as information management, data mining, digital libraries and information retrieval.

3   Characteristics of the EVENTS Dataset

EVENTS dataset covers historical information about 25 top-prestigious events of the last five decades, including (where available) an event's full title, acronym, start date, end date, number of submissions, number of accepted papers, city, state, country, event type, field and homepage. These global indicators have been used to spot and interpret peculiarities on the temporal and geographical evolution of event series. There are two types of events: conferences and symposia[6]. Table 1 provides high-level statistics for the 25 event series in the five CS communities of IS, SEC, AI, CSO, and SE. Entries refer to all available attributes of all events.

Use Cases. Using EVENTS dataset, event organizers and chairs will be able to assess their selection process, e.g., to keep, if desired, the acceptance rate stable even when the submissions increase, to make sure the event is held around the same time each year, and to compare against other competing events. Furthermore, we believe that EVENTS will assist researchers who want to submit a paper to be able to decide to which events they could submit their work, e.g., answering questions, such as "which events have a high impact in a particular CS field?". Moreover, when a specific event is held each year, it helps them to prepare their research within the event's usual timeline. Section 5 presents a part of the analysis that could be performed by using the EVENTS dataset.

Extensibility. EVENTS can be extended in three dimensions to meet future requirements by (1) adding more events in each community, (2) adding events in other communities, (3) creating a unified Knowledge graph of top-prestigious events based on scientific events ontologies found in the literature, and (4) adding more attributes, such as hosting university or organization, sponsors, and event steering committees or program committee chairs.

---

[6] It would be correct to label a symposium as a small scale conference as the number of participants is smaller.

Table 1. EVENTS dataset: high-level statistics.

Metrics	Value	Metrics	Value
Series	25	Event types	2
Editions	718	Communities	5
Entries	9,460	Duration (years)	50
Attributes	15	Available formats	3

Availability. EVENTS is published at http://sda.tech/EVENTS-Dataset/ EVENTS.html and is registered in the GitHub repository https://github.com/ saidfathalla/EVENTS-Dataset. It is subject to the Creative Commons Attribution license, as documented at https://saidfathalla.github.io/EVENTS-Dataset/ EVENTS_Licence.html. The RDF version has been validated using W3C Validation Service[7]. The following listing[8] shows metadata of AAAI conference of 2017 in turtle.

Listing 1. An event description using the SEO ontology

```
### http://purl.org/seo/ISWC2017
eventskg:ISWC2017 rdf:type owl:NamedIndividual ,
    conference-ontology:Conference ;
    seo:belongsToSeries eventskg:ISWC ;
    seo:acceptanceRate "0.253" ;
    seo:submittedPapers 300;
    seo:acceptedPapers 76 ;
    seo:city "Vienna" ;
    seo:country "Austria" ;
    seo:field "Semantic Web" ;
    conference-ontology:acronym "ISWC2017" ;
    conference-ontology:startDate "2017-10-21T00:00:00.0000000+00:00"^^xsd:dateTime ;
    conference-ontology:endDate "2017-10-25T00:00:00.0000000+00:00"^^xsd:dateTime ;
    seo:EventWebpage "https://iswc2017.semanticweb.org/" .
```

4 Data Curation

During data acquisition, we faced several technical problems, such as irrelevant and redundant data, event name change over time, and missing and incorrect data. Therefore, a data curation process is required. The EVENTS dataset is being maintained over time according to the curation process described later in this section.

4.1 Data Acquisition

After identifying top events, metadata (raw data) of these events is collected either from structured or unstructured data sources. The metadata of the

---

[7] https://www.w3.org/RDF/Validator/.

[8] Prefixes are used as defined at http://prefix.cc. "seo" is used for OR-SEO, the Scientific Events Ontology.

selected events has been manually collected from various sources, such as IEEE Xplore Digital Library[9], ACM Digital Libraries[10], DBLP, OpenResearch.org[11] and events websites. The selection is based on several criteria, such as CORE ranking, Qualis ranking, GII ranking and Google h-index (the largest number h such that h articles published in the last 5 complete years have at least h citations each).

4.2 Data Preprocessing

The main objective of the data preprocessing phase is to fill in missing data, identify and correct incorrect data, eliminate irrelevant data and resolve inconsistencies. In order to prepare the raw data for analysis, we carried out four preprocessing tasks: *data integration*, *data cleansing*, *data transformation* and *Event name unification*.

Data Integration. This process involves combining data from multiple sources into a meaningful and valuable information. In addition, this process also involves eliminating redundant data which might result during the integration process.

Data Cleansing. This process involves detecting and correcting incorrect or inaccurate records. For instance, we found several websites providing incorrect information about events' submissions and accepted papers. We double checked this information against the events' official websites or proceedings published in digital libraries.

Data Transformation. This process involves converting cleaned data values from unstructured formats into a structured one. For instance, data collected from events websites as text (i.e. unstructured format) is manually transformed to CSV (i.e. structured format) and consequently to XML and RDF. **Event Name Unification.** This process involves integrating all editions of an event series, which had changed its name since the beginning under its most recent name because it is important for the researchers to know the recent name rather than the old name. However, the old name remains important for a researcher who wants to get an overview of the history of an event. For example, PLDI is the unified name of the *Conference on Programming Language Design and Implementation*, which was named *Symposium on Compiler Construction* in the period 1979–1986, *Symposium on Interpreters and Interpretive Techniques* in 1987 and finally it assumed its recent name in the period 1989–2018, i.e., for 30 years. With the completion of these steps, we are now ready to perform our exploratory data analysis.

5   Data Analysis and Results

Over the last 50 years, we have analyzed metadata of CS events in the EVENTS dataset including the h5-index, the average acceptance rate, the number of editions of each event, the country that hosted most editions of the event, the month

---

[9] http://ieeexplore.ieee.org.
[10] https://dl.acm.org/.
[11] http://openresearch.org.

in which the event is usually held each year, the year of the first edition, and the publisher of the proceedings. Table 2 shows the scientometric profile of all events in the EVENTS dataset in the five considered CS communities ordered by descending h5-index for each community.

Submissions and Publications. Figure 1 presents accepted and submitted papers measures for the top events, i.e. high-ranked events in terms of h5-index and events ranking services, in the five CS communities from 1985 to 2017. For the CVPR conference, the numbers of submitted and accepted papers were very close in the first edition in 1985, and the gap between them began to slightly increase until 2000, then it increased noticeably until the end of the time span, i.e., 2017. The gap between submissions and accepted papers refers to how far the number of submissions from the accepted papers.

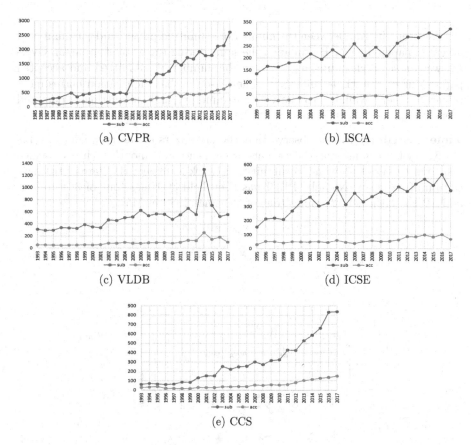

(a) CVPR

(b) ISCA

(c) VLDB

(d) ICSE

(e) CCS

Fig. 1. Variation of the number of submitted and accepted papers of the top event in each CS community.

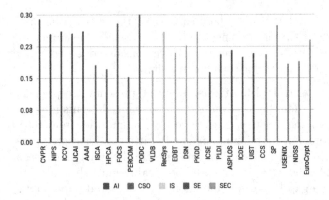

Fig. 2. Average acceptance rate of all events

However, the gap between the number of submitted papers and the number of accepted papers in VLDB remained the same during the whole time span. Overall, we can see a clear upward trend in the number of submitted and accepted papers during the whole time span. The reason is that digitization makes more research papers available to the whole community and submitting papers and even contacting papers' reviewers has become much easier and efficient.

Time Distribution. We observe that the organizers of the prestigious events always try to keep holding their events around the same month each year, which helps researchers who want to submit their work to expect the date of the next edition of an event. Namely, PLDI has been held 30 times (out of 36) in June and SP has been held 31 times (out of 39) since 1989 in May.

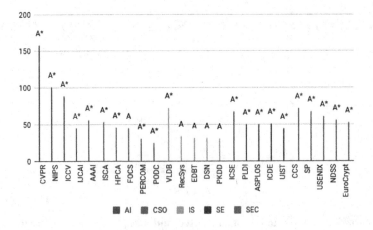

Fig. 3. H5-index of all events along with CORE 2018 ranking

Acceptance Rate. We analyze the acceptance rate of the events involved in the study over the last 50 years. As shown in Fig. 2, for each event, we compute the average of the acceptance rate of each event since beginning[12]. Interestingly, we found that the average acceptance rate for all events, since the first edition, falls into the range 15% to 31% in the time window of 50 years. Overall, the largest acceptance rate is the one of PODC of 31%, while PERCOM has the smallest one of 15%.

H5-Index. Figure 3 presents the h5-index of all event series along with their CORE 2018 ranking. The highest h5-index is the one of CVPR of 158, while PODC has the smallest one of 25.

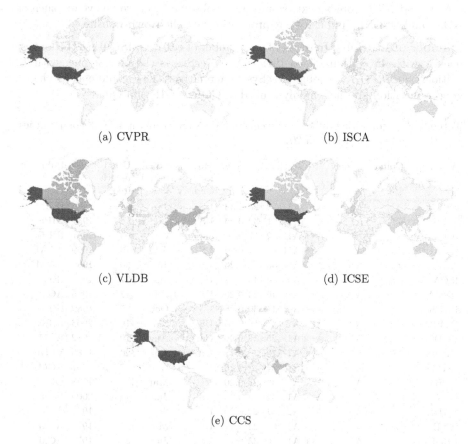

(a) CVPR

(b) ISCA

(c) VLDB

(d) ICSE

(e) CCS

Fig. 4. Geographical distribution of the top event in each CS community since 1973.

Geographical Distribution. We analyze the geographical distribution of each event in the dataset. The key question is which countries hosted most of the top events in the EVENTS dataset, and how frequently a country has hosted

---

[12] these values are included into the dataset, so that others wouldn't have to recompute them.

an event during the last five decades. Figure 4 shows how frequently different countries around the world have hosted a top event in the five CS communities considered in the study. We observe that USA leads by far, having hosted most editions of CVPR, ISCA, VLDB, ICSE, and CCS. Canada comes in second, hosting most editions of ISCA, VLDB, and ICSE.

H5-Index. AI community has the largest average h5-index of 89.9; SEC comes second with 62. Surprisingly, despite the Qualis ranking of RecSys as *B1*, the h5-index of RecSys is relatively high, and it is ranked as *A* by CORE and as *A-* by GII.

Publishers. We observe that ACM publishes most of the proceedings of CS events, and IEEE comes next. However, we observed that some events, such as NDSS and USENIX publish their proceedings on their own website.

Number of Editions. In terms of the number of editions, ISCA has the longest history with 45 editions since 1969, while RecSys is the newest one, with 12 editions since 2007. Although RecSys is a relatively new conference, it has a good reputation and it is highly-ranked in CORE, GII, and Qualis.

Table 2. Scientometric profile of all events in EVENTS dataset in five CS communities. N is the number of editions in 2018

Acronym	Comm.	CORE 2018	GII	Q	h5	N	Avg. AR	Most freq. country	Usual month	Usual month freq.	Since	Publisher
CVPR	AI	A*	A+	A1	158	28	0.33	US	Jun	26	1985	IEEE
NIPS		A*	A++	A1	101	32	0.25	US	Dec	18	1987	NIPS
ICCV		A*	A++	A1	89	17	0.26	Japan	Oct	5	1987	IEEE
IJCAI		A*	A++	A1	45	27	0.26	US	Aug	16	1969	AAAI
AAAI		A*	A++	A1	56	32	0.26	US	Jul	20	1980	AAAI
ISCA	CSO	A*	A++	A1	54	45	0.18	US	Jun	27	1973	IEEE
HPCA		A*	A+	A1	46	24	0.20	US	Feb	17	1995	ACM
FOCS		A	A++	A1	45	30	0.28	US	Oct	25	1989	IEEE
PERCOM		A*	A+	A1	31	16	0.15	US	Mar	16	2003	IEEE
PODC		A*	A+	A1	25	37	0.30	Canada	Aug	19	1982	ACM
VLDB	IS	A*	A++	A1	73	33	0.18	US	Aug	20	1985	VLDB
RecSys		A	A−	B1	34	12	0.26	US	Oct	7	2007	ACM
EDBT		A	A	A2	32	21	0.20	Italy	Mar	21	1988	OP
DSN		A	A	A1	32	19	0.23	US	Jun	18	2000	IEEE
PKDD		A	A	A2	31	22	0.25	France	Sep	19	1997	ACM
ICSE	SE	A*	A++	A1	68	24	0.17	US	May	25	1975	ACM
PLDI		A*	A++	A1	50	33	0.21	US	Jun	33	1979	ACM
ASPLOS		A*	A++	A1	50	23	0.22	US	Mar	10	1982	ACM
ICDE		A*	A+	A1	51	34	0.20	US	Feb	14	1984	IEEE
UIST		A*	A+	A1	44	31	0.21	US	Oct	18	1988	ACM
CCS	SEC	A*	A++	A1	72	25	0.22	US	Oct	12	1993	ACM
SP		A*	A++	A1	68	39	0.28	US	May	31	1980	IEEE
USENIX		A*	A−	A1	61	27	0.19	US	Aug	17	1990	USENIX
NDSS		A*	A+	A1	56	25	0.20	US	Feb	24	1993	NDSS
EuroCrypt		A*	A++	A1	53	37	0.24	France	May	23	1982	Springer

6 Conclusions and Future Work

In this paper, we present a dataset (EVENTS) of metadata about conferences and symposia, containing historical data about 25 top prestigious events in five computer science communities. We present the curation process of creating the dataset, starting from identifying prestigious events, data acquisition and pre-processing to finally publishing the dataset. To the best of our knowledge, this is the first time a dataset is published that contains metadata of top presti-gious events in Information systems, Security and privacy, Artificial intelligence, Computer systems organization and Software and its engineering. This dataset is used to compare scientific events in the same community, which is useful for both events organizers and less-expertise researchers. In summary, the most remarkable findings are:

- During data acquisition, we observed that there is not much information about events prior to 1990, in particular on the number of submissions and accepted papers,
- Organizers of the prestigious events try to keep the events held around the same month each year,
- There is a clear upward trend in the number of submitted and accepted papers during the whole time span due to the digitization of scholarly com-munication. However, the digitization of scholarly communication also has negative impacts, most significantly the proliferation of submissions, which significantly increases the reviewing workload,
- Among all countries, USA hosted about 76% of the events in the dataset in the last five decades.

To further our research, we are planning to systematically investigate review quality, to update EVENTS to meet future requirements by publishing it as a knowledge graph and by adding more events in each community and more attributes, such as hosting university or organization, sponsors, and event steer-ing committees or program committee chairs. Furthermore, we are planning to perform more exploratory analysis by applying more metrics, such as geograph-ical distribution and publications by continents, event continuity, event progress rate and acceptance rate stability.

Acknowledgments. Said Fathalla would like to acknowledge the Ministry of Higher Education (MoHE) of Egypt for providing a scholarship to conduct this study and Heba Mohamed for her support in data acquisition. This work has been supported by the DFG under grant agreement AU 340/9-1 (OSCOSS).

References

1. Agarwal, S., Mittal, N., Sureka, A.: A glance at seven ACM SIGWEB series of conferences. ACM SIGWEB Newsl. **6**(Summer), 5 (2016)
2. Ameloot, T.J., Marx, M., Martens, W., Neven, F., van Wees, J.: 30 years of PODS in facts and figures. SIGMOD Rec. **40**(3), 54–60 (2011)

3. Aumüller, D., Rahm, E.: Affiliation analysis of database publications. SIGMOD Rec. **40**(1), 26–31 (2011)
4. Barbosa, S.D.J., Silveira, M.S., Gasparini, I.: What publications metadata tell us about the evolution of a scientific community: the case of the Brazilian human-computer interaction conference series. Scientometrics **110**(1), 275–300 (2017)
5. Biryukov, M., Dong, C.: Analysis of computer science communities based on DBLP. In: Lalmas, M., Jose, J., Rauber, A., Sebastiani, F., Frommholz, I. (eds.) ECDL 2010. LNCS, vol. 6273, pp. 228–235. Springer, Heidelberg (2010). https://doi.org/10.1007/978-3-642-15464-5_24
6. Bryl, V., Birukou, A., Eckert, K., Kessler, M.: What's in the proceedings? Combining publisher's and researcher's perspectives. In: SePublica, vol. 1155. CEURWS.org (2014)
7. Fathalla, S., Vahdati, S., Lange, C., Auer, S.: Analysing scholarly communication metadata of computer science events. In: Kamps, J., Tsakonas, G., Manolopoulos, Y., Iliadis, L., Karydis, I. (eds.) TPDL 2017. LNCS, vol. 10450, pp. 342–354. Springer, Cham (2017). https://doi.org/10.1007/978-3-319-67008-9_27
8. Fathalla, S., Vahdati, S., Auer, S., Lange, C.: Towards a knowledge graph representing research findings by semantifying survey articles. In: Kamps, J., Tsakonas, G., Manolopoulos, Y., Iliadis, L., Karydis, I. (eds.) TPDL 2017. LNCS, vol. 10450, pp. 315–327. Springer, Cham (2017). https://doi.org/10.1007/978-3-319-67008-9_25
9. Fathalla, S., Vahdati, S., Auer, S., Lange, C.: SemSur: a core ontology for the semantic representation of research findings. In: Proceedings of the 14th International Conference on Semantic Systems. ACM (2018, in press)
10. Hiemstra, D., Hauff, C., De Jong, F., Kraaij, W.: SIGIR's 30th anniversary: an analysis of trends in IR research and the topology of its community. In: ACM SIGIR Forum, vol. 41, no. 2, pp. 18–24. ACM (2007)
11. Vasilescu, B., Serebrenik, A., Mens, T.: A historical dataset of software engineering conferences. In: Proceedings of the 10th Working Conference on Mining Software Repositories, pp. 373–376. IEEE Press (2013)

OSCAR: A Customisable Tool for Free-Text Search over SPARQL Endpoints

Ivan Heibi[1]([✉]), Silvio Peroni[2], and David Shotton[3]

[1] Department of Computer Science and Engineering, University of Bologna, Bologna, Italy
ivan.heibi2@unibo.it
[2] Department of Classical Philology and Italian Studies, University of Bologna, Bologna, Italy
silvio.peroni@unibo.it
[3] Oxford e-Research Centre, University of Oxford, Oxford, UK
david.shotton@oerc.ox.ac.uk

Abstract. SPARQL is a very powerful query language for RDF data, which can be used to retrieve data following specific patterns. In order to foster the availability of scholarly data on the Web, several project and institutions make available Web interfaces to SPARQL endpoints so as to enable a user to search for information in the RDF datasets they expose using SPARQL. However, SPARQL is quite complex to learn, and usually it is fully accessible only to experts in Semantic Web technologies, remaining completely obscure to ordinary Web users. In this paper we introduce OSCAR, the OpenCitations RDF Search Application, which is a user-friendly search platform that can be used to search any RDF triplestore providing a SPARQL endpoint, while hiding the complexities of SPARQL. We present its main features and demonstrate how it can be adapted to work with different SPARQL endpoints containing scholarly data, *vis* those provided by OpenCitations, ScholarlyData and Wikidata. We conclude by discussing the results of a user testing session that reveal the usability of the OSCAR search interface when employed to access information within the OpenCitations Corpus.

Keywords: OSCAR · OpenCitations · OpenCitations Corpus
SPARQL · Free-text search · Scholarly data

1 Introduction

The amount of data available on the World Wide Web (the Web) keep increasing rapidly, and finding relevant information by searching the Web is a daily challenge. Traditional search techniques rely on a textual matching of words, and do not take into consideration the semantic information behind the textual content. The Semantic Web is an approach which tries to overcome these disadvantages

© Springer Nature Switzerland AG 2018
A. González-Beltrán et al. (Eds.): SAVE-SD 2017/2018, LNCS 10959, pp. 121–137, 2018.
https://doi.org/10.1007/978-3-030-01379-0_9

by representing knowledge on the World Wide Web in a way that can be interpreted by machines. In particular, these data are stored using RDF [1], a data model that enables one to express information in form of *subject-predicate-object* statements. Usually these RDF statements are stored in a particular kind of RDF database called a *triplestore*, and can be queried by means of SPARQL [2], the query language for RDF data.

SPARQL is a very powerful query language, that can be used to look for data that follow specific patterns. When institutions such as the British Library[1] and the British Museum[2], and projects such as Wikidata[3] and DBpedia[4], want to make available their RDF data to the public, they usually provide a specialised Web interface to a SPARQL endpoint of their triplestore, so as to enable users to conduct programmatic searches for particular information, which is returned in one or more formats (usually HTML, XML, JSON, and CSV). However, this SPARQL query language is quite complex to learn, and is normally usable only by experts in Semantic Web technologies, remaining completely obscure to ordinary Web users. The SPARQL service which we have developed for the OpenCitations Corpus[5] [11] is no exception.

The main work of OpenCitations is the creation and current expansion of the OpenCitations Corpus (OCC), an open repository of scholarly citation data made available under a Creative Commons public domain dedication, which provides in RDF accurate citation information (bibliographic references) harvested from the scholarly literature. The whole OCC is available for querying via its SPARQL endpoint, but hitherto it has not had a query interface that would permit ordinary Web users to undertake free text queries in order to search and explore OCC data.

To address this issue, we have developed an application that can be reused in different contexts for any type of RDF data, not just scholarly RDF data. This is *OSCAR, the OpenCitations RDF Search Application*, which is a user-friendly search platform that can be used with **any** RDF triplestore providing a SPARQL endpoint, and which is entirely built without the integration of external application components. OSCAR provides a configurable mechanism that allows one to query a triplestore by means of a user-input free-text string, while in the background one or more SPARQL queries are actually executed. The involvement of experts in Semantic Web technologies remains crucial. However, their involvement is reduced to an initial once-for-all-time configuration of the system to work with a particular triplestore, by customizing the script that provides the text-search interface and enables users to filter the returned results by means of appropriate facets and values.

In this paper, we present the main features of OSCAR and the most significant parts of its configuration file. In order to show how it can be adapted to work

---

[1] http://bnb.data.bl.uk/.
[2] https://collection.britishmuseum.org/.
[3] https://www.wikidata.org/.
[4] http://dbpedia.org/sparql.
[5] http://opencitations.net/.

with different SPARQL endpoints, we provide three distinct configuration files which implement free-text query interfaces over the SPARQL endpoints of the OpenCitations Corpus [11], ScholarlyData[6] [8] and Wikidata (See footnote 3) [13], respectively. In addition, we report the results of a user testing session in order to understand the perceived usability of one of the aforementioned implementations, namely that for searching the OpenCitations Corpus.

The rest of this paper is organized as follows. In Sect. 2 we describe some of the most important existing SPARQL-based searching tools. In Sect. 3, we describe OSCAR and discuss its model definition and architectural form. In Sect. 4, we demonstrate its reusability in different contexts, while, in Sect. 5, we assess the usability of the search interface of this application when querying the OpenCitations Corpus. Finally, in Sect. 6, we conclude the paper and sketch out some future developments.

2   Related Works

In the past, several projects that customize SPARQL queries according to user needs have been released. They can be classified into two categories.

On the one hand, there are the tools that generate and apply SPARQL queries starting from a free text search input, hiding the complexities of the SPARQL query behind a simple and familiar-looking search interface. We say that these interfaces are *unaware-user tools*, since they permit users to make textual queries without needing to understand the complexity of the languages used for storing and querying the data.

Scholia[7] [5] is a tool which is in this category. It is a Web application to expose scientific bibliographic information through Wikidata. In particular, its Web service creates on-the-fly scholarly profiles for researchers, organizations, journals, publishers, individual scholarly works, and research topics, by querying the SPARQL-based Wikidata Query Service. A search field on the front page of Wikidata permits a user to look for a particular name and displays its data by means of well-structured visual interfaces.

Another tool of this type is BioCarian[8] [14]. It is an efficient and user-friendly search engine for performing exploratory searches on biological databases, providing an interface for SPARQL queries over RDF triplestores, and providing a graphical interface for the results based on facets. It allows complex queries to be constructed, and has additional features like filtering and ranking the results according to user-selected facet values.

OSCAR is, of course, also in this category of tools.

On the other hand, there are tools which aim at helping the user to build a SPARQL query by using specific visual constructs that mimic the various operations made available by SPARQL (filters, values selections, etc.). In this case, the users are very aware that they are using Semantic Web technologies,

---

[6] http://www.scholarlydata.org/.

[7] https://tools.wmflabs.org/scholia/.

[8] http://www.biocarian.com/.

and that the function of the tools is only to be a support for guiding the user in creating the particular query of interest. These tools are grouped under the label *aware-user tools*.

Within this category, we have the Wikidata Query Service (WDQS)[9], which is a Web interface that enable the creation of a SPARQL query by writing the actual label associated to each item and property, instead of employing the URL customarily used for identifying it. In addition, it makes available several visualisation interfaces for the results, from a simple table to very complex diagrams and graphs.

Along the same lines is the Visual SPARQL Builder (VSB)[10], a tool which allows users to create and run SPARQL queries with a browser's graphical interface. While WDQS exposes the SPARQL query to the user, VSB hides it entirely behind blocks which explicitly represent all the SPARQL constructs, including filters. Upon execution, the visual queries are translated to SPARQL code, which is made accessible to the user, and the results are shown in structured tables.

3   OSCAR, the OpenCitations RDF Search Application

OSCAR, the OpenCitations RDF Search Application, is an open source stand-alone javascript tool which can be embedded in a webpage so as to provide a human-friendly interface for searching for data within RDF triplestores by means of SPARQL queries. It is possible to configure OSCAR to work with a particular SPARQL endpoint, by configuring a JSON document which specifies how the SPARQL queries are sent to that endpoint, and how the returned query results should be visualized, according to the predefined tabular view that OSCAR provides. The source code and documentation for OSCAR are available on GitHub at https://github.com/opencitations/oscar.

OSCAR has been developed to meet the following requirements:

- it must enable a free text search, such as is common to Web search engines;
- it must permit filtering of the result set, filtering operations being applied to one or more of the result fields presented in the tabular results interface, and these operations must be applied dynamically and handled without the need for any further querying of the triplestore;
- its interface, functionalities and queries must be customizable according to the user needs;
- although originally developed to work with the OpenCitations SPARQL endpoint, it must be easily configured to work with any other RDF triplestore, and must also be easily integrated as a new module within that system's website.

The above list of requirements is based on our observations and experience of user requirements while working on the OpenCitations project, and on informal feedbacks from potential users interviewed during OSCAR's development. In the following subsections we describe the general architecture of the OSCAR system.

---

[9] https://www.mediawiki.org/wiki/Wikidata_query_service.
[10] https://leipert.github.io/vsb/.

3.1   Architecture of OSCAR

All the functionalities implemented by OSCAR are executed in the browser (client side), so as to make it easily reusable in different contexts and with different Web sites without the need of handling specific programming languages for running the back-end scripts. In particular, OSCAR is defined by three files:

1. *search.js*, which is the main core of the tool, handling all its behaviour and define its model;
2. *search-conf.js*, which is the configuration file that defines all the parameters and customisation used by the tool to access data within a particular triple-store;
3. *search.css*, which is a stylesheet that defines the layout and other stylistic aspects of its user interface.

All these files need first to be imported into an HTML page that will provide the user with the text query interface. In addition, a skeleton HTML snippet should be included in such page, that will be populated with the result of such a search operation. This snippet is defined as follows:

```
<div id="search" class="search">
  <div id="search_extra" class="search-extra"></div>
  <div id="search_header" class="search-header">
    <div id="rows_per_page"></div>
    <div id="sort_results"></div>
  </div>
  <div id="search_body" class="search-body">
    <div id="search_filters" class="search-filters">
      <div id="limit_results"></div>
      <div id="filter_btns"></div>
      <div id="filter_values_list"></div>
    </div>
    <div id="search_results" class="search-results"></div>
  </div>
</div>
```

The skeleton layout of the aforementioned OSCAR results interface (element div with attribute @id = search) is composed of three main sections, defined by specific div elements: the section *extra* (@id = search_extra), the section *header* (@id = search_header), and the section *body* (@id = search_body).

The *extra* section can be used for applying additional functionalities and operations to the results of a search operation. Currently, it includes a mechanism for exporting the results shown as a CSV file. The *header* section contains components that allow one to modify the table of results from a visual perspective – e.g. by specifying the maximum number of rows to be visualized per page, and by sorting the results according to a specific column or field. Finally, the *body* section is where the results are actually shown. It contains a table populated with the results obtained from the query execution, and a series of filters that enable a user to refine the results, so as to keep or excluding specific values.

The organisation of the structure of the aforementioned sections (and of all the subsections they contain) can be customized according to particular needs. In particular, one can decide which components are to be included within or excluded from the results Web page by keeping within that Web page the relevant

HTML fragment, or by omitting it. Furthermore, while OSCAR provide a set of basic layout rules for all the components, these can be freely customized so as to align them with the particular style required by the Web site under consideration.

3.2   The Workflow

The workflow implemented by OSCAR is described in Fig. 1, where we introduce all the operations that OSCAR enables, and the various steps it runs as consequences of such operations. The process starts with the generation of the search interface, which is the mechanism used to permit someone to input a textual query within in the text search box provided by the interface.

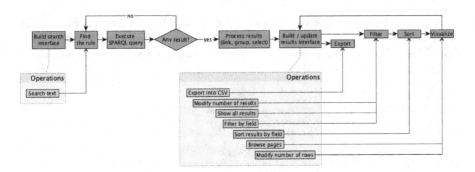

Fig. 1. The workflow implemented by OSCAR (in blue, at the top) and the set of operations that a user can perform by using the search interface and the results interface. Each operation is connected to the particular step within the workflow that will be executed as a consequence of that operation. The set of operations are possible only after precise steps in the workflow (the dashed lines specify these steps). After the execution of an operation, the workflow execution will move on the linked step. (Color figure online)

When a query is run (by pressing the "enter" key or by clicking on the lens provided in the interface to the right of the free-text field), OSCAR determines which SPARQL query it has to execute in order to provide results to match the particular textual input specified. As described in more detail in Sect. 3.3, the configuration file allows one to specify a sequence of rules, each defining a SPARQL query and a particular regular expression. OSCAR iterates each rule as they appear in the sequence, and it runs the related SPARQL query *only* if the input text matches the regular expression specified in the rule under consideration. If no results are returned by that particular SPARQL query, OSCAR iterates to the next rule and its associated SPARQL query until a result is returned, or until no result at all is found.

Once a result is returned, three additional operations are executed. First, OSCAR checks if some fields returned in the result table actually represent URL links for values of other fields – as specified in the configuration file – and, if that is the case, it creates explicit links in the resulting Web page. For instance, if we consider a simple two-column table where each row describes the title of an article and the URL from which one can retrieve its full metadata, then OSCAR can be configured to show the article title as a clickable link that allows one to go to the descriptive page for that article, by incorporating into the title the related URL that would otherwise have been displayed in the second column.

OSCAR then performs all the grouping operations indicated in the configuration file. This operation allows one to group rows in the result set according to a particular field, when all the other fields of the rows under consideration contain the same values (as shown in the last results row of Fig. 2). For instance, if we extend the two-column table mentioned above with an additional field for expressing author names, in case a certain article has more than one authors, the SPARQL-endpoint would return several rows (one for each author of the article), each repeating the title and the article URL in the first two fields and listing one of its authors in the third field. This makes for uncomfortable reading of the table. The grouping operation performed by OSCAR allows us to group all these authors into one 'author' cell in the third column, so as to provide just one row per article in the result table.

Finally, OSCAR selects a subset of the fields returned by the SPARQL endpoint to display in the Web page, according to the specification given within the configuration file. For instance, using the example given above, at this phase of the operation we can exclude the second column depicting the URLs of the articles, since those URL have already been incorporated into the clickable links added to the article titles in the first column.

All the data obtained by the aforementioned operations are initialized and stored internally in four different forms, called *native data*, *filtered data*, *sorted data* and *visualized data* respectively. Native data are the complete original result-set after the execution of the aforementioned operations. Filtered data are the subset of the native data after the application – brought about by a user interacting with the OSCAR interface – of filtering operations upon them (e.g. to show only the articles published in 2016). Sorted data are the subset of the filtered data after the execution – again brought about by a user interacting with the OSCAR interface – of sorting operations (e.g. sorting the rows in descending order according to the number of citations that the articles have received). Finally, visualized data are the subset of the sorted data that are displayed in the Web page (for example, the first twenty results), while the others are hidden behind a pagination mechanism so as to avoid filling up the entire page with all the results. It is worth mentioning that, in the initialization phase, before filtering and sorting, all the 'filtered' and 'sorted' data are equivalent to the native data, while the visualized results (i.e. those actually shown in the webpage) are a subset of the sorted data initially created using the display parameters specified in the configuration file. The filtered and sorted data are then subsequently modified as consequence of the filtering and sorting operations undertaken by using the OSCAR interface, as described above.

Once all the various data are initialized, OSCAR builds the layout components introduced at Sect. 3.1, and thus enables the user to interact with the results by executing certain type of operations on the data – i.e. exporting, filtering, sorting and visualizing, briefly introduced above. All the aforementioned operations, with the exception of the exporting operation, result in updating the user interface, which shows only the new subset of visualized data obtained as consequence of each operation, as summarized in Fig. 1 (Table 1).

Table 1. All the possible operations that a user can perform on the results returned by a free-text search, arranged by the steps in the OSCAR workflow in the order that they are executed.

Step	Operation	Data modified	Description
Export	Export into a CSV file	Sorted data	The sorted data are exported into a CSV file
Filter	Show all results	Filtered data	The filtered data are reset to the native data
Filter	Modify number of results	Filtered data	Reduce the filtered data to a specified number of rows
Filter	Filter by field	Filtered data	Exclude or show only the filtered data equal to some specific values of a certain field
Sort	Sort results by field	Filtered data	Sort (in ascending or descending order) all the filtered data according to the value of a particular field
Visualize	Browse pages	Visualized data	Show the visualized data, organized into pages, page by page
Visualize	Modify number of rows	Visualized data	Increase or decrease the number of visualized data row shown at any one time in the Web page

3.3   Customizing OSCAR

OSCAR offers a flexible way for customizing its behaviour according to different needs. In particular, an adopter has to modify a particular configuration file (*search-conf.js*, which contains a JSON object) so as to customize the tool – as illustrated in the documentation of the tool available on the GitHub repository. An excerpt of an exemplar configuration file is shown as follows:

```
{
    "sparql_endpoint": "https://w3id.org/oc/sparql",

    "prefixes": [
      { "prefix":"cito", "iri":"http://purl.org/spar/cito/" },
      { "prefix":"dcterms", "iri":"http://purl.org/dc/terms/" },
      ...
    ],

    "rules": [
      {
        "name":"doi",
        "category": "document",
        "regex":"(10.\\d{4,9}\/[-._;()/:A-Za-z0-9][^\\s]+)",
        "query": "SELECT DISTINCT ?iri ?short_iri ..."
      },
      ...
    ],

    "categories": [
      {
        "name": "document",
        "fields": [
          {
            "value":"short_iri", "title": "Corpus ID",
            "column_width":"15%", "type": "text",
            "sort": { "value": true },
            "link": { "field":"iri", "prefix":"" }
          },
          ...
        ]
      },
      ...
    ]
}
```

This configuration file allows one to specify the *SPARQL endpoint* to connect with for running SPARQL queries, and the *SPARQL prefixes* to use in the various queries. In addition, it enables the specification of the *rules* for executing the appropriate SPARQL queries. In particular, each rule includes a *name*, an *activator* (i.e. a regular expression shaping a particular string pattern), a *category* describing the types of data that will be collected (see below), and the *SPARQL query* to be executed if the activator matches with the free-text search query provided by the user.

Finally, the configuration file also comprises the *categories*, i.e. particular descriptive operation that are applied to the results returned by a SPARQL query defined in a rule. In particular, each category includes a *name* and a set of SPARQL query SELECT *variables*. Each of these variables is accompanied by information about its presentation mechanisms (e.g. the label to use for presenting it in the Web page, and the width of the table column in which to put the related values) and about other filtering operations that can be applied to the values associated to that variable (e.g. the operations *link*, *group* and *select* described in Sect. 3.2).

4   Configuring OSCAR for Use with Different RDF Datasets

In order to demonstrate the flexibility that OSCAR offers in terms of its customizability and adaptability to a particular triplestore, we have developed three configuration files that provide free-text search interfaces to three different RDF datasets (each with a separate SPARQL endpoint): those of OpenCitations Corpus, Scholarly Data and Wikidata.

The OpenCitations Corpus (OCC, http://opencitations.net) [9,11] is an open repository of scholarly citation data bibliographic information that we have developed, which has been the main target and incentive for the development of OSCAR. The OCC triplestore contains such open scholarly citation and bibliographic data. The OSCAR search interface for the OpenCitations Corpus can be seen and used at http://opencitations.net/search. The use of OSCAR in this context enables the search for two basic entities included in the OCC: documents (bibliographic resources) and authors. Currently, the free-text search allows the recognition of two different types of input: unique global identifiers (specifically DOIs and ORCIDs, that identify published works and people, respectively), and any other textual string which can be used to identify the title of a document or the name of an author. It is worth mentioning that this text search string do not match against the abstracts and the keywords of documents since these data are not currently stored within the OCC. In Fig. 2, we depict a screenshot of OSCAR after the execution of a free text search using the string "machine learning".

A similar instantiation has been made for the SPARQL endpoint provided by Scholarly Data (http://www.scholarlydata.org) [8]. Scholarly Data provides an RDF dataset of the papers, people, organisations and events related to Web and Semantic Web academic conferences. The current version of the project has a SPARQL endpoint, but it does not include a free-text search interface for discovery of the entities included in the dataset. We have created an *ad hoc* configuration file for OSCAR so as to enable such search operation on the Scholarly Data triplestore. The Web interface for OSCAR searches over the SPARQL endpoint for Scholarly Data is available at http://opencitations.net/static/savesd2018/oscar/scholarlydata.html. Figure 3 shows a screenshot of OSCAR with ScholarlyData results.

Finally, we have prepared a configuration files to enable free-text searches within Wikidata (https://www.wikidata.org) [13]. Wikidata is a free open knowledge base which acts as a central store for the structured data of Wikimedia Foundation projects including Wikipedia, and of other sites and services. Wikidata offer a SPARQL query service and already has its own powerful Web graphical user interface for facilitating the users to construct SPARQL queries, Scholia, as mentioned above. Our OSCAR interface to the Wikidata SPARQL endpoint is thus entirely for demonstration purposes, rather than to provide new functionality for Wikidata users. While Wikidata contains a wide variety of information, for the Wikidata customisation of OSCAR we decided to limit the range of data to be searched to bibliographic entities within the scholarly

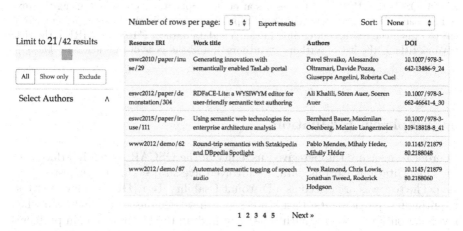

OpenCitations

machine learning   Q

Home   About   Corpus   Model   Download   Sparql   **Search**   Publications   Licenses   Contacts

Number of rows per page: 5 ↕   Export results   Sort: None ↕

Limit to 155/311 results

All | Show only | Exclude

Select **Year**   ∧

Select **Authors**   ∧

Corpus ID	Year	Title	Authors	Cited by
/br/6096958	2009	Machine Learning	Peter Flach	1
/br/40929		Machine Learning		0
/br/2713223		Machine Learning		0
/br/4231671	2008	Gaussian Processes for Machine Learning	Songthip T Ounpraseuth	1
/br/4453459	2014	DaDianNao: A Machine-Learning Supercomputer	Yunji Chen, Tao Luo, Shaoli Liu, Shijin Zhang, Liqiang He, Jia Wang, Ling Li, Tianshi Chen, Zhiwei Xu, Ninghui Sun, Olivier Temam	1

1 2 3 4 5 6 7 8 9 10 11 ...   Next »

Fig. 2. The results interface of the OSCAR tool in the OpenCitations Corpus website: the results shown are those obtained after the application of a search using the text string "machine learning". Each row represents a publication, while the fields represent (from left to right): the resource identifier in the OpenCitations Corpus ("Corpus ID"), the year of publication ("year"), the title ("title"), the list of authors ("Authors"), and how many times the publication has been cited by other publications documented within the OCC ("Cited by").

Number of rows per page: 5 ↕   Export results   Sort: None ↕

Limit to 21/42 results

All | Show only | Exclude

Select **Authors**   ∧

Resource IRI	Work title	Authors	DOI
eswc2010/paper/inuse/29	Generating innovation with semantically enabled TasLab portal	Pavel Shvaiko, Alessandro Oltramari, Davide Pozza, Giuseppe Angelini, Roberta Cuel	10.1007/978-3-642-13486-9_24
eswc2012/paper/demonstation/304	RDFaCE-Lite: a WYSIWYM editor for user-friendly semantic text authoring	Ali Khalili, Sören Auer, Soeren Auer	10.1007/978-3-662-46641-4_30
eswc2015/paper/inuse/111	Using semantic web technologies for enterprise architecture analysis	Bernhard Bauer, Maximilan Osenberg, Melanie Langermeier	10.1007/978-3-319-18818-8_41
www2012/demo/62	Round-trip semantics with Sztakipedia and DBpedia Spotlight	Pablo Mendes, Mihaly Heder, Mihály Héder	10.1145/2187980.2188048
www2012/demo/87	Automated semantic tagging of speech audio	Yves Raimond, Chris Lowis, Jonathan Tweed, Roderick Hodgson	10.1145/2187980.2188060

1 2 3 4 5   Next »

Fig. 3. OSCAR with ScholarlyData: results after the application of a search using the text string "semantic". Each row represents a publication, while the fields represent (from left to right): the resource identifier in the ScholarlyData dataset ("Resource IRI"), the title ("Work title"), the list of authors ("Authors"), and the corresponding DOI for that publication ("DOI").

domain. The configuration file thus includes rules for detecting DOIs, ORCIDs and free textual inputs, and classifies the information returned according to two categories: documents and authors, as is done for the OSCAR search interface over the OpenCitations Corpus. The Web interface for OSCAR searches over the SPARQL endpoint of Wikidata is available at http://opencitations.net/static/savesd2018/oscar/wikidata.html. Figure 4 shows a screenshot of OSCAR with Wikidata results.

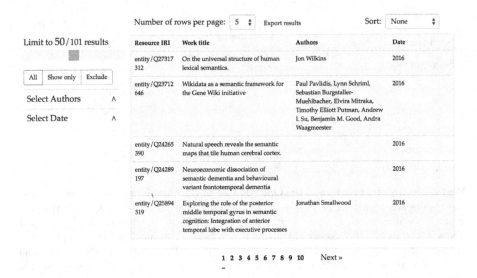

Fig. 4. OSCAR with Wikidata: results after the application of a search using the text string "semantic". Each row represents a publication, while the fields represent (from left to right): the resource identifier in the Wikidata dataset ("Resource IRI"), the title ("Work title"), the list of authors ("Authors"), and the year of publication ("Date").

5   Empirical Evaluation

In order to measure the perceived usability of the OSCAR search interface over the OpenCitations Corpus data, we involved five subjects in a user testing session. The test was organized as a Discount Usability Test (DUT): a low-cost test requiring few participants. Past studies [6, 7] have demonstrated that even when involving only five people, such a test can find up to 80% of the main problems of a system. In the next subsections, we first discuss the settings of our tests and then we show the outcomes. All the material and outcomes of the test are available at [3].

5.1   Settings

We asked five different subjects to perform five unsupervised tasks during the month of January 2018. The tasks were defined as result of informal brainstorming with academics interested in retrieving similar information using existing tools such as Google Scholar and Scopus. All the subjects were volunteers who responded to personal e-mails. At the very beginning of the user testing session, we provided the subjects with a quick description of OSCAR and its main features, and then we just left the testers to execute their tasks individually, without observing them during the performance of these tasks. The tasks we asked them to undertake are as follows:

1. Search the corpus with the Digital Object Identifier (DOI) "10.1002/cncr. 28414", and write down the title of the document.
2. Search for the author with an ORCID "0000-0001-5506-523X", and write down the author's name.
3. Search for all the document titles with matches to the term "chemical classification system", and sort the results obtained according to the year of publication in descendent order. Write down the "Corpus ID" value of the document in the first row in the table of results.
4. Refine the result table to retain only the documents that have "Dae-Jong Song" as one of their authors. Write down the number of rows in the table.
5. Look for the 10 most cited documents published in 2015 and 2016 that have titles containing the string "clinical review". Export the details of these as a CSV, and copy and paste the content of this downloaded CSV file into your results sheet.

After these tasks, we asked the participants to fill out two questionnaires and answer some questions according to their experience. The first questionnaire was a SUS (System Usability Scale) questionnaire [10], while the second one contained the following four questions relating to the user experience while using OSCAR to accomplish the tasks, i.e.:

- How effectively did the tool support you in completing the required tasks?
- What were the most useful features of the tool that helped you accomplishing your tasks?
- What were the main weaknesses exhibited by the tool while executing your tasks?
- Can you think of other additional features that would have helped you accomplish your tasks?

Finally, we asked all the participants for some background information, including their ages and their current work positions.

5.2   Outcomes

The five people involved – one professor, two post-doctoral researchers, one Ph.D. student and one master-degree student (all from Italy, four Computer Scientists and one Digital Humanist) – responded positively to our invitation, and we received five full feedback forms concerning their experience of using of OSCAR to explore the OpenCitations Corpus, according to the aforementioned tasks. The first four tasks were successfully executed by all the subjects. The final task was the most complex and was not fully completed by two subjects, one of whom forgot to report only those papers published in 2015 and 2016, and the other of whom failed to restrict the results to the ten most cited papers meeting the textual search criterion. Thus, for Task 5, we received only 3 correct answers, as shown in Table 2. We then questioned the subjects who answered the last task incorrectly, so as to learn about possible shortcomings of the OSCAR interface, and discovered that their problems were mainly caused by some ambiguity in the interface and the operation of the filtering option buttons/triggers, which we have since addressed.

Table 2. The accuracy of the answers returned by the subjects for the five tasks.

Subject	Task 1	Task 2	Task 3	Task 4	Task 5
1	OK	OK	OK	OK	OK
2	OK	OK	OK	OK	OK
3	OK	OK	OK	OK	X
4	OK	OK	OK	OK	X
5	OK	OK	OK	OK	OK
Fraction correct	5/5	5/5	5/5	5/5	3/5

The usability score for OSCAR under these circumstances was computed using the *System Usability Scale* (SUS) [10], a well-known questionnaire used for the perception of the usability of a system. This has the advantage of being technology independent (it has been tested on hardware, software, Web sites, etc.) and it is reliable even with a very small sample size. In addition to the main SUS scale, we also were interested in examining the sub-scales of pure *Usability* and pure *Learnability* of the system, as proposed recently by Lewis and Sauro [4].

The mean SUS score for OSCAR was 87 (within the range from 0 to 100), surpassing by a high margin the target score of 68 that demonstrates a good level of usability [10]. The mean values for the SUS sub-scales Usability and Learnability were 84.37 and 97.5 respectively. This result was expected, since the operations provided by OSCAR are close to the common operations of any either generic (e.g. Google) or domain-specific (e.g. Scopus) search engine applications.

Axial coding [12] of the personal comments expressed in the second questionnaire by all the five participants revealed some widely perceived issues, as shown in Table 3.

Table 3. Axial coding of the personal comments of the participants expressed in the second questionnaire.

Category	Positive	Negative
Filters	4	1
Operation behaviour	3	3
User's satisfaction	3	2
Interface	2	2

We generally received a large number of positive comments regarding the variety of the filters and of the operations (e.g. search and sort) that can be applied on the data. Notable features of the OSCAR tool that attracted praise were first the fact that it is able to recognise different kinds of unique identifiers (i.e. DOI and ORCID) automatically, and second that fields of the results table are customized according to the particular kind of objects returned (i.e. documents or people). The main weakness identified lied mainly in the ambiguity of part of the OSCAR interface and of the "show all" operation, and in its efficiency, since often it spent several seconds before returning the result to a query. While this latter aspect is crucial to user satisfaction, in our test it was unsatisfactory mainly due to the poor performance offered by our previous (very limited) OpenCitations infrastructure hosting the SPARQL endpoint. However, this specific issue is currently being addressed by migrating the OpenCitations Corpus to the new infrastructure, which includes a powerful physical server.

6 Conclusions

In this paper we have introduced OSCAR, the OpenCitations RDF Search Application, a user-friendly searching tool for use with RDF triplestores presenting a SPARQL endpoint. In particular, we have presented its main features and we have shown how it can be adapted to work with different SPARQL endpoints, including those of the OpenCitations Corpus, Scholarly Data and Wikidata. Finally, we have discussed the outcomes of user testing undertaken in order to understand the perceived usability of the OSCAR search interface when used to interrogate the OpenCitations Corpus.

We are currently working on some extensions of OSCAR, particularly an advanced search interface, so as to permit complex combinations of field-oriented queries by means of logical connections (*OR*, *AND*, etc.). For a more accurate usability analysis, we would like to strengthen our evaluation by involving a larger number of participants from different fields of study, and also to evaluate OSCAR in a comparative test with other similar tools. In addition, we are presently developing a related tool, named LUCINDA, to **browse** the resources inside a triplestore. In particular, LUCINDA will have the ability to visualize the resources attributes directly, providing detailed information about bibliographic resources such as journal names, page numbers, and additional identifiers. As with OSCAR, this new browsing tool will be integrated within the OpenCitations Web site so as to provide human-readable descriptions of the OpenCitations Corpus entities, and will equally be made publicly available for customization and implementation over the triplestores of other RDF data repositories.

We recommend the use of OSCAR, which is a fully open source application provided by OpenCitations for general community use, to permit free-text queries over the SPARQL endpoints of other triplestores. We would be grateful to receive feedback (to contact@opencitations.net) from its users.

Acknowledgements. We gratefully acknowledge the financial support provided to us by the Alfred P. Sloan Foundation for the OpenCitations Enhancement Project (grant number G-2017-9800).

References

1. Cyganiak, R., Wood, D., Lanthaler, M.: RDF 1.1 concepts and abstract syntax. W3C Recommendation, 25 February 2014. https://www.w3.org/TR/rdf11-concepts/
2. Harris, S., Seaborne, A.: SPARQL 1.1 query language. W3C Recommendation, 21 March 2013. https://www.w3.org/TR/sparql11-query/
3. Hiebi, I., Peroni, S., Shotton, D.: Material and outcomes of the OSCAR user testing session. Figshare (2018). https://doi.org/10.6084/m9.figshare.5849724
4. Lewis, J.R., Sauro, J.: The factor structure of the system usability scale. In: Kurosu, M. (ed.) HCD 2009. LNCS, vol. 5619, pp. 94–103. Springer, Heidelberg (2009). https://doi.org/10.1007/978-3-642-02806-9_12
5. Nielsen, F.Å., Mietchen, D., Willighagen, E.: Scholia, scientometrics and wikidata. In: Blomqvist, E., Hose, K., Paulheim, H., Lawrynowicz, A., Ciravegna, F., Hartig, O. (eds.) ESWC 2017. LNCS, vol. 10577, pp. 237–259. Springer, Cham (2017). https://doi.org/10.1007/978-3-319-70407-4_36
6. Nielsen, J.: Why you only need to test with 5 users (2000). https://www.nngroup.com/articles/why-you-only-need-to-test-with-5-users/. Accessed 30 Jan 2018
7. Nielsen, J.: Discount usability: 20 years (2009). https://www.nngroup.com/articles/discount-usability-20-years/. Accessed 30 Jan 2018
8. Nuzzolese, A.G., Gentile, A.L., Presutti, V., Gangemi, A.: Conference linked data: the ScholarlyData project. In: Groth, P., et al. (eds.) ISWC 2016. LNCS, vol. 9982, pp. 150–158. Springer, Cham (2016). https://doi.org/10.1007/978-3-319-46547-0_16
9. Peroni, S., Shotton, D., Vitali, F.: One year of the OpenCitations Corpus. In: d'Amato, C., et al. (eds.) ISWC 2017. LNCS, vol. 10588, pp. 184–192. Springer, Cham (2017). https://doi.org/10.1007/978-3-319-68204-4_19
10. Sauro, J.: A Practical Guide to the System Usability Scale: Background, Benchmarks & Best Practices (2011). ISBN 978-1461062707

11. Peroni, S., Dutton, A., Gray, T., Shotton, D.: Setting our bibliographic references free: towards open citation data. J. Doc. **71**(2), 253–277 (2015). https://doi.org/10.1108/JD-12-2013-0166. http://speroni.web.cs.unibo.it/publications/peroni-2015-setting-bibliographic-references.pdf

12. Strauss, A., Corbin, J.: Basics of Qualitative Research Techniques and Procedures for Developing Grounded Theory, 2nd edn. Sage Publications, London (1998). ISBN: 978-0803959408

13. Vrandečić, D., Krötzsch, M.: Wikidata: a free collaborative knowledgebase. Commun. ACM **57**(10), 78–85 (2014). https://doi.org/10.1145/2629489

14. Zaki, N., Tennakoon, C.: BioCarian: search engine for exploratory searches in heterogeneous biological databases. BMC Bioinform. **18**, 435 (2017). https://doi.org/10.1186/s12859-017-1840-4

Storing Combustion Data Experiments: New Requirements Emerging from a First Prototype
Position Paper

Gabriele Scalia[1]([envelope]), Matteo Pelucchi[2], Alessandro Stagni[2], Tiziano Faravelli[2], and Barbara Pernici[1]

[1] Department of Electronics, Information and Bioengineering, Politecnico di Milano, Milan, Italy
{gabriele.scalia,barbara.pernici}@polimi.it
[2] Department of Chemistry Materials, and Chemical Engineering Giulio Natta, Politecnico di Milano, Milan, Italy
{matteo.pelucchi,alessandro.stagni,tiziano.faravelli}@polimi.it
http://www.polimi.it

Abstract. Repositories for scientific and scholarly data are valuable resources to share, search, and reuse data by the community. Such repositories are essential in data-driven research based on experimental data. In this paper we focus on the case of combustion kinetic modeling, where the goal is to design models typically validated by means of comparisons with a large number of experiments.

In this paper, we discuss new requirements emerging from the analysis of an existing data collection prototype and its associated services. New requirements, elaborated in the paper, include the acquisition of new experiments, the automatic discovery of new sources, semantic exploration of information and multi-source integration, the selection of data for model validation.

These new requirements set the need for a new representation of scientific data and associated metadata. This paper describes the scenario, the requirements and outlines an initial architecture to support them.

Keywords: Experimental data · Explorative approaches
Combustion modeling

1 Introduction

The collection of experimental data for scientific research is becoming more and more important for the validation of the research results. One of the current goals is also the ability and effectiveness of sharing experimental data among researchers, in order to increase their quality and reproducibility and to derive and validate new research results.

© Springer Nature Switzerland AG 2018
A. González-Beltrán et al. (Eds.): SAVE-SD 2017/2018, LNCS 10959, pp. 138–149, 2018.
https://doi.org/10.1007/978-3-030-01379-0_10

In particular, in this paper we focus on experimental data in the combustion domain, and in particular in chemical kinetics, where a number of initiatives have been developed to collect experimental data in a systematic way, to be shared in the research community. Recent developments of experimental data repositories for chemical kinetics (e.g., ReSpecTh [4], CloudFlame [2], ChemKED [1], PrIMe [3]) aim to collect and store the increasing number of basic and complex experimental measurements of reacting and non-reacting combustion phenomena (or properties) in more efficient machine-readable formats (e.g. XML, YAML etc.). In parallel, EU-funded projects are pursuing the challenging goal of defining community data reporting standards[1] to overcome instances of incomplete, inaccurate, or ambiguous descriptions of fundamental data, both in the past and in the recent scientific literature. Based on the Open Science Cloud strategy of the EU[2], *every* project financed within the H2020 framework has to deal with FAIR data policy and Data Management Plan.

Even if the requirements described in this paper arise in a specific scenario, they are shared among many different domains, both in other scientific fields and in other different areas, as discussed in the following.

The urgent need of improving the infrastructure supporting the reuse of experimental data has been highlighted in literature. To facilitate this effort, general guidelines have been proposed for creating and managing repositories, like the FAIRness [32] (being findable, accessible, interoperable and reusable) or the "pyramid" of needs for data management that span from being simply *saved* to being *shared* to ultimately being *trusted* [12].

On top of these needs for data, new analytics requirements arise. The new requirements are mainly related to the *semantics of data*. Taking into consideration the semantics of the stored data, necessary to improve tasks like acquisition, exploration and validation, brings new challenges. For example, "this necessitates machines to be capable of autonomously and appropriately acting when faced with the wide range of types, formats, and access-mechanisms/protocols that will be encountered during their self-guided exploration" [32].

If a scientific repository with its basic tools for import/export can improve the efficiency of many tasks, like structurally retrieving certain experiment types, on the other side taking into account the semantics allow improving the *effectiveness* of data management. For example, many different functionalities that can exploit the scientific information conveyed by data and evaluate it not only for the quality of the available data/information itself, but with respect to the available models for that particular scientific experiment described by those data.

Others emerging requirements are arising in terms of the ability of retrieving data in an exploratory way [13,14,30]. This involves searching non obvious relations among data exploring possible research directions, and being able to assess the quality of the retrieved information.

The goal of the present paper is to discuss on new requirements emerging from the development and use of existing repositories of experimental data in

---

[1] http://www.smartcats.eu/wg4/task-force/.

[2] https://ec.europa.eu/research/openscience/index.cfm?pg=open-science-cloud.

the domain of kinetic modeling of chemical processes such as combustion [23, 29]. While these new requirements are investigated in this specific domain, they are general and may be extended to many other fields in the wider domain of scientific experimentation.

The paper is structured as follows. Section 2 introduces the domain presenting the scenario, Sect. 3 presents the emerging requirements and Sect. 4 sketches an a proposed architecture to support them.

2   Scenario

In this section is described the scenario: combusion kinetic modelling. Since the requirements which arise from this scenario are certainly shared among many other domains, the section ends with a discussion on the challenges that can be generalized.

Combustion kinetic modelling has been driving the development of more efficient fuels and combustion technologies (e.g. internal combustion engines, gas turbines, industrial furnaces etc.) for the last 30 years. As a matter of fact, chemical kinetics determines the reactivity of a given fuel or a fuel mixture; thus, a better understanding of the effects of a specific chemical compound on combustion performances and emissions allows the tailoring of a fuel or a fuel blend for an existing infrastructure or vice versa [5].

The Chemical Reaction Engineering and Chemical Kinetics (CRECK) research group at Politecnico di Milano deals on a daily basis with the development and update of such kinetic models.

The development and update of reliable kinetic models is a rather challenging task, directly reflecting the intrinsic complexity of combustion phenomena, and is one of the fields of research of the CRECK modeling group[3]. Such models typically involve $\sim 10^2 - 10^3$ chemical species connected by a network of $\sim 10^3 - 10^4$ elementary reaction steps. Moreover, a combustion kinetic model hierarchically develops from small chemical species (e.g. hydrogen, methane, etc.) up to heavier compounds typically found in commercial fuels (gasoline, diesel and jet fuels). For this reason, any modification in the core mechanism significantly propagates its effects to heavier species making continuous revisions and updates mandatory to preserve the reliability of the model.

From an operational perspective, the iterative validation of such models (Fig. 1) strongly relies on extensive comparisons of results from numerical simulations with an enormous number of experimental data covering conditions of interest for real combustion devices. The key step in such procedure consists in the objective and automatic assessment of model performances, properly taking into account experimental uncertainties, and avoiding time consuming and unsustainable qualitative comparisons. Analysis tools (e.g., sensitivity analysis) allow highlighting relevant model parameters and drive their refinement by means of more accurate estimation methods.

---

[3] http://creckmodeling.chem.polimi.it/.

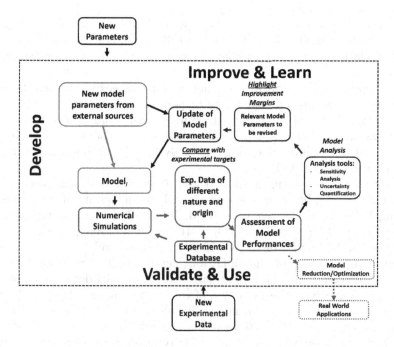

Fig. 1. Standard development, validation and refinement procedure of a chemical kinetic model for combustion applications [20].

Many different tools have been developed within the CRECK research activity. The OpenSMOKE++ [10] code is used to perform kinetic simulations of typical facilities such as jet stirred and flow reactors, 1D-2D laminar flames, shock tubes and rapid compression machines. The variables of interest are typically ignition delay times or laminar flame speeds of fuel/oxidizer mixtures, fuel consumption, intermediate and product species formation/disappearance at specific conditions of temperature (T) and pressure (p). Experimental measurements, typically stored in ASCII, CSV, XML formats on remote servers are compared to outputs from numerical simulations.

Beyond classical graphical comparisons (i.e., those typically reported in publications) the "Curve Matching approach" [6] allows for an objective, quantitative and automatic evaluation of model capability of predicting the variables of interest. If the model provides satisfactory agreement, subsequent steps of optimization and reduction [28] make the model suitable for large scale computations of interest for industry. On the contrary, if the model shows deviations outside of the experimental uncertainties, relevant pathways can be identified by means of analysis tools and model parameters are further refined with better estimates. Indeed, the recent developments coupling high performance computing and theoretical chemistry allow the automatic generation of highly accurate parameters [8,21].

While the efficient integration of the above tools in a fully automatized system is one of today's challenges in kinetic modelling [18], efficient and smart data collection, formatting, analysis, conversion and storage is the new frontier for the domain.

The exponential growth in the number and complexity of scientific information in the combustion community (experimental data, models, theoretical investigations etc.) and the improved accuracy of experimental techniques and theoretical methods can be beneficial at best only if coupled with extremely efficient tools for acquiring, storing and analyzing of such information, thereof allowing real advances in knowledge.

Several initiatives to enable effective and structured data collection of experimental data for combustion science are available in the literature at present. Starting from the pioneering work of M. Frenklach and co-workers developing the PrIMe [3,15] database which is still under continuous update at DLR Stuttgart, the ReSpecTh repository largely improved and extended the previous approach by means of a more flexible, detailed and user-friendly structure [4,29]. At present ReSpecTh collects into XML files ~104 datasets (~105 data points) of relevance for the validation of combustion models. Despite the total number of combustion experiments is difficult to estimate, the extent of this collection is expected to increase more than linearly in the years to come. Additional data repositories such as ChemKED (Oregon State/Connecticut) [1,31] and CloudFlame (KAUST) [2] further extended the interest in better structuring experimental information and increased the number of experimental data systematically collected through machine readable formats. Interestingly, the COST Action CM 1404 (SMARTCATs) established a task force of scientist aiming at defining standards for data collection, allowing easy and effective coupling with the above systems. According to the Open Science Cloud strategy *every* project financed within the H2020 framework has to deal with the FAIRness of data [32] and the CRECK group is involved in several projects which include data production and management according to FAIR, like JetSCREEN[4], Residue2Heat[5], IMPROOF[6] and CLEAN GAS[7].

On top of the reference repositories mentioned above, one should consider a similar amount of experimental information stored in a less structured format into many institutional servers belonging to experimental or modelling groups working in the field of combustion. As an example, the CRECK repository, which is taken as the basis for defining the requirements illustrated in this paper, is the result of data collection in ~30 years of research efforts in modelling combustion phenomena. While the previous less systematic approach to data management relied on manual extraction and classification into spreadsheets or ASCII/txt files, a more accurate and very recent implementation relies on a relational database (MySQL) [23] with a structured interface for extracting experiments,

---

[4] https://www.jetscreen-h2020.eu/.

[5] https://www.residue2heat.eu/.

[6] https://www.spire2030.eu/improof.

[7] http://www.clean-gas.polimi.it/.

and a collection of related files. In its "beta" version it contains references to 30 scientific papers and their associated experimental data (~60 datasets and ~1000 data points). This tool is interoperable with the ReSpecTh repository and coupled with the OpenSMOKE++ suite of programs [10] for numerical replication of experimental data aiming at combustion models validation.

The challenges which arise from the scenario described can be easily generalized to other domains and contexts. First of all, the need of a continuous validation of models based on new experiments is shared among most scientific fields, and therefore the activities of acquiring, analyzing and evaluating models and experiments is certainly shared to other scientific domains. Moreover, the need of automatically acquiring inputs coming from different sources, integrate them and analyze them in order to validate them with respect to some model is very generalizable. For example, the inputs could be those coming from a set of processes and environment variables, and the evaluation could be with respect to a model of the quality that must be ensured. However, addressing the challenges presented in this paper also arises domain-specific requirements, in particular those related to the description (ontology) of the field.

3   Dynamic Analysis Requirements

Starting from the scenario described in the previous Section and wishes described in Sect. 1, a set of requirements has been formulated.

The goal of these requirements is to enhance the efficiency and the effectiveness of data management for this context.

Different analysis can be performed on the collected data, independently from one another. The analysis requirements are presented and discussed in the following paragraphs.

3.1   Continuous Multi-source Integration

The need for a continuous multi-source integration comes from the variability of the information sources, which could vary over time and cannot, therefore, be presumed a priori. This integration has many facets, most notably:

- The *format* of the data, which could vary.
- The *semantics*, since the same concepts could be described differently in different sources and datasets. This requires an ontology-based semantic layer—which is dynamic itself—and a conceptualization of the information already stored.
- The *information* conveyed by the data, which can be related to different types of experiments and settings and can largely vary in terms of *accuracy*, *precision* and *coverage*, from experimental uncertainty, parameters needed for correct simulations and/or replicability of the same measurement.

A continuous management of the already-acquired information is necessary in order to update data already stored according to new requirements for the analysis. The need for updates is also related to the *information quality* (IQ) management: as new data and metadata are acquired or generated through processing, the IQ—with each single dimension that defines it—evolves. Therefore, for example, the data associated to an experiment may have a certain accuracy (which impacts on the overall quality), but further acquired information and/or processing can improve it without changes in the data itself. Moreover, complex data not only are characterized by objects which change over time, enriching their information, but also by explicit (*complex networks*) or implicit (*articulated objects*) relationships of interdependencies among objects. The IQ of such articulated objects is a function of the information quality of the sub-objects and of the other objects for which a relationship exists. Indeed, besides managing the quality of raw data, which is a problem addressed in the literature, the focus is on introducing the management of the quality of complex information through their relationship. Such cases are typically characterized by *context-dependent* information and these dependencies are in general not simply additive. For example, there could be "partial views" expressed by sub-entities which bring to a meaningful information only when combined.

An open issue is represented by the lack of a complete domain ontology. To face this challenge, a solution could be the automatic generation of ontological relationships based on the acquired data and *data mining* techniques. For example, finding synonyms for the same entities starting from papers text [16] or attributes related to an experiment through clustering and other machine learning techniques on the data available.

3.2   Dynamic Acquisition

The requirement for the system is to continuously "find" and integrate new data automatically. This can be accomplished by a dynamic acquisition driven by the already stored data. The goal is to (potentially) enhance the IQ of the already stored data by finding new information about them or new related data (for example, new experiments for a stored model).

Given the continuous validation performed on the stored information, the acquisition ultimately aims at better assessing the IQ and in general enhancing the data coverage.

This is accomplished by extending the concept of "focused crawling" [33]. The best predicate for querying, in general, changes over time and depends on a background knowledge. Acquired data can drive the acquisition of new data in a *virtuous cycle*. The background knowledge is certainly composed by the already acquired information, but also by the list of preceding queries and their results. Indeed, when acquiring data from unreliable sources it is not possible to make strong assumptions about them and an *exploratory approach* must be employed (see the discussion in Subsect. 3.4).

Since the goal is to acquire as much information as possible, different source types must be taken into account. In particular, there are *structured* and *unstructured* source types. While the first include repositories or manual inputs and are handled mainly through the integration process illustrated in Subsect. 3.1, the second includes valuable sources like papers and web pages without or with little structured information. This requires to *extract* information from unstructured text and images, using mining techniques (e.g. [11,25]) and image analysis (e.g. [22]). Semi-automatic techniques can also be employed (e.g. [17]).

3.3   Continuous Validation

The process of continuous validation entails the matching of already stored information with new information as it is acquired.

This requirement mainly comes from the need of validating *models* and *experimental data*, one respect to the others through curve matching techniques, as described in Sect. 2, but could be extended also to validations based on other kinds of data and metadata, e.g., authors, experiment types, and information quality.

Validation is performed through *cross-comparisons* which require efficient means of *extracting* the right data, *comparing* them taking into account the differences and the lacks that could exist in their representations and *enriching* the entities (models, experimental data, etc.) with the results.

This is a continuous process: for example, a model must be tested against new experimental data as they become available over time and therefore the validity of the model itself evolves over time.

Validating means also *verifying* data and models. However, there are many different situations that must be handled. For example:

- There could be a set of models that fails in a particular condition because there are no data for that condition and therefore new data should drive the refinement of models ("experimental design").
- There could be data for an experiment that is not congruent with other data for the same experiment and therefore should be repeated and verified.
- There could be that *all* models fail for an experiment because they are ignoring something. In this case the experiment is correct and instead the models should be improved.

3.4   Data Exploration

Articulated (meta)data can provide support for interactive and evolving data exploration [13].

This has to do with the need of automatically or manually querying for information which are in general incomplete, heterogeneous or may not exist at all.

In particular, manual interventions are key to maintain an overall high IQ resolving conflicts and enriching domain knowledge, and they need to be supported by effective query techniques. These include summarization [9], result refinement, iterative exploration [30] and a *top-k* query processing environment [27], thus improving the returned "manageable" results.

4   Proposed Architecture

After listing the analysis requirements in Sect. 3, this section outlines an initial architecture to support them, focusing on architectural requirements.

The goal here is to show how the requirements could be combined in an architecture and highlight the main challenges. A detailed architectural design, together with its development and testing, are not the scope of this paper and represent the ongoing work started with the requirements formulated here.

The main components are sketched in Fig. 2.

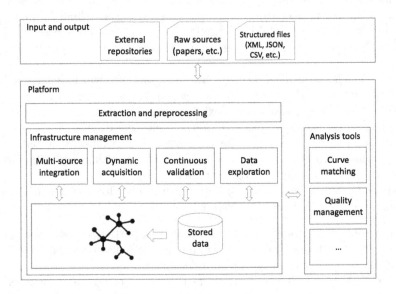

Fig. 2. Sketch of an initial architecture for the infrastructure.

A service-based approach has two advantages: the integration of legacy components with new components and the autonomous development of each of the services. Analysis tools need to be wrapped in services uniforming their interfaces to interact with infrastructure management components.

All the services access a common database. The database should optimize the functionalities of the components. This can be obtained first of all using a graph structures as conceptual-modeling. This allows to store and query data based on the relationships among objects, which is necessary to model interdependencies among entities (required by the continuous multi-source integration) and for data exploration—also through faceted search [24]—which is key in all the requirements. Graphs can also be exploited for mining activities [24] and to model varying precision and accuracy. Graph modeling can be accomplished through a graph database [19] or via mappings that enable graph reasonings over traditional relational databases [7,26]. A main challenge here is represented by the conversion and management of the various inputs in the property graph structure underpinning.

Another important requisite for the database is *indexing* to efficiently search and retrieve data based on the patterns of the acquisition/validation/exploration cycle and the metadata. For example, to validate an experiment, all the models for that particular experiment should be retrieved. This is also related to *top-k* query processing for data exploration.

Latency should be limited by parallelizing and putting in background tasks which not require to be responsive.

Finally, given the variety of existing formats and standards, the import/export interfaces should provide conversion tools.

5   Concluding Remarks

The effective integration of data science in current approaches and techniques for science and engineering is one of today's societal challenges, potentially allowing rapid and extremely significant technological advancements. Despite the generality of this perspective, this work focused on the well defined domain of combustion science, typically dealing with the investigation and development of new, cleaner and more efficient combustion technologies (i.e. fuel and engines). Even though a consistent delay exists compared to other industrial or research areas (e.g., pharmaceutics, organic chemistry etc.), recent implementation of data repositories specifically conceived for combustion kinetic modelling activities [2–4,31], ongoing initiatives within the community and incentives from the EU, further encourage the activity outlined in this work. After a qualitative analysis of the domain, requirements for the dynamic analysis of the large amount of information available have been discussed, focusing on the continuous multisource integration, the dynamic acquisition, the continuous validation and data exploration, with the related issues. Finally, a preliminary architecture has been defined, setting the basis for its refinement, development and testing in future activities.

References

1. ChemKED repository. http://www.chemked.com/
2. CloudFlame repository. https://cloudflame.kaust.edu.sa/
3. PrIMe repository. http://primekinetics.org/
4. ReSpecTh repository. http://respecth.hu/
5. Bergthorson, J.M., Thomson, M.J.: A review of the combustion and emissions properties of advanced transportation biofuels and their impact on existing and future engines. Renew. Sustain. Energy Rev. **42**, 1393–1417 (2015)
6. Bernardi, M., et al.: Curve matching, a generalized framework for models/experiments comparison: an application to n-heptane combustion kinetic mechanisms. Combust. Flame **168**, 186–203 (2016)
7. Calvanese, D., et al.: Ontop: answering SPARQL queries over relational databases. Semant. Web **8**(3), 471–487 (2017)

8. Cavallotti, C., Pelucchi, M., Klippenstein, S.: EStokTP: electronic structure to temperature and pressure dependent rate constants (2017, unpublished)

9. Cohan, A., Goharian, N.: Scientific article summarization using citation-context and article's discourse structure. arXiv preprint arXiv:1704.06619 (2017)

10. Cuoci, A., Frassoldati, A., Faravelli, T., Ranzi, E.: OpenSMOKE++: an object-oriented framework for the numerical modeling of reactive systems with detailed kinetic mechanisms. Comput. Phys. Commun. **192**, 237–264 (2015)

11. Daudaravicius, V.: A framework for keyphrase extraction from scientific journals. In: González-Beltrán, A., Osborne, F., Peroni, S. (eds.) SAVE-SD 2016. LNCS, vol. 9792, pp. 51–66. Springer, Cham (2016). https://doi.org/10.1007/978-3-319-53637-8_7

12. de Waard, A.: Research data management at Elsevier: supporting networks of data and workflows. Inf. Serv. Use **36**(1–2), 49–55 (2016)

13. Di Blas, N., Mazuran, M., Paolini, P., Quintarelli, E., Tanca, L.: Exploratory computing: a comprehensive approach to data sensemaking. Int. J. Data Sci. Anal. **3**(1), 61–77 (2017)

14. Francalanci, C., Pernici, B., Scalia, G.: Exploratory spatio-temporal queries in evolving information. In: Doulkeridis, C., Vouros, G.A., Qu, Q., Wang, S. (eds.) MATES 2017. LNCS, vol. 10731, pp. 138–156. Springer, Cham (2018). https://doi.org/10.1007/978-3-319-73521-4_9

15. Frenklach, M.: Transforming data into knowledge-process informatics for combustion chemistry. Proc. Combust. Inst. **31**(1), 125–140 (2007)

16. Gábor, K., Zargayouna, H., Tellier, I., Buscaldi, D., Charnois, T.: A typology of semantic relations dedicated to scientific literature analysis. In: González-Beltrán, A., Osborne, F., Peroni, S. (eds.) SAVE-SD 2016. LNCS, vol. 9792, pp. 26–32. Springer, Cham (2016). https://doi.org/10.1007/978-3-319-53637-8_3

17. Jung, D., et al.: ChartSense: interactive data extraction from chart images. In: Proceedings of the 2017 CHI Conference on Human Factors in Computing Systems, pp. 6706–6717. ACM (2017)

18. Keçeli, M., et al.: Automated computational thermochemistry for butane oxidation: a prelude to predictive automated combustion kinetics. Proc. Combust. Inst. (2018). Elsevier

19. Libkin, L., Martens, W., Vrgoč, D.: Querying graphs with data. J. ACM (JACM) **63**(2), 14 (2016)

20. Pelucchi, M.: Development of kinetic mechanisms for the combustion of renewable fuels. Ph.D. thesis, Politecnico di Milano (2017)

21. Pelucchi, M., Cavallotti, C., Faravelli, T., Klippenstein, S.: H-abstraction reactions by OH, HO_2, O, O_2 and benzyl radical addition to O_2 and their implications for kinetic modelling of toluene oxidation. Phys. Chem. Chem. Phys. **20**, 10607–10627 (2018)

22. Poco, J., Heer, J.: Reverse-engineering visualizations: recovering visual encodings from chart images. Comput. Graph. Forum. **36**, 353–363 (2017)

23. Rigamonti, A.: Automatic modeling system: a database based infrastructure to develop, validate and evaluate scientific models. An application to combustion kinetic models (2017)

24. Ristoski, P., Paulheim, H.: Semantic web in data mining and knowledge discovery: a comprehensive survey. Web Semant.: Sci. Serv. Agents World Wide Web **36**, 1–22 (2016)

25. Ronzano, F., Saggion, H.: Knowledge extraction and modeling from scientific publications. In: González-Beltrán, A., Osborne, F., Peroni, S. (eds.) SAVE-SD 2016. LNCS, vol. 9792, pp. 11–25. Springer, Cham (2016). https://doi.org/10.1007/978-3-319-53637-8_2

26. Schätzle, A., Przyjaciel-Zablocki, M., Skilevic, S., Lausen, G.: S2RDF: RDF querying with SPARQL on spark. Proc. VLDB Endow. **9**(10), 804–815 (2016)

27. Soliman, M.A., Ilyas, I.F., Chang, K.C.-C.: Top-k query processing in uncertain databases. In: DIEEE 23rd International Conference on Data Engineering, ICDE 2007, pp. 896–905. IEEE (2007)

28. Stagni, A., Frassoldati, A., Cuoci, A., Faravelli, T., Ranzi, E.: Skeletal mechanism reduction through species-targeted sensitivity analysis. Combust. Flame **163**, 382–393 (2016)

29. Varga, T., Turányi, T., Czinki, E., Furtenbacher, T., Császár, A.: ReSpecth: a joint reaction kinetics, spectroscopy, and thermochemistry information system. In: Proceedings of the 7th European Combustion Meeting, vol. 30, pp. 1–5 (2015)

30. Wasay, A., Athanassoulis, M., Idreos, S.: Queriosity: automated data exploration. In: Carminati, B., Khan, L. (eds.) 2015 IEEE International Congress on Big Data, New York City, NY, USA, 27 June–2 July 2015, pp. 716–719. IEEE (2015)

31. Weber, B.W., Niemeyer, K.E.: ChemKED: a human-and machine-readable data standard for chemical kinetics experiments. Int. J. Chem. Kinet. **50**, 135–148 (2017)

32. Wilkinson, M.D., et al.: The FAIR guiding principles for scientific data management and stewardship. Scientific Data **3** (2016)

33. Yu, R., Gadiraju, U., Fetahu, B., Dietze, S.: Adaptive focused crawling of linked data. In: Wang, J., et al. (eds.) WISE 2015 Part I. LNCS, vol. 9418, pp. 554–569. Springer, Cham (2015). https://doi.org/10.1007/978-3-319-26190-4_37

Investigating Facets to Characterise Citations for Scholars

Angelo Di Iorio[1]($\boxtimes$), Freddy Limpens[1], Silvio Peroni[1], Agata Rotondi[1],
Georgios Tsatsaronis[2], and Jorgos Achtsivassilis[2]

[1] Department of Computer Science and Engineering, University of Bologna,
Bologna, Italy
{angelo.diiorio,freddy.limpens,silvio.peroni,agata.rotondi2}@unibo.it
[2] Elsevier B.V., Amsterdam, The Netherlands
{g.tsatsaronis,j.achtsivassilis}@elsevier.com

Abstract. Citations within academic literature keep gaining more importance both for the work of scholars and for improving digital libraries related tools and services. We present in this article the preliminary results of an investigation on the characterisations of citations whose objective is to propose a framework for globally enriching citations with explicit information about their nature, role and characteristics. This article focuses on the set of properties we are studying to support the automatic analysis of large corpora of citations. This model is grounded on a literature review also detailed here, and has been submitted to a group of several hundreds of scholars of all disciplines in the form of a survey. The results confirm that these properties are perceived as useful.

Keywords: Citation functions · Citations · Semantic publishing

1 Introduction

Citations are fundamental tools for scholars, anytime during their career. Everyone focuses on different aspects and looks for them while working. A PhD student surveying the literature for her thesis exploits citations to find relevant articles; a senior researcher deepening his research exploits citations to continuously find new material; a reviewer reads citations to understand if the citing works are up-to-date and well-connected to others; a professor writing a project proposal uses citations to spot recent works and useful links; and several other examples could be listed here.

A research line about citations that have been studied for long time, and is increasingly re-gaining importance, is about the identification of authors' motivations for citation. Several schemas of what they are often called *citation functions* have been proposed by the community towards this goal, very heterogeneous in terms of number of options, granularity and, above all, type of classification: some schemas focus on structural features (position in the article, section, etc.),

A. González-Beltrán et al. (Eds.): SAVE-SD 2017/2018, LNCS 10959, pp. 150–160, 2018.
https://doi.org/10.1007/978-3-030-01379-0_11

some on semantic aspects (negative or positive citations, rhetorical aspects, etc.); some on objective properties, some others on more subjective ones; moreover characterisations also differ a lot among disciplines.

We present here a review of these schemas trying to identify common traits and suggestions for new models, and the results of a survey we conducted with more than three hundred scholars to investigate which characterisations are really useful for the final users. To the best of our knowledge, this is the first quantitative study on how users perceive qualified citations, with the aim of deriving which aspects are considered more important and why.

This work is part of a larger project on enriching citations, called SCAR - Semantic Colouring of Academic References. In our vision, each citation (both references in bibliographies and incoming citations) is treated as an individual, first-class entity, which can be classified, accessed, filtered and grouped with other references according to different criteria.

This work is in fact a first step to identify a suitable set of properties for characterising citations, that will be used as reference for automatic classification in the SCAR project. Our goal here is also to collect further feedback from the community, so as to incrementally refine our model.

The article is structured as follows. Section 2 reviews the related works, from which we derived a data model for characterisations presented in detail in Sect. 3. The scholars survey is presented in Sect. 4 before drawing some conclusions in Sect. 5.

2   Characterising Citations: A Literature Review

Nowadays, the impact of authors, the comparative evaluation of scientists and other research evaluations are mostly based on quantitative metrics for citations (e.g. *h-index*). The validity of these approaches has been often criticised (see for e.g. [41]) as it does not account for different qualitative aspects of citations. Negative or self-citations should be weighted in a different way compared for example to affirmative or methodological citations. White in [39] however tackles the penalisation of negative citations saying that it is anyway an achievement to have one's work noticed by others. It is clear that some cases might be controversial but this is not always the case. A famous example reported by [17] is the case of a South Korean research scientist, Hwang Woo-suk, whose faked research gained popularity with its 200 citations, most of which were negative. Negative citations in this last example have a significant weight.

Authors might show ambivalent opinions regarding a cited work (as discussed by [3]), dissemble their real viewpoint for politeness and stylistic reasons and change their opinion over time.

Citations functions do not differ only in authors' motivations but they depend also on the research domain where the use of citations varies from discipline to discipline (see [14]) both on motivational and structural level. The question of qualitative bibliometrics is gaining interest in literature and researchers are suggesting different approaches to the problem (see [1,7]).

152   A. Di Iorio et al.

One of the first step in this direction is the delineation of a citation functions schema which works as a basis for an automatic citation characterisation tool. This is not an easy task considering the different features and aspects that have to be taken into account.

One of the first work on the topic is Garfield [12] whose list of authors' motivations for citation behaviour has been widely cited in literature. Garfield is also one of the first authors to envisage a machine able to automatically identify such motivations. In fact, most of the existing citation functions schemas are the result of theoretical studies and manual analysis more than basis for automatic tools.

Existing schemas differ in the number of citation functions they include and consequently in degree of detail. For example, [8] propose four categories of citations (*background, fundamental idea, technical basis and comparison*) while [13] more than thirty. A detailed and well formed classification model is CiTO [28] whose 41 citations properties are hierarchically structured and divided into factual and rhetorical (further classified as negative, neutral, positive). CiTO has been already used in different tools and other projects like CiteULike[1] and Data.open.c.uk[2] as well as reference scheme to annotate citations directly via browser[3] or CMS plugins[4].

Several studies on the citation functions (See for e.g. [18]) refer to the four-categories schema proposed by Moravcsik and Murugesan [25]: *conceptual* (theoretical) vs. *operational* (methodological); *evolutionary* (build on cited work) vs. *juxtapositional* (alternative to cited work); *confirmative* or *negational* and *organic* (necessary to understand the current work) vs. *perfunctory* (not really necessary for the development of the current work). The last pair is interesting because it introduces the concept of information utility of a citation. The *perfunctory* function has been pursued in different citation functions schemas such as [20,40] and [13].

The question of the utility and importance of a citation compared to others is a recurrent topic in literature. [11] divides his different categories in *primary* and *secondary* sources, [24] conceive citation to be *central* or *peripheral*, [8] figures *background* citation and *fundamental background* ideas and one of [21] citation functions is *significant* i.e. the cited work is important for the current article.

The relevance of a citation is also related to the difference between *constituent* and *parenthetical* citations (See [38]); does a citation in brackets has the same value of a citation with a syntactic role in the sentence? This is a question it might be interesting to investigate. In the same way, single citations and groups of citations, especially when redundant (in the Moravcsik's concept of redundant, i.e. several articles each of which makes the same point), should be accurately considered.

Besides the shared comparison axis, existing schemas have other recurrent properties both on semantic and objective level. Since [22] two of the most con-

---

[1] CiteULike homepage: http://www.citeulike.org.
[2] Open Linked Data from The Open university: http://data.open.ac.uk.
[3] CiTO Reference Annotation Tools for Google Chrome.
[4] Link to Link Wordpress plugin: https://wordpress.org/plugins/link-to-link/.

templated semantic properties concern the use of a citation in order to *affirm* or *negate/criticise* a cited or citing work. [25] named them *confirmative* and *negational* functions, [10] *confirmational* and *negational*; for [32] a cited source can be *positively* or *negatively* evaluated; [21] put in their fine-grained citation function classification schema a *negative* function (when the weakness of the cited work is discussed) and a *positive* function (when the cited work is successful). These two authors' motivations are strictly related to the work of polarity analysis of citations (see [16]).

Other recurrent semantic features are the idea of *supporting* and we found it for example in [6,13,27] (who classifies it as a sub-category of the affirmation property), [35] and [14] and those of *extending*, see for example [24] and [37].

On the objective side, two main aspects arise from the majority of the schemas: citations used as *background* and those which are references to *methods* and *data* sources. Among the ones who adopt the background function, [23] distinguish *generalbackground* from *specific background* and like other colleagues define the background as *historical* (e.g. [26]). *Methods* and *data*, seen both as a single [1] or separated [9] properties, are the most recurrent functions from Garfield 1965 to Dong 2011 where they are named *technical basis*.

While some properties like *methods* and *data* seem to be highly related to the scientific domain most of the schemas belong to, the other properties are more interdisciplinary and thus can be applied to different domains (see [33] for an overview). Our analysis is further confirmed by Tahamtan's study of the most used citation functions in literature [34].

A scholar browsing references, or a list of *cited by* works, would also be interested in knowing other aspects of the citations, for instance where each citation appears in the article. Sections bring important information about a citation as well as its location in a broader sense (beginning, central, final part). As [34] point out "the citation location might reveal the reasons and decision rules for citing a specific document". Hernández et al. affirm and show in their 2016 survey [15] the existing relationship between the location of a citation and its polarity. Moreover, different locations often mean different relevance. For example [2] note that citations outside the introduction are perceived to be more valuable since this section often contains general background information and the highest number of citations (compared to other sections). These aspects can also help the automatic identification of citation functions (see [35]) but their validity depends on disciplinary structures which might differ among domains.

3   Facets for Characterising Citations

The characterisations discussed so far constitute a valuable background for this work. We continue our past research as part of a new project called SCAR, whose goal is to enrich lists of citations with explicit information about their role, features and impact. The basic idea is to let scholars access enhanced publications in which the bibliography is not a monolithic unit, as it happens today, but a collection of entries that can be shown, filtered and aggregated according to multiple properties. The same capabilities can be added to the lists of incoming citations: these are very common in digital libraries and citation indexes that often show lists of related articles when reading one. Characterising both outgoing and incoming citations is the main goal of our research. We also plan to build interfaces and tools to exploit these characterisations.

Some questions arise naturally: which properties shall we use to characterise citations? How are these properties related to each other? Which information is most interesting for the users?

This section introduces our initial list of properties, derived from the literature review and our past studies in this area.

Table 1 summarises our data model, organised in seven classes, shown in the first column of the table. Single characterisations are listed in the right column and identified by a label composed of a letter corresponding to the class and a progressive number. These references will be used throughout the article.

Table 1. The SCAR set of facets for characterising citations

Class	Options and details
Citation metrics	Global citation count (m1) | number of times cited in the current article (m2)
Author metrics	Self-citation (a1) | most cited authors (a2)
Type of cited work	Type of venue (s1) | type of contribution (s2) | awarded (s3)
Citation context	Sentence/paragraph (c2) | section name (c2) | single or grouped citation (c3)
Temporal information	Time span (t1)
Citation functions	Extends (f1) | same research (f2) | suggests or critiques (f3) | use method in (f4) | data source (f5) |...
Citation polarity	Positive (p1) | negative (p2) | neutral (p3)

The first class is named citation metrics. In fact, one of the most common task citations are used for is to identify the most relevant articles in a research area: the more an article is cited the higher its impact. Thus, despite the very basic nature of this feature, we believe it is helpful to enrich bibliographies with the global citation count of each cited article (m1). This metrics count does not consider for example that an article might be cited many times by the same source, a situation that might indicate that the cited article was very influential for the citing one (See [40] and [17]). This is captured as (m2).

The considerations about the impact of cited articles can be easily extended to the authors: a list of citations that also include data about each author, in fact, might be used to identify potentially interesting works written by the experts of a given domain (a2). The authors metrics class is completed by hints about self-citations (a1): their identification is often needed to picture the scientific production of an author and for evaluation purposes.

Citations can also be classified according to the publication venue of the cited work (s1) differentiating for instance between workshop, conference and journal articles. Such a characterisation is helpful when evaluating research contributions. Another interesting dimension is the actual contribution of the cited work (s2): citations could be annotated as citing research articles, surveys, in-use reports, and so on. This is helpful when exploring a research topic: the ability to easily spot surveys or application reports makes searches much easier and faster; similarly it is useful to identify full research articles when searching contributions within scientific events. The fact that an article was awarded is a further information that could be exploited by the scholars (s3).

Temporal information about cited or citing articles are also relevant here. Consider, for instance, the task of checking the freshness of references while reviewing an article: this could be done automatically providing users with filtering widgets that work on annotated references and their time-related data (t1).

Citations could also be enriched with information about their textual context. The term 'citation context' has been introduced to indicate the sentence of the paragraph in which an article is cited but different conceptions of its size window have been investigated during the past years (See [31] and [19]). Showing such context has been proved to be useful for the readers and several platforms already include it (c1) (e.g. CiteSeerX and ResearchGate).

Other contextual information could be provided about the section containing the citation (c2). As previously shown, several studies confirm the significance of the location of citations as an important feature for the authors' motivations identification, see also the Teufel's Argumentative Zoning theory [36] and the work of Abu-Jabara [1] where article section is used as one of the features to identify citation purpose and polarity. In the same work, Abu-Jabara considers also the difference between single and group of citations as an important aspect for citation classification (labelled as c3 in the table).

The last two classes of our list comprise the most challenging characterisations: citation functions and polarity. As seen in a previous section, several citation functions schemas have been proposed through the years which converge in different aspects. In [4] we studied how CiTO ontology is perceived and used by users. The idea of the study came for the observation that the projects which adopt CiTO employ a sub-set of its properties. For example the Link to Link Wordpress plugin allow users to specify ten of its properties, while the Pensoft Publishers enable authors to use only six properties. In fact, the richness of CiTO ontology can be seen also as a hindrance by annotators and a less fine grained functions set seems to be more usable. In our previous experiment, two groups of ten subjects with different backgrounds and skills were asked to annotate citations whose contexts were automatically extracted from the proceedings of the Balisage Conference[5]. The first group was provided with the full list of 41 CiTO properties while the second one performed the same task by using a subset of 10 CiTO properties (selected with a preliminary experiment, see [5]).

---

[5] Balisage Conference WebPage: http://www.balisage.net.

Results show that besides the most generic and neutral functions such as *citesForInformation* or *citesAsRelated* both groups of annotators mainly used some specific functions: *obtainsBackroundFrom*, *citesAsDataSource*, *citesAsReccomandationReading*, *Credits*, *usesMethodIn*, *Critiques* and the first group employed only a sub-set of the 41 properties (See [4] for the detailed results). The most used functions of the human annotation experiment and also those selected by other projects are in line with the most common citation features we found in literature and are the ones we included in our citation functions list (f1–f5).

The last class of our model regards polarity of citations. This type of sentiment analysis, meant to classify positive (p1), or negative (p2), or neutral (p3) categories, has been proved to be related to the article sections. Furthermore it can provide a broad pattern of agreement and disagreement among authors (see [33]). In addition to providing a straightforward view of authors opinions to scholars, polarity can help survey generation systems [29] and citation-based summarisation systems [30].

In the next section we will show how our model is perceived by scholars, investigated through an ad-hoc questionnaire. This step was conceived in order to sharpen and finalise our analysis on citation characterisations.

4   Surveying Scholars on Characterisations of Citations

We designed and scripted a survey in SurveyMonkey. We then invited all members of the Elsevier's CDI Researcher Innovation Community to fill in the survey by e-mailing a direct link. From the 1200+ members of the community, we received 318 completed responses. The CDI Researcher Innovation Community is an in-house, carefully curated panel composed of researchers with wide representation across career phases, disciplines and regions. Elsevier has built this community up over 3 years, it is by invitation only and utilised for both qualitative and quantitative research.

We asked the respondents to our questionnaire to figure themselves as a user of a platform which gives access to full texts articles together with bibliographic references, and additional information on the articles cited by a given one (outgoing citations) as well as on articles citing that one (incoming citations). The full text of the questionnaire is available on-line[6].

The first part consisted in rating the relevance (from 0 to 5) of 13 characterisations for both incoming and outgoing citations, as well as impact factors of the articles authors, with the possibility each time to suggest other information through a free text box. We did not show all properties covered in previous section merely to keep duration of the test as low as possible. The characterisations submitted are: *is extended by, same research problem, supported by or criticised by, use method in, global citation count, data sources, most cited authors, type of publication venue, type of content, self-citations, citation context, in paper*

---

[6] See http://scar.disi.unibo.it/survey/ for the full text of the questionnaire.

citation count, section in which cited. Each of these characterisations can be used for outgoing and incoming citations, and within the questionnaire, both cases were presented each in a different section and a detailed explanation was given for each characterisation.

A final part of the survey was collecting info about the background of the respondents, focusing on the research domain, role, and habits regarding the use of digital scholar libraries.

To compare the different characterisations, we calculated, for each of them, the weighted score of relevance, the score's possible value ranging from 0 (not relevant) to 5 (very high relevance). Given the percentage $p(s)$ of response for each score s, the weighted score S is obtained by summing for each score value s the product $p(s) * s$. Figure 1 reports the weighted score for all citation characterisations for outgoing and incoming citations.

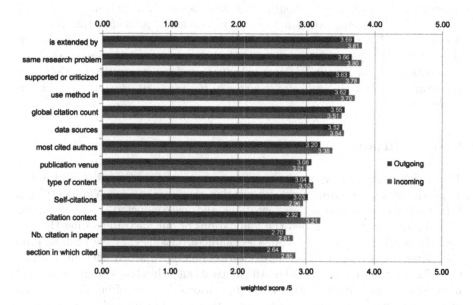

Fig. 1. Weighted score of characterisations for outgoing and incoming citations

The values of the weighted score range from 2.61 (*section in which cited* for outgoing citations) to 3.78 (*is extended by* for incoming citations). Therefore all characterisations remain around the medium score, i.e. 3. The standard deviation for each calculation of the weighted score range from 1 to 1.3 across all the cases. This level of standard deviation accounts for the relatively flat distribution of the ratings of all respondents.

Several remarks can be drawn from the global results:

– Due to the small amplitude and to a standard deviation not negligible, it is not straightforward to establish a significant ranking among the highest scored characterisations, nor to discard the characterisations with the smallest score. This means that all of them can be considered of relative interest for the majority of the respondents.

- Looking at the group of 7 chracterisations whose weighted score is above 3, one can observe that the 4 most highly scored characterisations (both for incoming and outgoing citations) are citation functions and that the only factual features are all related to the global citation count (global citation count and most cited author).
- The highest gap between the weighted score value of incoming and outgoing citations for a given characterisation is found for the citation context (3.21 for incoming, 2.92 for outgoing). This shows that this information is more valuable when given for the citing articles than for the cited ones.

The free text box inviting testers to suggest additional characterisations was skipped or given a "none" or equivalent response by 95% (incoming citations) and by 85% (outgoing citations) of the respondents. Although this does not demonstrate that the above list of 13 citation characterisations is complete, it gives us a pretty good hint in showing that the most wanted characterisations were covered in our listing. We were only suggested two properties to add to our list: *year of publication* and *impact factor of the venue in which cited work was published*.

5   Conclusions

This article presented the results of an investigation of the SCAR project aimed at providing a global framework for citation characterisations. We identified a list of properties to characterise citations and we conducted a survey among scholars in order to strengthen the foundations of our idea. Regarding the survey, the main outcome is that all the characterisations that we proposed are considered interesting. Furthermore, citation functions, which offer an information of a substantial higher level on the motivations behind a citation, clearly got more interest than more factual characterisations that are often already found in currently available tools. This confirms that scholars are willing to see these features coming to the digital libraries they often use, and that our model covers the usage we envision.

There is a lot of way to go for the SCAR project. We are currently working on algorithms to characterise the most wanted citation functions, in order to integrate them in a Semantic Web-based technological stack, so as to produce a large dataset connected to other sources of information. In the long-run we also target a higher level of user engagement in accessing bibliographies and list of citations.

References

1. Abu-Jbara, A., Ezra J., Radev, D.: Purpose and polarity of citation: towards NLP-based bibliometrics. In: Proceedings of the 12th Hlt-Naacl, Atlanta, GA (2013)
2. Boyack, K.W., Van Eck, N.J., Colavizza, G., Waltman, L.: Characterising in-text citations in scientific articles: a large-scale analysis. J. Informetr. **12**(1), 59–73 (2018)
3. Brooks, T.A.: Evidence of complex citer motivations. J. Am. Soc. Inf. Sci. **37**(1), 34–36 (1986)
4. Ciancarini, P., Di Iorio, A., Nuzzolese, A.G., Peroni, S., Vitali, F.: Evaluating citation functions in CiTO: cognitive issues. In: Presutti, V., d'Amato, C., Gandon, F., d'Aquin, M., Staab, S., Tordai, A. (eds.) ESWC 2014. LNCS, vol. 8465, pp. 580–594. Springer, Cham (2014). https://doi.org/10.1007/978-3-319-07443-6_39
5. Ciancarini, P., Di Iorio, A., Nuzzolese, A.G., Peroni, S., Vitali, F.: Characterising citations in scholarly articles: an experiment. In: Proceedings of the 1st AIC 2013. CEUR Workshop, Aachen, Germany (2013)
6. Cole, S.: The growth of scientific knowledge: theories of deviance as a case study. In: Idea of Social Structure, New York, pp. 175–220 (1975). Papers in Honour of Robert K Merton
7. Ding, Y., Zhang, G., Chambers, T., Song, M., Wang, X., Zhai, C.: Content-based citation analysis: the next generation of citation analysis. J. Assoc. Inf. Sci. Technol. **65**(9), 1820–1833 (2014)
8. Dong, C., Schäfer, U.: Ensemble-style self-training on citation classification. In: Proceedings of 5th IJCNLP, Chiang Mai, Thailand (2011)
9. Duncan, E.B., Anderson, F.D., Mc Aleese, R.: Qualified citation indexing: its relevance to education technology. In: Proceedings of the 1st Symposium on Information Retrieval in Education Technology, Aberdeen (1981)
10. Finney, B.: The reference characteristics of scientific texts. M.Sc. thesis, London City University, Centre for Information Science (1979)
11. Frost, C.O.: The use of citations in literary research: a preliminary classification of citation functions. Lib. Q. Inf. Commun. Pol. **49**(4), 399–414 (1979)
12. Garfield, E.: Can citation indexing be automated? In: Statistical Association Methods for Mechanized Documentation, Symposium Proceedings, vol. 269, pp. 189–192 (1965)
13. Garzone, M.: Automated classification of citations using linguistic semantic grammars. M.Sc. thesis, The University of Western Ontario (1996)
14. Harwood, N.: An interview-based study of he functions of citations in academic writing across two disciplines. J. Pragmat. **41**(3), 497–518 (2009)
15. Hernández-Alvarez, M., Gomez, J.M.: Survey about citation context analysis: tasks, techniques, and resources. Nat. Lang. Eng. **22**(3), 327–349 (2016)
16. Hernández-Alvarez, M., Gomez-Soriano, J.M., Martínez-Barco, P.: Citation function, polarity and influence classification. Nat. Lang. Eng. **23**(4), 561–588 (2017)
17. Hou, W.R., Li, M., Niu, D.K.: Counting citations in texts rather than reference lists to improve the accuracy of assessing scientific contribution. BioEssays **33**(10), 724–727 (2011)
18. Jochim, C., Schütze, H.: Towards a generic and flexible citation classifier based on a faceted classification scheme. In: Proceedings of the 24th COLING, Bombay, India (2012)
19. Kaplan, D., Tokunaga, T., Teufel, S.: Citation block determination using textual coherence. J. Inf. Process. **24**(3), 540–553 (2016)

20. Krampen, G., Becker, R., Wahner, U., Montada, L.: On the validity of citation counting in science evaluation: content analyses of references and citations in psychological publications. Scientometrics **71**(2), 191–202 (2007)
21. Li, X., He, Y., Meyers, A., Grishman, R.: Towards fine-grained citation function classification. In: Proceedings of Ranlp, Hissar, Bulgaria (2013)
22. Lipetz, B.A.: Improvement of the selectivity of citation indexes to science literature through inclusion of citation relationship indicators. J. Assoc. Inf. Sci. Technol. **16**(2), 81–90 (1965)
23. Magee, M.: How research biochemists use information: an analysis of use of information from cited references. M.Sc. thesis, Graduate Library School, University of Chicago (1966)
24. McCain, K.W., Turner, K.: Citation context analysis and aging patterns of journal articles in molecular genetics. Scientometrics **17**(1–2), 127–163 (1989)
25. Moravcsik, M.J., Murugesan, P.: Some results on the function and quality of citations. Soc. Stud. Sci. **5**(1), 86–92 (1975)
26. Oppenheim, C., Renn, S.P.: Highly cited old papers and the reasons why they continue to be cited. J. Am. Soc. Inf. Sci. **29**(5), 225 (1978)
27. Peritz, B.C.: A classification of citation roles for the social sciences and related fields. Scientometrics **5**(5), 303–312 (1983)
28. Peroni, S., Shotton, D.: FaBiO and CiTO: ontologies for describing bibliographic resources and citations. J. Web Semant. **17**, 33–43 (2012)
29. Qazvinian, V., Radev, D.R., Mohammad, M.S., Dorr, B., Zajic, D., Whidby, M., Moon, T.: Generating extractive summaries of scientific paradigms. J. Artif. Intell. Res. **46**, 165–201 (2013)
30. Qazvinian, V., Radev, D.R.: Identifying non-explicit citing sentences for citation-based summarization. In: Proceedings of the 48th ACL Annual Meeting, Uppsala, Sweden (2010)
31. Ritchie, A., Robertson, S., Teufel, S.: Comparing citation contexts for information retrieval. In: Proceeding of the 17th CIKM, Napa Valley, CA (2008)
32. Spiegel-Rosing, I.: Science studies: bibliometric and content analysis. Soc. Stud. Sci. **7**(1), 97–113 (1977)
33. Sula, C.A., Miller, M.: Citations, contexts, and humanistic discourse: toward automatic extraction and classification. Lit. Linguist. Comput. **29**(3), 452–464 (2014)
34. Tahamtan, I., Bornmann, L.: Core elements in the process of citing publications: conceptual overview of the literature. J. Informetr. **12**(1), 203–216 (2018)
35. Teufel, S., Siddharthan, A., Tidhar, D.: Automatic classification of citation function. In: Proceedings of the 11th EMNLP Conference, Sydney, Australia (2006)
36. Teufel, S., Siddharthan, A., Batchelor, C.: Towards discipline-independent argumentative zoning: evidence from chemistry and computational linguistics. In: Proceedings of the of the 2009 EMNLP, Singapore (2009)
37. Tuarob, S., Mitra, P., Giles, C.L.: A classification scheme for algorithm citation function in scholarly works. In: Proceedings of the 13th JCDL, Indianapolis, IN (2013)
38. Whidby, M., Zajic, D., Dorr, B.: Citation handling for improved summarization of scientific documents, Technical report (2011)
39. White, H.D.: Citation analysis and discourse analysis revisited. Appl. Linguist. **25**(1), 89–116 (2004)
40. Zhao, D., Cappello, A., Johnston, L.: Functions of uni- and multi-citations: implications for weighted citation analysis. J. Data Inf. Sci. **2**(1), 51–69 (2017)
41. Zhu, X., Turney, P., Lemire, D., Vellino, A.: Measuring academic influence: not all citations are equal. J. Assoc. Inf. Sci. Technol. **66**(2), 408–427 (2015)

Striving for Semantics of Plant Phenotyping Data

Hanna Ćwiek-Kupczyńska[(✉)]

Institute of Plant Genetics, Polish Academy of Sciences, Poznań, Poland
hcwi@igr.poznan.pl

Abstract. Addressing the goal of the workshop, i.e. to bridge the gap between academic and industrial aspects in regard to scholarly data, we inspect the case of plant phenotyping data publishing. We discuss how the publishers could foster advancements in the field of plant research and data analysis methods by warranting good quality phenotypic data with foreseeable semantics.

Examining of a set of scientific journals dealing with life sciences for their policy with respect to plant phenotyping data publication shows that this type of resource seems largely overlooked by the data policymakers. Current lack of recognition, and resulting lack of recommended standards and repositories for plant phenotypic data, leads to depreciation of such datasets and their dispersion within general-purpose, unstructured data storages. No clear incentive for individual researchers to follow data description and deposition guidelines makes it difficult to develop and promote new approaches and tools utilising public phenotypic data resources.

Keywords: Phenotypic and environmental traits · Plant data
Reporting guidelines · Research data policy · Semantic publishing

1 Background

Understanding plant phenotypes is the ultimate goal of plant research, motivated by the desire to improve plants with respect to such traits like yield, taste or disease resistance for the benefit of mankind. To discover complex biological mechanisms behind certain phenotypic traits, a large number of elementary analyses must be done and eventually integrated. To allow this, sufficient amount of constitutive datasets with adequate experimental metadata must be available.

Quality publications and supplementary dataset submissions should ensure that the published data is fully comprehensible, and thus replicable and reusable. Validation against a set of established requirements, deposition in open repositories, and indexing of datasets should guarantee that good quality plant phenotyping datasets are accessible for both researchers studying biological phenomena and developers of new methodological approaches to data analysis.

© Springer Nature Switzerland AG 2018
A. González-Beltrán et al. (Eds.): SAVE-SD 2017/2018, LNCS 10959, pp. 161–169, 2018.
https://doi.org/10.1007/978-3-030-01379-0_12

Surprisingly, despite being a valuable and very basic type of resource in plant research, plant phenotypic data tend to be overlooked by the publishers and their policy-makers. Among the journals examined for requirements and recommendations with respect to plant phenotyping datasets, only one names this kind of data explicitly and mentions a repository where phenotyping results can be stored. As a consequence, the published data get dispersed among general-purpose, unstructured repositories and lose its chance to stimulate new discoveries and development of dedicated methodologies.

2   Research Data Publication Guidelines

Having selected a (non-exhaustive) set of popular life science journals where plant research involving phenotypic data has been published or submitted within the previous months, we have examined their current data policies with respect to plant phenotyping datasets. A summary of the journals' guidelines is shown in Table 1.

Most of the journals declare adoption of some research open data and data archiving policy, and *'data availability statement'* is usually required in a paper. With minor exceptions of confidential data, *'data not shown'* statements are no longer accepted; instead, the research data underlying all claims and conclusions formulated by the authors must be provided. If the data cannot be included in the paper itself, its deposition in public repositories is suggested. Institutional or private repositories are rarely allowed. In some cases attaching a small dataset as size-constrained supplementary information to the online article is also accepted.

Only a few specific data types are governed and validated against domain-specific metadata standards or reporting guidelines. A set of required repositories are usually explicitly given for well established measurement types resulting in homogeneous data such as nucleotide sequences (DDBJ, ENA, GeneBank), amino acid sequences (UniProt/Swiss-Prot) and structures (PDB), microarrays (ArrayExpress), metabolites (MetaboLights) or chemical structures (ChemSpider, PubChem). More heterogeneous submissions of specific species are appointed to dedicated repositories, e.g. Arabidopsis genome functional annotation data (TAIR) or human genome-phenome interactions (dbGaP, EGA). Other data types are expected to be put into general-purpose repositories such as Dryad[1], figshare[2] or Zenodo[3], or a more scientific-oriented GigaDB[4]. For all but one journal, this is the case of plant phenotyping data, not being explicitly mentioned in the data policies described on their websites.

The only publisher accounting for plant data covering phenotypes is Giga-Science[5], that directs to a dedicated public repository of PGP[6] [1]. Another

---

[1] https://www.datadryad.org.
[2] https://figshare.com.
[3] https://zenodo.org.
[4] http://gigadb.org.
[5] https://academic.oup.com/gigascience.
[6] https://edal.ipk-gatersleben.de/repos/pgp.

Table 1. A summary of data policy of selected life science journals towards plant phenotyping data. PR = Public Repository; SI = Supplementary Information; IR = Institution Repository; AuR = Available upon Request; () = if need be; n/a - information not available. *Finding definitive information about data policies was not straightforward due to the information being frequently scattered across journals' and publishers' websites and submission portals. At different locations there appear multiple declarations about journal-specific data policy, policy of the publisher, supported or adopted external initiatives, recommended data repositories, reporting standards, and data archiving policies. Having this information published in a standardised form and place would greatly improve the access and comprehensibility.*

Journal Title	Data category covering plant phenotypic data	Suggested data location	Suggested reporting standards
Plant Journal	Other	PR; SI; IR/AuR	
New Phytologist	n/a	SI; (PR)	
Journal of Applied Genetics	Other	PR: Figshare, Dryad	
Euphytica	Other	PR: Figshare, Dryad; (SI)	
Scientific Data	Other	PR: Dryad, Figshare, Harvard Dataverse, Open Science Framework, Zenodo	
Plant Methods	Other	PR: Dryad, Figshare, Harvard Dataverse, Open Science Framework, Zenodo; IR	Field-specific standards reported at BioSharing website
Theoretical and Experimental Plant Physiology	n/a	n/a	"By data we mean the minimal dataset that would be necessary to interpret, replicate and build upon the findings reported in the article"
Genetic Resources and Crop Evolution	Other	PR: Figshare, Dryad; SI	
GigaScience	**Plant**; other	**PGP**; GigaDB, FigShare, Dryad, Zenodo; IR	Minimum reporting guidelines at FAIRsharing Portal
Integrative Biology	Other	PR: Figshare, Dryad; IR, SI	MIBBI checklists for reporting biological and biomedical research
BMC Plant Biology	Other	PR: Dryad, Figshare, Harvard Dataverse, Open Science Framework, Zenodo	
Plant Science	Life science; other	PR: Dryad; Mendeley Data, Data in Brief	
Frontiers in Plant Science	Other; **traits**	PR: Dryad; **TRY**	
Genetics	Other	PR: Figshare, Dryad; (SI)	
Plos One	Other	PR: Dryad, Figshare, Harvard Dataverse, Open Science Framework, Zenodo	Prescriptive checklists for reporting biological and biomedical research at FAIRsharing Portal
Journal of Experimental Botany	Other	PR: Dryad, Figshare or Zenodo	

(*continued*)

Table 1. (*continued*)

Journal Title	Data category covering plant phenotypic data	Suggested data location	Suggested reporting standards
The Plant Journal	Other	PR: Dryad, Figshare or Zenodo; (SI)	"Reporting standards for large-scale omics datasets are constantly evolving and TPJ will follow common sense standards currently accepted in the field"
Nature Plants	Other	PR: Dryad, Figshare, Harvard Dataverse, Open Science Framework, Zenodo	Life Sciences Reporting Summary (internal of Nature Publishing Group)
Nature Genetics	Other	PR: Dryad, Figshare, Harvard Dataverse, Open Science Framework, Zenodo	Life Sciences Reporting Summary (internal of Nature Publishing Group)
Scientific Reports	Other	PR: Dryad	
Heredity	Other	PR: Dryad, Figshare, Harvard Dataverse, Open Science Framework, Zenodo	Life Sciences Reporting Summary (internal of Nature Publishing Group)

type-specific repository assigned to a broad category of 'trait data' is the TRY[7] database. Although the storage is indeed dedicated to a wide range of plant trait information, its purpose advertised in [2] is not to be a running repository for experimental datasets, but an analytical processing database for environmental compilations.

Some journals guide an ambitious author to a policy register FAIRsharing[8] (formerly MIBBI and BioSharing, still referenced to as such in the guidelines) to identify and follow a suitable standard on their own. Some other links provided by the journals lead to DataCite[9]'s re3data.org[10] repository catalogue that lists institutional, project- or community-specific resources, where some phenotyping databases of different scope and governed by diverse requirements can be found.

Alas, dataset publishing alone does not ensure sufficient data comprehensibility or reproducibility. No systematic validation of whether a supplementary dataset complies with the recognised standards seems to be done by the journals. General-purpose storages, contrary to the dedicated databases, do not impose any constraints on the content and quality of the submissions, whereas some dedicated repositories for phenotypic data might be governed by provisional guidelines appropriate for current applications rather than long-term storage with the view of replicability and interoperability. The obligation to publish combined with the lack of journals' consistent data validation policy poses a threat of missing out important metadata qualities, at the same time letting the storages fill with non-reusable datasets.

---

[7] https://www.try-db.org/TryWeb/Home.php.

[8] https://fairsharing.org.

[9] https://www.datacite.org.

[10] https://www.re3data.org.

3   Plant Phenotypic Data

3.1   Data Characteristics

Plant phenotypic data constitute one of the fundamental bricks of plant science. Phenotypes result from the interaction of organism's genotype and environment, and are manifested as organism's observable characteristics. Phenotypic traits can be of different nature (qualitative or quantitative) and scope (e.g. cellular or whole plant properties); they can be determined by diverse techniques (e.g. visual observation, manual measurement, automated imaging and processing, or analysis of samples by sophisticated devices) in different time regimes (one-time capture, repeated, time-series or continuant monitoring), and expressed in different scales and units. Thus, the general notion of plant phenotyping encompasses many types of observations and pertains to a huge fraction of plant research.

In plant experiments, the relationships between the phenotypes and environmental conditions are to be explained. Thus, a precise and exhaustive characterisation of the experiment's environment constitutes an integral part of all plant phenotyping studies. Together with environmental data, phenotypes serve in genome-environment interaction[11] analysis, and in conjunction with genomic marker data, they make a crucial part of QTL[12] or GWAS[13] analyses. Plant dataset can also be used on their own by researchers, breeders and farmers to simply screen plant varieties and identify genotypes that behave in a special way in certain conditions. It is the accurate and comprehensive set of metadata that makes experimental data usable and unique. The well-documented plant phenotyping datasets are valuable not only due to specific environmental conditions that contribute to the observed phenotype but also because they are frequently expensive and time-consuming to produce. Thus each experiment deserves scrupulous data handling.

As mentioned before, many types of measurements that produce a homogeneous set of specific, in-depth observations are well-standardized; they have a dedicated standard for data description and formatting, as well as measurement-specific data repositories. Meanwhile, apart from them, a wide range of "traditional" measurements done with a variety of non-standardised, non-automated or low-throughput methods are collected and analysed in laboratories every day. Frequently they apply to basic plant qualities like yield, fruit taste and colour, or disease resistance. Those basic phenotyping data are indispensable for interpretation of the in-depth "-omics" analyses by providing the ultimate observable result of the biological mechanisms under study. The lack of explicit consideration (in recommendations, validation process, encouragement to publish, and access to databases or keywords) for this non-specific yet important data type, even in biological journals, makes it dissipate in the general repositories and limits the possible biological research findings.

---

[11] https://en.wikipedia.org/wiki/Gene-environment_interaction.
[12] https://en.wikipedia.org/wiki/Quantitative_trait_locus.
[13] https://en.wikipedia.org/wiki/Genome-wide_association_study.

The huge diversity of plant studies performed by researchers to investigate mechanisms of plant reactions to different stimuli makes it difficult to establish one fixed approach to handling all aspects of the description of all the processes and their results. While standardising experimental procedures is undesirable, as it could restrict scientific findings and hinder innovative approaches and methodologies, some standardisation of the description of experimental procedures is necessary. It should be done in a way that is both precise and flexible, so that it is possible to interact with datasets of different types in a similar way, and yet the standardisation does not impose constraints leading to losing details of non-standard aspects of particular research. In case of plant phenotyping, irrespective of the type of organisms, their treatments and measurements done, a set of common abstract properties of such experiments can be recognised. A number of common organism properties, environmental properties and foreseeable steps in the preparation of the plant material and its growth can be identified, named and described; and eventually used for data validation, searching, processing and analysis. Identification and providing of those general common experimental metadata is a step towards taming the broad field of plant phenotyping data.

3.2   Plant Phenotyping Community

In the community of plant researchers dealing with phenotyping data, the work on new improved approaches to plant experimental data description, modelling and processing is ongoing. Numerous project- or organism-specific databases and tools exist, and many smart solutions are successfully implemented to describe and store plant phenotyping datasets at individual institutions, organisations, and companies. In many of them care is taken of appropriate data description by requesting from users to use specific data submission forms, models or ontologies, according to their internal standards.

Lately, the work of many groups in plant phenotyping community has been aimed at facilitating plant phenotypic data exchange and reuse through improvement of experimental data standardisation and description guidelines.

Proposed Solutions and Ongoing Efforts. In the absence of common standards addressing the description of plant phenotyping experiments, the Minimum Information About a Plant Phenotyping Experiment (MIAPPE)[14] recommendations have been proposed in [3,4] by a joint effort of big projects dedicated to plant infrastructure development: transPLANT[15] and EPPN[16], followed by Elixir-Excelerate[17]. MIAPPE constitutes a checklist of general properties needed to accurately describe a plant experiment. To enable standardisation of the wording used in the description of all elements specified in MIAPPE, a set of ontologies and taxonomies for their semantic annotation has been recommended.

---

[14] http://www.miappe.org.

[15] http://www.transplantdb.eu.

[16] http://www.plant-phenotyping-network.eu.

[17] https://www.elixir-europe.org/about-us/how-funded/eu-projects/excelerate.

Specific vocabularies to use, e.g. with environment characterisation, are being collaboratively developed by phenotyping community projects (EPPN2020[18], EMPHASIS[19]).

The MIAPPE recommendations are implemented in a number of databases (PGP, EphesIS[20], PlantPhenoDB[21] and GWA-Portal[22]). There is an ongoing work on harmonising implementations of MIAPPE and Breeding API[23], another community initiative developing a standard interface for plant phenotype/genotype databases. A semantic representation[24] of MIAPPE-compliant plant phenotyping experiment model is being developed. A reference implementation for flat file data exchange has been proposed in ISA-Tab format[25].

On top of the phenotyping dataset description standard, a number of data processing, validation, quality assessment and statistical analysis tools exist or are being constructed, e.g., MIAPPE-based configuration to use with ISA-Tools[26] for dataset creation and validation, data parsers in online tools provided by COPO[27] infrastructure, or individual institutions' data processing tools for importing and exporting datasets from their systems. Common semantics has proved beneficial for the implementation of distributed search tools for plant data resources, like transPLANT search[28] or WheatIS search[29]. As a follow-up, applications taking advantage of the enhanced data semantics will be built, conceivably offering advanced and innovative approaches for data exploration and analysis.

Limitations. The above-mentioned solutions proposed by the plant phenotyping community work towards establishing best practices in data management across phenotyping facilities. Although the Minimum Information approach might not be sufficient to cover all aspects of specific research types, it helps ensure the presence of the basic common properties in the description of heterogeneous phenotyping studies. Using MIAPPE as a checklist for preparing a dataset to release should provoke the researchers to think of documenting all related, meaningful aspects of the experiment. Frequent situations where certain metadata is forgotten or omitted as 'obvious' should be reduced, both in case of the supplementary datasets and in the main papers.

The checklist-based approach could become even more relevant if individual researchers, also those with small amounts of phenotypic observations possibly

---

[18] https://eppn2020.plant-phenotyping.eu.
[19] https://emphasis.plant-phenotyping.eu.
[20] https://urgi.versailles.inra.fr/ephesis.
[21] http://cropnet.pl/plantphenodb.
[22] https://gwas.gmi.oeaw.ac.at.
[23] https://brapi.org.
[24] https://github.com/MIAPPE/MIAPPE-ontology.
[25] http://isa-tools.org/format/specification.
[26] http://isa-tools.org/software-suite.
[27] https://copo-project.org.
[28] http://www.transplantdb.eu/search/transPLANT.
[29] https://urgi.versailles.inra.fr/wheatis.

linked to other data types, were incentivised to provide good quality phenotyping datasets to repositories and papers. So, are there not enough reasons for publishing good research data? As shown by Piwowar et al. in [5] for microarray clinical trial publications, there is a correlation between public availability of the research data and the number of paper citations, which should work as a natural motivation for both the researchers and the publishers. Moreover, citations of the dataset itself and its reuse, leading to the increase of author's indices or altmetrics statistics could be another measurable benefit for the researcher. Finally, availability of datasets with good quality metadata should enable conducting new interesting research involving integrative and comparative studies or meta-analyses. Additionally, accessible data are bound to result in the development of data-driven applications for managing and analysis of datasets to facilitate researchers' work. Unfortunately those benefits might be intangible for many plant phenotypic data producers, not having their research field recognized by the journals, and thus discouraged from publishing such data and its reuse due to perceived unsure reliability. The potential benefits might be also unconvincing compared to the amount of work necessary from researchers to individually look for and follow the metadata guidelines for the field.

To facilitate data reuse independently of data providers, some approaches assume automatic discovery of scientific data. Search companies attempt to build datasets by collecting the metadata and by capturing the semantics of the data from other unstructured data resources [6]. For some purposes, the approach might provide a considerable number of good quality datasets to use, and spare a lot of work to the data curators. Assuming that the obtained results are made publicly available, plant phenotyping datasets constructed from plain text publications could be useful to identify general aspects of the research. However, there is a big chance that it would not suffice to replicate an experiment or reanalyse its data. A precise set of adequate metadata, together with their explicit description, roles and relationships, must be ensured to allow answering domain-specific questions.

It appears that without journals' putting more stress on the publication of complete and well-described phenotypic datasets, the work on harmonising phenotyping resources and tools taking advantage of data semantics will be restricted only to huge players, i.e. research institutions administering own permanent storage systems and implementing own solutions. Meanwhile, smaller scientific units and researchers unable or not motivated to publish the phenotyping observations together with the standardised and adequate metadata will keep producing single-use-by-author-only datasets.

4 Conclusions

The field of plant phenotyping data publishing, lacking explicit recommendations, dedicated public repositories, and curation, is likely to generate lots of datasets whose storage might be questionable. Unsupervised data publications tend to be incomplete, and thus provide data unsuitable for understanding, replication or re-analysis of the original experiment. To avoid data loss and confusion by single-use-by-author-only datasets, individual researchers should be encouraged and assisted in publishing phenotypic observations with the standardised and adequate metadata.

Despite the variety of plant phenotyping studies and difficulties in pointing to one, unequivocally accepted data description standard, some approach of the publishers to systematically validate the quality of the phenotyping data submissions would be beneficial. Discussing the approach with plant phenotyping community is advisable. Initially, it could be required of the authors to follow some phenotyping-specific reporting guidelines (possibly one of a few reasonable ones), or explicitly stating if this cannot be done in some respects and why. Thus the gaps in the existing recommendations should be identified and a commonly accepted standard would be successively shaped.

An explicit consideration of plant phenotypic data by the biological journals, especially the plant-focused ones, is desirable. Recommendations for data-aware storages and a registry of phenotyping datasets could be made available to stimulate progress in both biological research and development of smarter tools and algorithms to deal with it.

Hopefully, with the ongoing initiatives of the plant phenotyping community, and with the raising awareness of both publishers and researchers, the presence of public phenotyping datasets in complex and innovative analyses will be facilitated and promoted. Introducing better semantics to public plant phenotyping data will trigger the development of smarter integrative analyses methods, expectantly leading to great new discoveries.

Acknowledgements. The work was funded by National Science Centre, Poland, project No. 2016/21/N/ST6/02358.

References

1. Arend, D., Junker, A., Scholz, U., Schüler, D., Wylie, J., Lange, M.: PGP repository: a plant phenomics and genomics data publication infrastructure. Database **2016**, 1 January 2016. https://doi.org/10.1093/database/baw033. (baw033)
2. Kattge, J., et al.: A generic structure for plant trait databases. Methods Ecol. Evol. **2**, 202–213 (2011). https://doi.org/10.1111/j.2041-210X.2010.00067.x
3. Krajewski, P., Chen, D., Ćwiek, H., et al.: Towards recommendations for metadata and data handling in plant phenotyping. J. Exp. Bot. **66**, 5417–5427 (2015). https://doi.org/10.1093/jxb/erv271
4. Ćwiek-Kupczyńska, H., Altmann, T., Arend, D., et al.: Measures for interoperability of phenotypic data: minimum information requirements and formatting. Plant Methods **12**, 44 (2016). https://doi.org/10.1186/s13007-016-0144-4
5. Piwowar, H.A., Day, R.S., Fridsma, D.B.: Sharing detailed research data is associated with increased citation rate. PLoS One **2**(3), e308 (2007). https://doi.org/10.1371/journal.pone.0000308
6. Noy, N.: Facilitative discovery of scientific data. In: SAVE-SD 2018 Workshop, Lyon, France, 24 April 2018. https://save-sd.github.io/2018/keynote.html#noy-talk

Author Index

Printed in the United States
By Bookmasters